The
Selection
of Parliamentary
Candidates

At a time when politicians are increasingly
becoming subject to criticism, it is important to
throw light on one of the most difficult hurdles the
would-be politician has to surmount. Ostensibly
this hurdle is election to the House of Commons,
but since about two thirds of the seats are
securely in the hands of the Conservative and
Labour parties, the nomination of the appropriate
party in any one constituency makes the actual
election a formality: *selection* often becomes
tantamount to *election*. Dr Rush's new book
examines in depth the machinery by which
candidates are selected in the Conservative
and Labour parties and seeks to uncover the
factors which influence their selection. It forms
an important and original investigation into the
whole machinery of parliamentary democracy,
and is essential source reading for all students of
political science and for anyone actively or
potentially involved in the political arena.

NELSON'S POLITICAL
SCIENCE LIBRARY
Editor: K. W. Watkins, PH.D.

The Selection of Parliamentary Candidates

MICHAEL RUSH, Ph.D.

NELSON

THOMAS NELSON AND SONS LTD
36 Park Street London W1
P.O. Box 2187 Accra
P.O. Box 336 Apapa Lagos
P.O. Box 25012 Nairobi
P.O. Box 21149 Dar es Salaam
77 Coffee Street San Fernando Trinidad

THOMAS NELSON (AUSTRALIA) LTD
597 Little Collins Street Melbourne 3000

THOMAS NELSON AND SONS (SOUTH AFRICA) (PROPRIETARY) LTD
51 Commissioner Street Johannesburg

THOMAS NELSON AND SONS (CANADA) LTD
81 Curlew Drive Don Mills Ontario

First published 1969

17 138037 1

PRINTED AND BOUND IN ENGLAND BY
HAZELL WATSON AND VINEY LTD
AYLESBURY, BUCKS

To My Parents

Contents

Preface

This book is largely the result of research carried out for a Ph.D. at the University of Sheffield between 1962 and 1964, the thesis for which was presented in 1965. Since then, however, I have substantially revised and brought up to date the statistical data and other aspects of the study.

Apart from various articles in popular and academic journals[1] and a chapter in Dr Peter Richards's book *Honourable Members*,[2] only two books have been devoted to the selection of parliamentary candidates in Britain. One by Peter Paterson[3] is more concerned with the case for introducing primary elections into Britain than with investigating the process of selection itself, so that the only major work on the subject is *Pathways to Parliament* by Professor Austin Ranney, published in September 1965. This book is not intended as a refutation of Professor Ranney's work. Though I find myself disagreeing with a number of his conclusions, particularly on the factors which influence selection in the two major parties, and also feel that there are a number of important omissions in his book, I have not attempted to deal with Professor Ranney's conclusions in any systematic fashion, since I feel the reader must be left to judge for himself.

No preface would be complete without some acknowledgement of the debts that I owe to those who have helped me in this research and the subsequent writing of this book. In particular the research itself could not have been undertaken without the generous financial assistance granted by the Research Fund Committee of the University of Sheffield during a two-year tenure of a University Postgraduate Scholarship at Sheffield, and the further assistance afforded by the University of Exeter.

A greater debt, however, is owing to Mr W. Thornhill, of the University of Sheffield, who supervised the original research and was a constant source of advice and encouragement. Grateful thanks are also due to my colleagues at Exeter, especially Professor H. V. Wiseman, who made many useful suggestions during the formative stage of the work; to Miss Niâ Mann and Mrs Alex Bentley, who endured the

1. e.g. J. Critchley, 'Candidates: How They Pick Them', *New Statesman*, 5 February 1965; D. Watt, 'Picking and Choosing', *Spectator*, 1 May 1965; 'The Selection of Parliamentary Candidates', *Political Quarterly*, 30, July–September 1959.
2. First edition, London, 1959; second edition, London, 1963.
3. *The Selectorate*, London, 1967.

typing of a difficult manuscript; to Dr K. W. Watkins, who was instrumental in persuading me to write this book and who very kindly carried the burden of negotiating with the publishers during my absence in Canada; but above all to my wife, without whose help neither the original research nor the book could have been completed.

Many people have assisted me in the research which preceded this book, including national and local party officials, trade union officials, M.P.s and candidates, the majority of whom prefer to remain anonymous. None the less, the research could not have been completed without their patient co-operation. Some of them may disagree with the views expressed in the book, but I, of course, accept sole responsibility for those views and any errors which may have occurred.

M.D.R.

Department of Politics,
University of Exeter
  June 1969

List of Abbreviations

A
A.E.U.: Amalgamated Engineering Union
A.P.C.R.: Annual Party Conference Report (of the Labour party)
A.S.L.E.F.: Associated Society of Locomotive Engineers and
 Firemen
A.S.W.: Amalgamated Society of Woodworkers
A.U.B.T.W.: Amalgamated Union of Building Trade Workers
A.U.F.W.: Amalgamated Union of Foundry Workers

B
B.I.S.A.K.T.A.: British Iron, Steel and Kindred Trades' Association
B.L.P.: Borough Labour party

C
C.A.W.U.: Clerical and Administrative Workers' Union
C.L.P.: Constituency Labour party

D
D.A.T.A.: Draughtsmen's and Allied Technicians' Association
 (formerly Association of Engineering and Shipbuilding
 Draughtsmen)
D.L.P.: Divisional Labour party
D.M.A.: Derbyshire Miners' Association

E
E.C.: Executive Committee (of a Constituency Labour party)
E.T.U.: Electrical Trades Union

G
G.M.C.: General Management Committee (of a Constituency
 Labour party)

I
I.L.P.: Independent Labour party

L
L.C.S.: London Co-operative Society
L.L.P.: Local Labour party

M

M.F.G.B.: Miners' Federation of Great Britain

N

National Union: National Union of Conservative and Unionist Associations
N.E.C.: National Executive Committee (of the Labour party)
N.U.A.W.: National Union of Agricultural Workers
N.U.D.A.W.: National Union of Distributive and Allied Trades (now U.S.D.A.W.)
N.U.G.M.W.: National Union of General and Municipal Workers
N.U.M.: National Union of Mineworkers
N.U.P.E.: National Union of Public Employees
N.U.R.: National Union of Railwaymen

R

R.A.C.S.: Royal Arsenal Co-operative Society

S

S.A.C.C.: Standing Advisory Committee on Candidates (of the National Union of Conservative and Unionist Associations)

T

T.G.W.U.: Transport and General Workers Union
T.S.S.A.: Transport Salaried Staffs' Association

U

U.P.W.: Union of Post Office Workers
U.S.D.A.W.: Union of Shop, Distributive and Allied Workers (formerly N.U.D.A.W. and the National Amalgamated Union of Shop Assistants, Warehousemen, and Allied Workers)
U.T.F.W.A.: United Textile Factory Workers' Association

Part One

CHAPTER ONE

Introduction

Between April 1950, when the first by-election of the 1950–1 Parliament took place, and March 1966, when Harold Wilson was returned to power with an overall majority of ninety-seven, there were 8,130 parliamentary *candidatures*.[1] Nearly four fifths (79·9 per cent) of these candidatures, however, were supported by the Conservative and Labour parties, and an even greater proportion (98·4 per cent) of those elected came from these two parties. Despite its support of over 1,200 candidatures, the Liberal party was able to secure the election of little more than one per cent of its candidates to Parliament; and the minor parties fared even worse. During the period 1950–66 the occasional Liberal success in constituencies like Torrington or North Devon, Orpington or Cheadle, Inverness or West Aberdeenshire, or the Colne Valley, did little to reduce the domination of the two major parties, whatever effect it may have had on the latters' self-esteem.

Thus for the aspiring politician, the would-be Member of Parliament, there is little doubt that the most promising vehicle of his ambition must be either the Conservative party or its Labour rival. To secure the Liberal nomination for a favoured few constituencies may ensure his election, but such opportunities are rare.[2] The alternative is the long and patient nursing of a non-Liberal constituency, at the end of which the prospect of success is invariably less than that of a Conservative or Labour challenger in a marginal seat. This was the achievement of Richard Wainwright in the Colne Valley, but he had to fight the constituency at two general elections and one by-election before he finally wrested the seat from Labour. It is true, of course, that from time to time Liberal candidates, with a minimum amount of nursing

1. i.e. including all sitting M.P.s seeking re-election and all candidates who fought one or more elections.
2. Since 1950 only one *newcomer*, Emlyn Hooson (Montgomery), has successfully retained a Liberal-held seat when it became vacant.

the constituency, have achieved dramatic by-election successes such as Torrington in 1958, where a Conservative majority of more than 9,000 was overturned, or the even greater triumph of Orpington, which saw the eradication of a majority of nearly 15,000. The victor of Torrington, however, did not survive the Conservative resurgence of 1959, whilst who can guarantee that Eric Lubbock's successor as the Member for Orpington will be a Liberal?

In theory all 630[3] seats in the House of Commons are at risk in a general election, but in practice there are two limiting factors on their availability: first, the number of sitting M.P.s seeking re-election, and second, overlapping to some extent, the degree to which certain seats may be described 'safe' for the party which holds them. The second of these two factors applies equally to by-elections, though not, of course, the first.

In the five general elections held between 1951 and 1966, over two-fifths (43·1 per cent) of the Conservative and Labour candidates were sitting M.P.s seeking re-election. Some, of course, sat for marginal constituencies and were subsequently defeated, but the majority were re-elected. Since statistical analysis of the relative marginality or safe-ness[4] of the constituencies held by the Conservative and Labour parties shows that at each of these general elections no less than two thirds could be regarded as secure in the hands of these two parties, it follows that nomination by the incumbent party is the strongest guarantee of election to Parliament; in short, *selection* is *tantamount* to election. The number of such seats which become available, however, is limited by the number of sitting M.P.s who choose to retire at the end of a parti-cular Parliament, and by the casual vacancies arising out of by-elec-tions. Table 1(1) shows the number of vacancies which occurred in constituencies held by the Conservative and Labour parties.

The table demonstrates that the number of vacancies available to prospective Conservative and Labour candidates between 1950 and 1966 was relatively limited by the small proportion of retirements (an average of 7·6 per cent at each of the five general elections), by the even smaller number of resignations for various reasons, and by the fairly limited turnover through by-elections.

Of the 469 vacancies mentioned in Table 1(1), only thirty-six[5] resulted in the defeat of the incumbent party, so that the vast majority

3. 625 between 1950 and 1955.
4. For definition, see Appendix A.
5. Twenty-four Conservatives and twelve Labour.

of gains by the two major parties were at the expense of sitting M.P.s. Between 1950 and 1966 there were, taking these gains and losses into account, 340 new Conservative and 303 new Labour M.P.s, making a total of 643, which amounts to rather more than a complete *numerical* turnover of the House of Commons. This figure may seem considerable, but not in relation to the total number of candidates who contested the elections of this period, nor in relation to the average length of service of the Members who retired at each of the five general elections. In both major parties the average length of service in the House of Commons on retirement, as opposed to defeat, was just over sixteen years: it is not therefore surprising to find that there was, roughly speaking, a complete numerical turnover in a *period* of sixteen years.

Table 1(1): *Vacancies in Conservative- and Labour-held constituencies, 1950–66*

	Conservative	Labour	Total
General Elections			
Retirements	140	98	238
Other causes*	30	14	44
By-elections	112	75	187
Totals:	282	187	469

* Appointments, succession to peerages, etc.

What is perhaps of greater interest is that the number of vacancies in Conservative-held seats was substantially greater than the number in Labour constituencies. This is not simply a reflection of the lower number of Labour constituencies during the 1950s: the *proportion* of Labour M.P.s retiring at a general election is normally lower than the *proportion* of Conservative M.P.s. The average proportion of Labour retirements between 1950 and 1966 was 7 per cent, compared with 9 per cent of Conservative M.P.s. This relative reluctance to retire is reflected in the average age at which M.P.s of both parties retire: for Labour M.P.s it is sixty-seven, for Conservatives fifty-nine years, and although there is common length of service between the two, there is a considerable differential *within* the various sections of the Labour party. The average age on retirement of trade union sponsored candidates was nearly seventy years between 1950 and 1966, that for

Co-operative M.P.s sixty-seven years, and that for non-sponsored M.P.s only sixty-four years. Similarly, the average length of service of trade union M.P.s was over eighteen years, for Co-operative M.P.s it was fifteen years, and for non-sponsored M.P.s only fourteen years.

The same point may be illustrated by examining the causes of by-elections between 1950 and 1966. In the first place there were again more by-elections in Conservative than Labour seats and this is largely a causal connection. Over a third of the Conservative vacancies were caused by elevation to the peerage, principally first creations, or life peerages after 1958. A further 12 per cent were caused by the appointment of M.P.s to various posts and offices incompatible with continued membership of the Commons, whilst another fifth were resignations for various reasons, such as ill-health, business commitments, or political disagreement. Little more than a quarter were caused by the death of the sitting M.P. The Labour party presents a marked contrast, however: no less than two thirds of the by-elections in Labour-held seats were brought about by the death of the sitting M.P., the remainder being attributable to the causes mentioned above.

The would-be Conservative M.P. appears to have some advantage over his Labour rival in so far as the turnover in Conservative-held constituencies is greater. This advantage is probably offset to some extent by the apparently fiercer competition for Conservative constituencies: of the lists of candidates maintained by the two party headquarters, the Conservative list is the larger, whilst for a local Conservative association in a safe seat to receive as many as a hundred applications is quite common, whereas few Constituency Labour parties will receive more than twenty nominations for the safest of seats. Even if account is taken of the individuals considered as *possible* nominees in a Labour selection, the total will seldom exceed fifty.

There is, of course, an alternative method of securing election to the House of Commons, and this is to capture a seat from the incumbent party. This method secured the election of eighty-two Conservative candidates and 128 Labour candidates between 1950 and 1966. There is, however, rather less guarantee of success: although it is easy enough to predict which constituencies can be expected to change hands given a sufficient electoral swing, it is rather more difficult to effect such a swing. To a large degree the candidate's fate is in the hands of his party: a favourable national swing to his party will *normally* be reflected in his constituency, but so will a swing against his party. Occasionally a constituency will defy the national swing from one party to the other, usually by falling substantially below or considerably exceeding the national average, or, more rarely, by actually registering a swing in the opposite direction. In the General Election of 1966, for example, six marginal seats and one semi-marginal seat should, statistically, have been Labour gains, but were not; similarly, in both 1964 and 1966, South-West Norfolk showed a swing to the Conservatives, despite a national swing to Labour.

The *relative* stability of electoral behaviour in Britain means that it is possible to classify constituencies statistically into a number of groups according to their relative safeness or marginality. For the purposes of this study the classification used by Finer, *et al.*,[6] has been used. This divides constituencies into five groups: marginal, semi-marginal, comfortable, safe and impregnable. Using these definitions to analyse the seats which the two major parties gained between 1950 and 1966 shows that more than two thirds of the seats gained by the Conservative and Labour parties were marginal, and nearly 96 per cent were either marginal or semi-marginal. In 1966, for example, only one non-marginal seat changed hands: this was the comfortable Conservative constituency of Cheadle, a *Liberal* gain. Conversely, over the same period, only one impregnable seat changed hands, and this too was a Liberal gain: Orpington.

For the large number of candidates who contest the comfortable, safe, and impregnable constituencies held by their opponents, the prospect of success is very slim indeed. They may, of course, subsequently secure selection in a more favourable constituency, one which is held by their own party or less securely by the opposition. The great majority of unsuccessful candidates are not, however, subsequently elected: only 17 per cent of the unsuccessful Conservative and Labour candidates at the General Election of 1951 (excluding defeated M.P.s) were subsequently elected, in spite of the opportunities presented by a further four general elections and 171 by-elections. The number of unsuccessful candidates at any one general election who are likely to be elected at or before the next is naturally even lower than this: of the unsuccessful candidates in 1959 only 10 per cent were elected between then and 1964, *including* the General Election of that year. Similarly, less than 8 per cent of the unsuccessful candidates of 1964 were elected at any of the thirteen by-elections between 1964 and 1966 or at the General Election of 1966. A substantial proportion of

6. S. E. Finer, *et. al.*, *Backbench opinion in the House of Commons, 1955–1959*, London, 1961; see also Appendix A.

these, moreover, are likely to be gains where the candidate benefited from a favourable electoral swing.

There is, therefore, an important dichotomy between the candidates selected by the party which holds the seat, the *incumbent* party, and the party which does not, the *non-incumbent* party. Two thirds of the candidates who became M.P.s between 1950 and 1966 were the beneficiaries of inherited majorities, having been selected by incumbent parties; one third were the beneficiaries of favourable electoral swings, having been elected by non-incumbent parties in marginal or semi-marginal constituencies. This dichotomy is important for two reasons: first, the nature of the relationship which is being established between the party and the candidate, between selectors and selected; and second, the possibility that there are substantive differences between the characteristics of the candidates selected by incumbent and non-incumbent parties respectively.

This is simply because in the latter case a candidate is normally selected to fight a particular election, sometimes a by-election, sometimes a general election, and once the basic obligation of the candidate to fight that election has been fulfilled then the relationship is terminated. It may, of course, be resurrected by re-selection, but this is a specific act which, in a sense, creates a fresh relationship. There are also those, of course, who gain seats from their opponents, but these constituted less than 7 per cent of the total number of unsuccessful candidates, and the overwhelming majority of the latter do not become Members of the House of Commons. Where a candidate successfully defends an inherited majority, however, and is elected to Parliament, then a long-term relationship is established. Indeed, one can go further and suggest that it is in many instances a case of a long-term relationship being *confirmed*, for where the candidate has been selected for a comfortable, safe, or impregnable seat, then, as it has already been pointed out, selection and election are almost synonymous. Selection by the incumbent party, therefore, is the beginning of a relationship which is normally terminated not by the election which follows, but by the resignation, defeat, or death of the Member five, ten, perhaps twenty years later.

The selectors of an incumbent party are, therefore, conscious that they are normally not only selecting a candidate, but a Member of Parliament. Consequently, they may apply criteria which differ considerably from those applied by the selectors of a non-incumbent party, which is seeking a 'standard-bearer' rather than a potential M.P.

Of course, selectors in a non-incumbent marginal constituency may feel that victory is within their grasp and select a candidate as a potential Member, but the majority of non-incumbent parties are faced with the less rewarding prospect of contesting the constituency unsuccessfully and thus selecting a candidate for a campaign rather than a political career. The criteria which these non-incumbent parties apply to the selection of their candidates are likely to be concerned far more with the ability of the applicants or nominees to represent the party locally, to 'nurse' the constituency during the pre-electoral period, and, above all, to fight an effective election campaign, than with their ability to represent the constituency at Westminster or to scale the heights of political power.

The importance of the selection of parliamentary candidates is emphasized, above all, by the fact that the normal path to ministerial office is through Parliament, and, moreover, the majority of those who achieve ministerial office serve their parliamentary apprenticeship in the House of Commons.[7] Furthermore, 93·5 per cent of the members of the House of Commons who held ministerial office and 98·4 per cent of those who held Cabinet office between 1918 and 1958, were supported by the Conservative and Labour parties.[8] For the majority of these men and women the first substantive step of their national political careers is selection as a parliamentary candidate by one of the two major parties. The power concentrated in the hands of the incumbent party's selectors in comfortable, safe, and impregnable seats is therefore considerable. Not only do they have it within their power virtually to confer the title of Member of Parliament on an individual, subject only to what is normally the formality of election, but they are selecting one member of the pool from which the majority of Ministers must be drawn.

It is therefore important to know to what extent the selectors are aware of their power, what criteria they apply, and, indeed, who the selectors themselves are. This study attempts to examine the selection of candidates within the context outlined above. Basically it is a study of the selection of all Conservative and Labour parliamentary candidates between 1950, beginning with the first by-election of the 1950–1 Parliament, and 1966, ending with the General Election of that

7. See P. W. Buck, *Amateurs and Professionals in British Politics 1918–59*, Chicago, 1963; F. M. G. Wilson, 'Routes of Entry of New Members to the British Cabinet, 1868–1958', *Political Studies* vol. VII, No. 3 (October 1959).
8. Buck, op. cit., pp. 84–5.

year.[9] This has entailed the examination of 3,760 selections, including a number of case studies in depth, some of which are discussed in the final chapter of each section. These case studies are preceded by a description of the machinery of selection and an assessment of the factors which influence its course.

9. The Conservative party here includes the Scottish Conservative (and Unionist) and Ulster Unionist parties. The Conservatives did not oppose the Speaker, a former Labour M.P., in 1966 and have in the past refrained from nominating candidates in certain Liberal-held constituencies in response to local electoral agreements. The Labour party does not contest the twelve seats in Northern Ireland, although it does have an electoral agreement with the Northern Ireland Labour party.

Part Two
The Conservative Party

CHAPTER TWO

The Machinery of Selection

'The selection of candidates is the responsibility of Constituency Associations'[1] commented Selwyn Lloyd in his report on the Conservative Party Organization in 1963. That this comment is taken from Lloyd's observations on the Standing Advisory Committee on Candidates[2] of the National Union of Conservatives and Unionist Associations[3] may seem incongruous, asserting that the right of selection belongs to local parties, whilst admitting that there is a national body which plays some part in selection. There are, moreover, many who would subscribe to the view that the Central Office of the Conservative Party Organization plays an informal but dominant role in the selection of Conservative candidates. In a letter to a national newspaper a member of East Grinstead Conservative Association wrote:

> I view with considerable disquiet the news ... that the acting chairman of the East Grinstead Divisional [Conservative] Association is also chairman of the Selection Committee, particularly as Sir Stephen Pierssené was until recently *a prominent figure at Central Office*.[4]

Similar views were expressed during the Salisbury by-election campaign early in 1965,[5] and were particularly prevalent immediately after the General Election of 1964, when a number of defeated ex-Ministers were looking for parliamentary seats. In fact, only one of these Ministers[6] was selected at his first attempt after the General Election and the remainder were rejected by one or more Conservative

1. The Selwyn Lloyd Report to the Chairman of the Party Organization and the Executive Committee of the National Union of Conservative and Unionist Associations, 1963, p. 17.
2. To be referred to as the S.A.C.C.
3. To be referred to as the National Union.
4. Letter to the *Daily Telegraph*, 29 December 1964. Sir Stephen Pierssené was General Director of the Conservative Central Office, 1945–57. (Author's italics.)
5. See *The Times*, 19 January 1965.
6. A. P. L. Barber, former Minister of Health, at Altrincham and Sale.

associations.[7] Whatever efforts Central Office may have made on their behalf seemed singularly unsuccessful; none the less, rumours of Central Office influence persist.

Unlike the Labour party, the Conservative party does not possess a formal constitution and this at least provides negative support, if not a source, for these rumours. The absence of a formal constitution renders it difficult to define the relative positions of national and local organizations although a series of pamphlets published by the Central Office describe in some detail the working of the party organization and the organization of local associations, and offer advice on the formation and maintenance of various political organizations at local level,[8] but not even these Model Rules[9] are obligatory: 'These Model Rules are intended *for the guidance of Constituency Associations* either in framing new rules or in amending existing ones.'[10] Similarly, the Central Office publishes a pamphlet on the selection of candidates,[11] and though the latter adopts a more authoritative tone than the Model Rules, there is no suggestion that every Conservative association *must* select its candidate in exactly the same way, following a clearly defined procedure laid down at national level as in the Labour party:

> *Subject to certain simple Party rules* each association has complete freedom to select the man or woman of its choice. *The purpose of this pamphlet is to assist associations* in discharging their responsibility in the interests both of the country and of the constituency.[12]

The fact remains, however, that the vast majority of Conservative associations select their candidates by a fairly uniform procedure, but it is a uniformity imposed by advice and long usage and not constitutional obligation. Though constitutionally impossible to define the roles of the National Union, the Central Office, and the local associations, it becomes necessary to describe their spheres of influence in the field of selection.

7. Three others, A. G. D. Rippon, former Minister of Public Buildings and Works, M. V. Macmillan, former Economic Secretary to the Treasury, and P. M. Kirk, former Parliamentary Under-Secretary for Defence for the Army, were subsequently selected for Conservative-held seats; and one other, A. Green, former Financial Secretary to the Treasury, fought his former constituency again in 1966.
8. Organization Series, Conservative and Unionist Central Office, 1946–56.
9. Organization Series No. 3 (1956): Model Rules.
10. ibid, p. 1. (Author's italics.) In fact most associations do adopt the Model Rules or something similar.
11. Notes on Procedure for the Adoption of Conservative Candidates in England and Wales, Central Office, 1960 edition. Henceforth called 'Selection pamphlet'.
12. Selection pamphlet, p. 1. (Author's italics.)

The National Sphere of Influence[13]

At national level the selection of candidates concerns both the National Union and the Central Office, the one representing the voluntary and the other the professional section of the Conservative party.

In 1935 the National Union established a Standing Advisory Committee on Candidates (S.A.C.C.).[14] The object of this committee was to control the quality of Conservative candidates by ensuring that all would-be candidates had their names on an approved list, the qualifications for which were decided by the S.A.C.C. The latter has the power 'to withhold or withdraw approval from any candidate or would-be candidate who is not considered suitable . . .',[15] and, although 'no member of the Conservative Party is debarred from submitting his or her name to the Advisory Committee, there is no onus on the S.A.C.C. to produce evidence to prove that a candidate is unsuitable'.[16]

The Maxwell Fyfe Committee on Party Organization re-examined the role of the S.A.C.C. whose authority had been endorsed by the Party Conference in 1948, and made a number of recommendations. The right of local associations to select someone who is not on the list of approved potential candidates was acknowledged, but the association 'should see that the Candidate receives approval of the S.A.C.C. before adoption as Prospective Candidate takes place'.[17] The Maxwell Fyfe Committee defined the aims of the S.A.C.C. as follows:

(a) To protect the good name of the Party by ensuring that no Candidate is adopted unless the Committee is previously satisfied as to:

    (i) Personal character.
    (ii) Party loyalty.
    (iii) Past record and experience.
    (iv) Political knowledge.
    (v) Speaking ability.
    (vi) Financial arrangements.

13. Scotland and Northern Ireland are separate, and what follows applies principally to England and Wales. See Appendix B.

14. Consisting of nine members: chairman of the Central Council of the National Union (Chairman); chairman of the Executive Committee of the National Union; the chairmen of the following National Union committees: Women's National Advisory Committee, Trade Unionists' National Advisory Committee, Young Conservatives National Advisory Committee; the chairman and deputy Chairman of the Party Organization; the chief whip in the House of Commons; and the honorary secretary of the National Union (Secretary).

15. Selection pamphlet, p. 3.

16. Final Report of the Maxwell Fyfe Committee on the Party Organization, 1949, p. 55.

17. ibid., p. 54. This occurred in the case of J. H. Osborn at Sheffield (Hallam) in 1958, and often occurs in the event of the selection of a local candidate.

(b) To avoid coming to adverse conclusions unless it is abundantly clear that they are not based on personal prejudices or on insufficient evidence.[18]

Furthermore, 'it should be the duty of the S.A.C.C. to ensure that it has a wide range of Candidates on its list, completely representative in every possible way'.[19]

There is no reason to believe that these criteria have changed in any way since the Maxwell Fyfe Report. Following the General Election of 1964, when the approved list was reconstituted, the criteria for inclusion on the latter were reported as follows:

Personal equipment, such as educational or professional qualifications;

Achievement, intended to indicate the use which the applicant has made of his natural gifts;

Strength as a candidate, which would include such assets as speaking ability or local authority experience;

Political capacity, such as knowledge of Conservative party policy and of current affairs at home and abroad.[20]

Most of the criteria are self-explanatory, but some comment is necessary in respect of the sixth condition listed in the Maxwell Fyfe Report: the question of *'financial arrangements'*. This does not refer to the ability or otherwise of candidates to subscribe to party funds or pay election expenses, nor is it a covert reference to financial influences in selection. On the contrary, it refers to the ability of candidates to 'nurse' a constituency and, in the event of his being elected, maintain himself as an M.P.[21] In its advice to local associations, Central Office points out:

It is the duty of the chairman and the selection committee [of the constituency association] to satisfy themselves that [candidates] *are in a position to nurse the seat* adequately and that they intend to do so. They should not however, be unreasonable in their demands or they may lose a first-class candidate. Character, ability and personality will prove much more important and electorally valuable than *unlimited leisure or the means to purchase a house in the constituency*.[22]

18. ibid., p. 54.   19. ibid., p. 55.
20. *Daily Telegraph*, 14 January 1965.
21. This was, of course, more applicable before the rise in salary granted to M.P.s in 1964.
22. Selection pamphlet, p. 8. (Author's italics.)

Moreover, 'where a candidate could not reasonably be expected to afford the personal expense to him of nursing a constituency, the Central Office Agent should be consulted'.[23]

Although the S.A.C.C. is responsible for deciding whether applicants are placed on the approved list, it does not itself interview candidates. Its decisions are based on information supplied to it by one of the two vice-chairmen of the Party Organization.[24] Anyone who wishes to be considered for the approved list may apply direct to the vice-chairman, who will then request the applicant to complete a candidate's form requesting biographical details and the names of three referees.

In addition to routine information about the applicant's name, address, date and place of birth, and education, candidates are asked to state their nationality, religion, and marital status. A note points out that the applicant's religion will not be revealed to a local association except on request.[25] There then follow ten further requests for information as follows:

(a) Present profession or occupation.
(b) Details of past career.
(c) Public offices held, including local government.
(d) Particulars of any social service undertaken.
(e) Particulars of political experience, including speaking experience and membership of any Conservative association.
(f) Specialized knowledge of political subjects.
(g) Whether the applicant agrees with party policy, and if not details of any difference.
(h) Type of constituency preferred and location.
(i) Capacity to give adequate time to a constituency and, if elected, as an M.P.; and willingness to undertake personal canvassing.
(j) Whether the applicant is a member of a trade union.

There is also provision for the applicant to add any other relevant information. Finally, the applicant is asked to give the names of three

23. ibid., p. 7.
24. 1945–51: J. P. L. Thomas, M.P. for Hereford.
    1951–5: J. H. Hare (Lord Blakenham), M.P. for Sudbury and Woodbridge.
    1955–61: (Sir) Donald Kaberry, M.P. for Leeds North-West.
    1961–5: P. E. O. Bryan, M.P. for Howden.
    April–August 1965: J. M. L. Prior, M.P. for Lowestoft.
    1965–7: Geoffrey Johnson Smith, M.P. for East Grinstead.
    1967– : R. C. Sharples, M.P. for Sutton and Cheam.
The vice-chairman is a personal appointee of the party leader. His term of office normally spans one Parliament and he usually resigns shortly after a general election.
25. See footnote 17, page 68 below.

referees, who should include, if possible, one M.P. and a constituency chairman. The whole form occupies two foolscap sheets.

In the meantime the applicant's local association is asked for a report through the Central Office area agent, and other reports may be forthcoming if the applicant has a variety of party contacts. It is also possible for a local association to suggest a person for the list and there are, of course, those candidates who are selected without first being on the list, but who must receive the approval of the S.A.C.C.

Applicants are interviewed twice: first by the vice-chairman and then by two M.P.s drawn from a panel established for this purpose. The M.P.s report back to the vice-chairman, who then sends a *report and recommendation* to the S.A.C.C. The latter will normally accept the report, although rejection is possible. Rejection is, in fact, more likely on the vice-chairman's recommendation: an applicant may be advised to seek more experience in local government or public speaking, for example.[26]

Following the 1966 election, when the list was again reconstituted, not only were possible applicants invited to consider whether they should re-apply, but one applicant was rejected on grounds of age, although his case was subsequently reconsidered.[27]

It is difficult to ascertain the extent to which the S.A.C.C. could, if at all, be described as a rubber-stamp of the vice-chairman's decisions. The fact that it seldom, if ever, rejects the advice of the vice-chairman would appear to support the view that it is no more than a rubber-stamp: Robert McKenzie describes the S.A.C.C. as 'a body of comparatively minor importance'.[28] Because the screening of candidates is a matter of *co-operation* between the vice-chairman and the S.A.C.C., however, the lack of disagreement between them probably confuses the issue: McKenzie speaks of the S.A.C.C. as appearing to have 'great potential influence', but concludes that it 'in no way ensures popular or non-professional control over policy with respect to candidates[29] ... [because] ... final authority lies with an official of the Central Office who is a direct personal nominee of the Leader'.[30] McKenzie's thesis rests on the fact that the S.A.C.C. accepts the advice of the vice-

26. One applicant, now an M.P., was rejected in 1954 and advised to seek nomination for the L.C.C. elections of 1955.
27. *Daily Telegraph*, 14 and 21 April 1967.
28. R. T. McKenzie, *British Political Parties* (second edition), London, 1963, p. 219. McKenzie also adds: '... it is difficult to understand in what respect the Standing Advisory Committee on Candidates is an advisory body, or to whom or what it advises' (p. 218).
29. ibid., p. 217. 30. ibid., p. 219.

chairman, but according to the Central Office it is *the S.A.C.C. and not the vice-chairman* which decides whether an applicant shall be placed on the approved list or endorses the selection of a candidate prior to his adoption by the local association.[31] In terms of the *distribution of power*, McKenzie is probably right, and to that extent the S.A.C.C. is superfluous, but this is not necessarily the case in the terms of *selection*. If the S.A.C.C. did not exist there would, at national level, be one screening process, in the person of the vice-chairman: at present there are two, the vice-chairman and the S.A.C.C. It is not surprising that the latter seldom rejects the advice of the former in view of their common aim and, probably, general views on the qualifications and qualities necessary for candidates. Furthermore, the vice-chairman is unlikely to recommend applicants who would be unacceptable to the S.A.C.C. unless he is in fundamental disagreement with the latter; in which case it is difficult to see how the vice-chairman can ensure that his will would prevail so long as the S.A.C.C. has the right to accept or reject any applicant. The Leader of the Conservative party can disregard the resolutions of the Annual Conference, he can ignore the advice of the National Union, but there is no evidence that his appointee, the vice-chairman of the Party Organization, can and does overrule the decisions of the S.A.C.C.

As far as selection is concerned, the importance of the S.A.C.C. is that it provides a screening process additional to that of the vice-chairman. It may be that it is little more than a safety mechanism designed to placate the National Union, but it probably acts as a check on the powers of the vice-chairman. The S.A.C.C.'s acceptance of the latter's advice is more likely to be an indication of its agreement with, than its subservience to, the vice-chairman.

In the event of a local association selecting a candidate who is unacceptable to the S.A.C.C. the

candidate will not be regarded as an official Party candidate at the next election. He will not receive the usual letter from the Leader of the Party commending his candidature to the electorate, nor will he be eligible for help from Central Office in the way of speakers or publications. If elected he will not receive the Party Whip.[32]

Such occurrences are, however, rare and there have been only two cases since the war. The first of these was at Chorley, where the local

31. Selection pamphlet, p. 3.   32. ibid., p. 4.

association selected Andrew Fountaine, a candidate with known strong right-wing views. Fountaine had not previously been approved by the S.A.C.C., largely because of these views, which had received considerable publicity at the Llandudno Annual Conference in 1948. Rumours that approval would be withheld did not deter the Chorley association and Fountaine was duly adopted, but the rumours became fact and Fountaine was subsequently denied recognition by the S.A.C.C. on the grounds that he refused to withdraw the extreme views he had expressed at Llandudno.[33] The local association refused to abandon Fountaine, however, and he fought the 1950 election, ostensibly as the Conservative candidate. The result was very close and Fountaine was only 362 votes from victory: it was no surprise, therefore, when there was strong local pressure to readopt him. The chairman of the Party Organization, Lord Woolton, made it clear, however, that the readoption of Fountaine would lead to the National Union withdrawing its recognition of Chorley Conservative Association. This caused a division in the association between those who supported Fountaine's candidature, those who saw the whole affair as a question of Central Office interference, and those who favoured the abandonment of Fountaine in order to avoid a local split which would help Labour. After a prolonged and bitter struggle, another candidate was selected and Fountaine eventually moved farther to the right, becoming president of the British National Party in 1962.[34]

The second case was that of Newcastle North in 1951.[35] A split occurred in the local association over the candidature of Major G. Lloyd George, formerly M.P. for Pembroke. Lloyd George was adopted by a breakaway association and the original association adopted another candidate, who stood as an Independent at the subsequent election. The S.A.C.C. refused to recognize the latter's candidature and he was denied official Conservative support, with the result that Lloyd George was elected.

Until the General Election of 1964, the list of approved candidates was not subject to any periodic reconstitution and names remained on the list indefinitely until election, resignation, or death removed them permanently. At any one time there were some 700 names on the list,

33. *Daily Telegraph*, 17 December 1949.
34. For a more detailed description of the Fountaine case, see Ranney, op. cit., pp. 42–8.
35. See P. G. Richards, *Honourable Members* (second edition), London, 1963, p. 21. Richards also quotes the case of Captain Cunningham-Reid, who was repudiated by his local association in 1942 (p. 156, footnote).

but this included many persons whose interest in becoming a parliamentary candidate was confined to a particular constituency. In the estimation of the vice-chairman, the operative length of the list, that is those persons who were willing to consider either any constituency or at least a substantial number, was about 300. After the 1964 election, however, the vice-chairman,[36] with the agreement of the S.A.C.C., cancelled the list and those on it were informed that a fresh application would be required. Over 300 applications were received and the vice-chairman enlisted the support of a former deputy chief whip[37] and took expert advice from a firm of management consultants.[38] A standardized interviewing technique was devised, and by the time Bryan resigned in April 1965 the list had been fully reconstructed.

The list was revised again after the 1966 election, largely because the electoral situation had changed: the next election was almost certainly several years away and the party managers wished to ensure that the list consisted of applicants who were prepared to adopt a long-term strategy. This meant principally imposing an age-limit, though not without protest,[39] whilst all former applicants were requested to consider their position seriously.

The list of approved potential candidates established and maintained by the national organization of the Conservative party provides the principal source of Conservative candidates. Apart from his role in relation to the list of potential candidates, the vice-chairman also plays an important part in helping local associations to secure suitable candidates, partly by offering advice and partly by supplying to the local party names from the approved list. This places the vice-chairman in a potentially powerful position: the meetings between the constituency representatives, usually the chairman and agent, and the vice-chairman are of an *ad hoc* nature, and it would not be difficult for the latter to bring pressure to bear on a local association in favour of a particular candidate. In practice, however, the vice-chairman tries to avoid any suggestion of support for particular individuals, if only because the merest hint of such support is often enough to damn any candidate in the eyes of the local association.

If the vice-chairman does bring any pressure to bear in favour of a particular individual then clearly he does not do it through the list of

36. Then Paul Bryan, M.P.
37. Lord St Helens, formerly Michael Hughes-Young, M.P. for Wandsworth Central, 1955–64.
38. See *Daily Telegraph*, 14 January 1965.   39. See above, page 18.

Table 2(1): *Number of applications received via the
Central Office in selected constituencies*

Constituency	Date	Number of applications Via Central Office	Total
Richmond (Surrey)	1958	131	135
Sheffield (Hallam)	1958	80	140
Woodford	1963	66	85

names he forwards to the local association,[40] as the figures in Table 2(1) demonstrate. Although the proportion of the total number of applications sent by Central Office varies considerably, it is in all cases too large to support any suggestion of *formal* favouritism. Any Central Office pressure must, therefore, be *informal*:

One of the [constituency] Chairman's first considerations must naturally be what type of candidate is most likely to win the seat and to serve the constituency with distinction. But he should also bear in mind (particularly if the seat is held with a good majority) the wider needs of the Party in Parliament. It may be that Conservative representation in the House would be greatly strengthened by the addition of another woman or trade unionist, or there may be some individual of exceptional qualifications whose experience would be of particular value. It may be that in the interests of the Party in that area some distinguished Party Leader should be invited to stand in order to give support to surrounding constituencies. *The Vice-Chairman will always be ready to advise on such matters.*[41]

There is little evidence, however, that the vice-chairman is regularly asked for such advice or that he frequently gives it: just as beauty is said to be in the eye of the beholder, so, it appears, Central Office influence is in the mind of the observer, particularly in the minds of members of local Conservative associations, who relish the power and independence which selection momentarily provides and resent any attempt by Central Office, real or imagined, to undermine their power or curtail their independence. In other words there are often sufficient grounds for *suspecting* that some pressure has been brought to bear on the local association simply because one or more of the applicants has some connection with Central Office, or it is known that his selection

40. The number is normally much lower for non-Conservative seats, often as few as ten or fifteen.
41. Selection pamphlet, p. 6. (Author's italics.)

22

would be welcomed by the latter. Nevertheless, such suspicions do not constitute a proven indictment against the Central Office and there is every reason to believe that it is a case of smoke without fire. An examination of the possible results of Central Office pressure supports this view.

Table 2(2): Number of by-elections in Conservative-held English and Welsh constituencies in which defeated Ministers, members of the government, or former M.P.s have been selected, 1945–66

Election	Defeated Ministers	Members of the government	Former M.P.s	Total	No. of by-elections
Post-1945	6	–	–	6	9
Post-1950	1	–	1	2	5
Post-1951	–	–	1	1	23
Post-1955	–	–	1	1	26
Post-1959	–	1*	1†	2	29
Post-1964	2	–	3	5	7
Total:	9	1	7	17	99

* Quintin Hogg on the renunciation of his peerage. (Hogg was, in fact, *approached* by a number of Conservative associations.)
† Former Labour M.P.

The figures for the English and Welsh constituencies shown in Table 2(2) do not suggest that there is any extensive use of by-elections to secure the return of individuals especially favoured by Central Office, at least between 1950 and 1964. In the ninety-nine by-elections in Conservative-held seats between 1945 and 1966 only seventeen candidates could be regarded as Central Office favourites in the sense that as ex-Ministers or former M.P.s their return to the House was strongly desired by the party managers. Even if the concentration of eleven of these 'favourites' in the post-1945 and post-1964 periods is regarded as at least prima facie evidence of Central Office influence, it should be noted that of the fifty-five Conservative Members defeated in 1964, only *eleven* were subsequently re-elected in the by-elections between 1964 and 1966 or in 1966.[42] Moreover, of those who were re-elected almost all were relatively young and likely, therefore, to

42. Several other ex-M.P.s have been re-elected at by-elections since March 1966, but with one exception they have all been under fifty years of age.

stand a chance of subsequent adoption. Older ex-Ministers, such as Peter Thorneycroft and Christopher Soames, who were defeated in 1966, failed to secure selection in fresh constituencies. In fact, the apparent use of by-elections at certain times to secure the return of former M.P.s in general, and ex-Ministers in particular, is as much prima facie evidence of the willingness of local associations to select them as it is of Central Office pressure.

None of the Ulster by-elections between 1945 and 1966 were used to return ex-Ministers, members of the government, or former M.P.s, and the corresponding figures for Scotland were: one ex-Minister, three members of the government, and one former M.P. in a total of seventeen by-elections. Of the members of the government, two were Solicitors-General for Scotland, and the other was Sir Alec Douglas-Home on the renunciation of his peerage. The post of Solicitor-General for Scotland must be filled by a member of the Scottish Bar, and since there are only about seventy Q.C.s in the Scottish Law List, the choice is inevitably limited. Although he need not be a member of the House of Commons, some effort is usually made to find the Solicitor-General for Scotland a seat should a non-member be appointed. Since the return of the Conservatives to power in 1951, none of the Solicitors-General for Scotland have initially been Members of Parliament. The first, W. R. Milligan, held the post from 1951 to 1954, serving the whole of his term outside Parliament, since he was not elected for Edinburgh North until January 1955. His successor, W. Grant, was appointed in January 1955 and was not elected to the Commons until the general election of that year. Grant's successor, D. C. Anderson, appointed in 1960, remained outside the Commons until his election for Dumfries in December 1963. Ironically, he resigned as solicitor-general in April 1964 (later leaving Parliament in October 1964), and was succeeded by N. R. Wylie, who was at that time prospective Conservative candidate for the Pentlands division of Edinburgh. Wylie was duly elected in October 1964, but his party lost office at the same time, of course. It is likely that some pressure is exerted to find the Solicitor-General for Scotland a seat, but it does not appear to be particularly strong: Milligan was not a member of the Commons at all during his tenure of the post; Grant's period of just under four months before becoming an M.P. would have been longer had the General Election been delayed beyond May 1955; Anderson became a member of the 1959 Parliament less than a year before its expiration; and Wylie, although a prospective candidate, spent the whole of his period of office outside the House. Moreover, it is known that Anderson was rejected by a number of associations before being adopted at Dumfries.

The case of Sir Alec Douglas-Home can hardly be attributed only to pressure from Unionist headquarters: for Kinross and West Perthshire Unionist Association to reject the Prime Minister would have been disastrous once the idea had been suggested, since the longer he remained in office without a seat in the Commons the more vulnerable his position became. It was not a case of *a* party leader seeking a constituency, but *the* party leader. Despite denials from the local association that the recently selected candidate, George Younger, would stand down in favour of Sir Alec,[43] the pressure to adopt the Prime Minister was overwhelming.

As far as Scotland is concerned, this leaves two further cases, one an ex-Minister, the other an ex-M.P., in which there may have been pressure from Unionist headquarters. There is no reason to believe that there was such pressure in either case, however: the ex-Minister was the late Walter Elliot, a popular member of the Unionist party, who was elected for the Scottish Universities in 1946, which were unlikely to be amenable to political pressure; and the ex-M.P. was J. H. R. Hutchinson, formerly M.P. for Glasgow Central, who was elected for the Scotstoun Division of Glasgow in 1950 with the advantage of being a former Glasgow M.P.

In fact, during the whole period from 1950 to 1966 only thirty-six of the 282 candidates selected for Conservative-held constituencies were former M.P.s. A similar picture emerges when other sources of possible Central Office 'favourites' are examined (Table 2(3)).

The number of candidates selected by Conservative-held constituencies who have held office in the national voluntary organizations of the Conservative party has tended to increase over the period, but even this accounts for only twenty of the 230 candidates selected by incumbent associations in England and Wales between 1950 and 1966. Far from being evidence of Central Office influence the increase is probably a reflection of the recognition of voluntary organizations as legitimate means of political ascent in the Conservative party, and less as symbols of prestige and party reward.

The staff of Central Office and the Conservative Research Department present a rather different problem. The largest single intake of professional party workers at any of the post-war elections was in 1950, when six such candidates were elected. Before the General

43. *Daily Telegraph*, 18 October 1963.

Table 2(3): Selection of members of national voluntary and professional organizations in Conservative-held constituencies in England and Wales, 1950–66

Election	Voluntary* organizations	Professional† organizations	Total	Selections in Conservative constituencies
1950–1	–	–	–	5
1951	1	–	1	17
1951–5	2	2	4	23
1955	3	3	6	31
1955–9	–	–	–	25
1959	2	1	3	39
1959–64	2	1	3	28
1964	8	3	11	34
1964–6	1	–	1	7
1966	1	2	3	21
Total	20	12	32	230

* Including the following: National Party officers, members of the Executive Committee of the National Union, National Advisory Committees of the National Union, National Executive Committee of the Young Conservatives, national officers of the Federation of University Conservative and Unionist Associations, and officers of the Bow Group.
† Including the following: staff of the Central Office and Conservative Research Department.

Election of 1950, however, Lord Woolton, then party chairman, became alarmed at the number of his staff who had been adopted for the forthcoming election. He therefore decided that 'in the event of any future adoptions occurring they must be accompanied by the resignation of the candidate from his position in the central organization'.[44] This action tended to reduce the rate at which members of the Central Office staff were adopted and none was elected between 1950 and 1954. There was also another factor involved, however: between 1945 and 1951 'the constituency organizations had many excellent candidates to choose from, the *"Central office label" was not regarded as a positive disadvantage for would-be candidates,* and the exigencies of the hour made selection committees extremely careful to ensure that they got a good candidate'.[45]

44. Rt. Hon. The Earl of Woolton, *Memoirs*, London, 1959, pp. 343–4.
45. The Earl of Kilmuir, *Political Adventure*, London, 1964, p. 158.

The figures shown in Tables 2(2) and 2(3) tend to support this view, and it would seem that the resentment at any suggestion of Central Office interference has grown since 1945. It is, in fact, difficult for the Central Office, either in the person of the vice-chairman or the area agent, to even attempt to secure the selection of a particular individual, and the stigma of the 'Central Office label' has interfered in the selection of people like Peter Goldman[46] and Eldon Griffiths[47] in recent years, whilst it has been little help to ex-Ministers, such as Maurice Macmillan and Geoffrey Rippon. Moreover, in April 1965 the vice-chairman admitted that, of thirty-five candidates selected since the General Election of 1964, there were three with whose selection he 'disapproved seriously',[48] but he was powerless to prevent their adoption.

Lord Woolton's comment on the attitude of local associations towards the national organization was: 'the Central Office was not allowed by the constituencies to have any influence in the selection of candidates',[49] to which Lord Kilmuir added: 'if the constituency association decides that it does not want a man as its candidate, there is very little that the party's headquarters and Leader can do about it, apart from letting their grave displeasure be known'.[50] He points out that the advice of Central Office has often resulted in the local party pointedly ignoring it, and asserts that 'even Churchill's immense popularity and authority were insufficient to secure safe seats for his son and Sir Roy Harrod in the early 1950s'.[51] It is true, of course, that a would-be candidate can, through Central Office, ask to be considered for a particular constituency or for a particular area, but Central Office can do little more than forward his name to the constituency or constituencies as one of many aspirants.

What of the 'simple Party rules'[52] which local associations must observe? For the most part, Central Office does not need to enforce these rules, all of which have had the approval of the National Union and the S.A.C.C., and local associations generally regard them as part of the normal framework and procedure of selection. In reminding constituencies of them, the Central Office pamphlet invariably assumes an authoritative tone, but there appears to be little significance in this beyond the ultimate power of veto which 'Central Office has naturally been very reluctant to exercise . . . except in extreme cases'.[53]

---

46. Former director of the Conservative Political Centre.
47. Formerly assistant to Sir Alec Douglas-Home.
48. *Observer*, 25 April 1965. 49. Woolton, op. cit., p. 332.
50. Kilmuir, op. cit., p. 159. 51. ibid., p. 159.
52. Selection pamphlet, p. 1. 53. Kilmuir, op. cit., p. 158.

There are five conditions which Central Office regards as obligatory upon local associations. First, throughout the selection the association must act 'strictly in accordance with the rules of the association, and the accepted rules of procedure at meetings. Any irregularity may invalidate the whole proceedings and lead to serious complications and internal disruption. **The Chairman should maintain complete impartiality'.**[54] This condition imposes nothing on the local party which it does not impose on itself and the principal deterrent is local dissension rather than a national veto.

Second, 'pressure from influential quarters and any form of canvassing, whether for or against [any applicant], should be severely discouraged'.[55] The non-federative nature of the Conservative party militates against any built-in form of canvassing or pressure and, apart from *ad hoc* pressure for a local applicant, there is seldom canvassing on any widespread basis.

Third, all applicants not previously vetted by the S.A.C.C. must receive the latter's approval before adoption. This has been accepted, in fact, throughout the party since the Maxwell Fyfe Report.

Fourth, once selected the candidate should be known as the 'prospective parliamentary candidate for the constituency'.[56] This is merely a device to avoid incurring legal election expenses over and above the maximum allowed under the Representation of the People Acts, a device used by all parties. Once the election date is known, the term 'prospective' is dropped.

Fifth, and by far the most important, there are strict rules governing the financial relationship between the candidate and the constituency association. These rules are based on the recommendations of the Maxwell Fyfe Committee.

Before the Second World War financial and social influence had often been paramount in the selection of Conservative candidates. Thus it was in 1873 that Lord Randolph Churchill could write to his future wife:

... You see, both he [his father] and my mother have set their hearts on my being member for Woodstock. *It is a family borough*, and for years a member of the family has sat for it. *The present member is a stranger*, though a Conservative, and is so unpopular that he is almost sure to be beaten if he

54. Selection pamphlet, p. 10 (bold type in original).
55. ibid., p. 7.
56. ibid., p. 5, original in heavy type. This does not apply, of course, to by-elections.

were to stand; and the fact of a Radical sitting for Woodstock is perfectly unsupportable to *my* family.[57]

Social influence in the form of 'pocket' boroughs in which the local party owed its existence to the local landowner declined with the extension of the suffrage, the increasingly political nature of the major parties, and the rise of a third major force on the left, assisted by the payment of members; but as late as 1924 the '17th Earl [of Devonshire] declared . . . that he was paying the expenses of three candidates and was also subscribing largely in five other seats'.[58] As social influences declined, however, financial influence remained, and may even have become more important:

> Mr Macmillan was fond of regaling younger members [of the Carlton Club] with an account of a selection committee he attended in the Twenties at which the chairman simply asked each applicant to write his name on a piece of paper together with the amount he was prepared to donate to the Association's funds. The highest bidder was adopted forthwith.[59]

'Up to 1935 there was no custom or regulation within the Party restricting the amount which a candidate might contribute annually towards the running of his association or the proportion of the election expenses which he might meet from his own pocket';[60] nor was there after 1935 nor indeed until 1944. As the chairman of the Maxwell Fyfe Committee recalls in his autobiography, following an invitation to become the candidate for the West Derby division of Liverpool:

> In the Liverpool seats in those days, the Conservative Member had to pay his own election expenses, amounting to something between £750 and £1,000, and also subscribe £200 a year to the central organization, apart from any other minor subscriptions. I was hesitant about accepting the association's invitation, because there would be two elections in that year of 1935.[61]

Jean Blondel reports a similar state of affairs in pre-war Reading,[62] where the M.P.'s subscription in 1935 was £200 and there was a prolonged tussle between the local association and the M.P. during which the latter sought to free himself of the annual subscription by giving a

---

57. W. S. Churchill, *Lord Randolph Churchill*, London,1896, p. 47. (Author's italics.)
58. W. L. Guttsman, *The British Political Elite*, London, 1963, p. 369, footnote.
59. D. Watt, 'Picking and Choosing', *Spectator*, 1 May 1964, p. 573.
60. Interim Report of the Maxwell Fyfe Committee, 1948, p. 11.
61. Kilmuir, op. cit., p. 42.
62. See J. Blondel, 'The Conservative Association in Reading', *Political Studies*, vol. VI (1958), pp. 104–5.

large sum to the association. The local executive tried to resist, but eventually realized 'that they would no longer be able to get large sums from their M.P., and after a time the issue was dropped'.[63]

In Reading the problem was solved by the pertinacity of the M.P., but the question of financial influence was not something which would solve itself: not all candidates and M.P.s were prepared to resist the monetary demands of their associations, whilst there were always others prepared to take the place of those who were. The scale of the problem was demonstrated by I. S. Harvey in 1939, who published an account of the financial considerations which influenced Conservative selections. He divided candidates into three classes: those willing to pay their election expenses and between £500 and £1,000 a year to the local association (Class A); those willing to pay half their election expenses and a subscription of £250 to £500 a year (Class B); and those unable to pay any election expenses and able to pay a maximum subscription of £100 (Class C).[64] 'According to present standards, 'A' class have always an excellent chance of being adopted, 'B' class a reasonable one, and 'C' hardly any chance at all. These standards are set up ... by the local Associations ...'[65]

The Conservative Party was conscious of the problem long before it made any attempt to solve it, and action was precipitated by the Report of the Speaker's Conference on Electoral Reform of 1944, which

> agreed to place on record the fact that they regarded with disapproval the direct or indirect payment or promise of payment of substantial contributions or annual subscriptions to party organizations (including local party organizations), designed *to influence the action of such organizations in selecting any particular individual as a Parliamentary candidate.*[66]

In response to this implied criticism of the Conservative party the S.A.C.C. laid down a number of rules governing the financial relationship between the local association and its candidate. First, the annual subscription of the M.P. or candidate to the association should not exceed £100; second, each association should establish an election fund and undertake to defray at least 50 per cent of the election expenses. Only if the S.A.C.C. was satisfied that circumstances existed in the

63. ibid., p. 105.
64. J. F. S. Ross, *Parliamentary Representation*, London, 1948, Appendix III, p. 297. See also pp. 129–31.
65. ibid., p. 130.
66. Report of the Conference on Electoral Reform and Redistribution of Seats, 1944, Cmd 6543, Section 9. (Author's italics.)

constituency which justified a departure from these two conditions, would it agree to a candidate making a larger contribution to association funds or to election expenses.[67] According to the Interim Report of the Maxwell Fyfe Committee, the position in 1948 was that '. . . 47 per cent of Candidates and M.P.s contribute less than the maximum of £100 and almost precisely the same proportion pay less than half the election expenses'.[68] It may therefore be assumed that, if the S.A.C.C. strictly enforced the conditions introduced in 1944, just over half the Conservative candidates and M.P.s of 1948 paid the maximum of £100 and half the election expenses, since it is doubtful whether there were many who made no contribution at all.

The Maxwell Fyfe Committee recommended a further reduction in candidates' subscriptions and sought to eradicate the influence of money in selections entirely. The recommendations were accepted by the Party Conference in 1948. In future the entire election expenses would be borne by the constituency associations, although this did not necessarily include the candidate's personal expenses of up to £100. Only in the event of obvious need would a grant be made to the constituency from national funds and the local association should make annual appropriations to its election fund. The agent's fee was to be paid by the association and not by the candidate and there was to be a maximum of £25 for candidates' subscriptions and £50 for M.P.s' subscriptions. Finally, and most important, 'in no circumstances shall the question of an annual subscription be mentioned by any constituency selection committee to any Candidate before he has been selected'.[69] These conditions were to apply to all candidates selected after 31 December 1948 and the limitation on subscriptions to all adopted candidates and M.P.s.

In its Final Report the Maxwell Fyfe Committee remarked: 'We understand that no Constituency has failed to observe our recommendations applicable to new Parliamentary Candidates selected after 31st December, 1948.'[70] The recommendations of the Maxwell-Fyfe Committee did not, of course, apply to either Scotland or Northern Ireland. In the case of the former, the financial rules which apply to England and Wales are generally observed, but in Ulster most of the election expenses are borne by the candidates themselves.[71]

67. Interim Report, Maxwell Fyfe Committee, p. 12.
68. ibid. These figures were based on 415 constituencies in England and Wales.
69. ibid., pp. 13–14.
70. Final Report, Maxwell Fyfe Committee, p. 26.
71. *Daily Telegraph*, 14 June 1963.

Apart from the financial rules which have come into operation since 1944, however, the Conservative party does insist that one other rule which falls into this category is observed:

... the Party does not approve the financing of its candidates by any trade union, trade association, or organization of employers.[72]

The term 'financing of its candidates' is somewhat ambiguous and it could be interpreted in the wider context of the retainers paid to some M.P.s by various pressure groups. There is no evidence, however, that the payment or prospective payment of these retainers in any way influences *selection*, since they constitute a relationship between the M.P. and the pressure group, rather than the constituency and the pressure group. The same cannot be said of grants towards election expenses, however. Since 1951 the National Union of Teachers has maintained a scheme by which the union may give financial support to a maximum of twelve candidates, drawn in equal numbers from the Conservative, Labour, and Liberal parties.[73] Under Section 1(c)[74] of the scheme, the Executive may give support to a union member who has not been adopted by a constituency party, but this has never yet been done. Although the Conservative party ruling that no outside body should be allowed to give financial support to any of its candidates is not strictly enforced in all cases, there is no evidence that the prospect of such support affects the selection of candidates. This is not necessarily the case in a few exceptional constituencies, where the predominance of a particular group may have important repercussions on selection, though not entirely for financial reasons.

Such a constituency is Rochdale, where a strong connection existed between the local Conservative association and the Rochdale and District Cotton Employers' Association. The latter body gave strong support to one of their number, Lieutenant-Colonel Wentworth Schofield, who fought the seat in 1950 and won it from Labour in

72. Selection pamphlet, p. 9.
73. In the General Election of 1959, the N.U.T. supported four Conservatives, four Labour candidates, and one Liberal, of whom two Conservative and four Labour candidates were elected. Four Labour Members were given financial support at the 1964 election, but this support ceased on three of the Members becoming Ministers, and the fourth deputy speaker, leaving only one Member, a Conservative, financially supported by the N.U.T. The N.U.T. pays 50 per cent of the election expenses up to a maximum of £400 and a retainer of up to £350 (£250 before 1958) is paid to M.P.s. The National Association of Schoolmasters also gives financial support to parliamentary candidates, and in 1964 spent approximately £600. Between 1959 and 1964 the association gave financial support to one Conservative M.P. See *Daily Telegraph*, 19 July 1965.
74. As approved by the Annual Conference of the N.U.T., 1958.

1951. The by-election caused by the death of Lieutenant-Colonel Schofield in 1957 enabled Labour, assisted by the termination of the Conservative-Liberal pact which had been in force for the 1951 and 1955 elections, to regain the seat, and the defeated Conservative candidate accused the Cotton Employers' Association of withholding their support and 'stabbing him in the back'.[75] It is doubtful, however, whether there are many cases of this sort: important pressure groups, such as the N.F.U. and the Country Landowners' Association no longer directly sponsor candidates, and, of course, with the notable exception of the N.U.T., sponsorship is confined to the Labour party.

Despite the authoritative tone which the Central Office often assumes in its pamphlet advising constituency associations on the selection of candidates, there is little or no machinery by which the national organization can coerce local parties. Such machinery as exists is of an entirely negative nature, providing Central Office with an overall control of the quality of candidates and an ultimate sanction on the selection of any candidate. The autonomy and independence of local associations is such, however, that this sanction can be applied only in extreme cases to the accompaniment of much unwelcome publicity, as the dispute between Bournemouth East and Christchurch Conservative Association and Nigel Nicolson forcefully demonstrated.[76] Unless the local association clearly contravenes national party rules or offends its own constitution, Central Office and the party leadership are powerless. It was not until the Bournemouth controversy had dragged on for nearly two years that Lord Hailsham, then chairman of the Party Organization, intervened, and then only to *suggest* a postal ballot of the members of the association. The latter accepted Lord Hailsham's advice, but there was no obligation to do so. In his study of relations between M.P.s and their local associations following the Suez crisis of 1956, Leon Epstein[77] has shown that those Members who survived disagreements with their local parties did so because there were circumstances peculiar to them or to their constituencies: some owed their survival to previously good relations with their associations, others to the fact that their seats were marginal, for instance. This is in part disputed by Lord Kilmuir, who asserts: *'Central Office worked very hard and successfully to save other Members from Mr Nicolson's fate* after Suez, but these successes were naturally

75. Quoted in *The Times*, 13 February 1958.
76. See N. Nicolson, *People and Parliament*, London, 1958.
77. L. Epstein, 'British M.P.s and their Local Parties: the Suez Cases', *American Political Science Review*, vol. 54 (1960), pp. 374–89.

kept secret, and remain so.'[78] It can only be assumed that those cases in which Central Office intervention enabled a Member to survive a dispute with his association, or were at least contributory to his survival, reflect informal rather than formal pressure, probably in the form of strongly worded advice from area officials, accepted by local parties in the knowledge that an open dispute with the M.P. could seriously damage the party in the constituency and the country.

The fact remains that Central Office can only seek to advise and arbitrate when disputes occur between M.P.s and their associations, and, furthermore, the circumstances in which any negative control over selection is possible (usually in refusing to recognize a candidate) are strictly limited. Any suggestion, therefore, that Central Office or the party leadership can secure a safe seat for a favoured individual is less than realistic: much can be done by judicious advice, even by earnest pleading, but Conservative associations 'are so independent that pressure from the centre in favour of a candidate is an almost certain method of getting someone else adopted'.[79] To the local Conservative association the right to select a parliamentary candidate is its most prized possession, a possession to be jealously guarded and independently exercised by the party activist, for whom it represents a brief moment of power and influence, the reward, perhaps, of many years of loyal service. Not only is it a brief moment, but, for many safe Conservative seats, an infrequent one, occurring perhaps once in ten or twenty years: selection therefore remains the prerogative of the local party and it was probably no coincidence that the local Unionist associations in Scotland accepted the reorganization of the party machine 'only on the condition that their autonomy in choosing candidates was re-emphasized'.[80]

The Local Sphere of Influence

Although the average membership of Conservative associations in England and Wales in 1953 was 4,488,[81] this figure gives little idea of the wide range of membership in local parties. Conservative associations have a higher average membership than Constituency Labour parties, although it is difficult to compare the individual and affiliated memberships of the latter with the straightforward memberships of the former. A Conservative association in a Labour-held constituency

78. Kilmuir, op. cit., p. 159.   79. ibid., p. 41.
80. *Observer*, 25 April 1964.
81. Based on Central Office Press Release 4085, 1953.

may have as few as 1,000 members, whereas that in a Conservative-held seat may boast as many as 10,000. There is some evidence to suggest that the safer the seat the greater the membership of the local association; Worthing, with a majority of over 18,000 in 1964, had 11,000 members; Bromley with a majority of 11,000, had 9,000 members; Woodford, with a majority of 10,000, had 8,000 members. Against this, the Conservative association in the Labour-held constituency of Erith and Crayford had only 1,500 members. Membership is liable to considerable variation: rural areas and divided boroughs often have a lower membership, urban and single boroughs a larger membership; or the challenge of a marginal seat may boost the membership, as in West Woolwich, which has 6,000 members in opposition to a similar number of local Labour party members. Despite the relatively large memberships in many constituencies, however, only a small minority of the members play any part in the selection of a candidate: the postal ballot used by Bournemouth East and Christchurch Conservatives and the more recent use of a mass meeting of members in the Kemptown division of Brighton[82] are the exceptions which prove the rule. Even in the latter case less than a third of those entitled to attend the meeting did so.[83] Similarly, the Conservative practice of *endorsing* the selection of a candidate by means of a general meeting of members of the association may involve a larger proportion of the membership than is common in the Labour party, but this proportion of the membership represents only a small minority: perhaps 500 out of several thousand. The major decisions in the selection of a Conservative parliamentary candidate are taken by a much smaller number of people representing a tiny proportion of the local membership.

Two organs of the local Conservative association are closely concerned with selection: the first is the executive council,[84] the governing body of the association; and the second is the selection committee, which may be appointed by the council as necessity demands. The size of both bodies varies considerably from association to association, but the council will normally consist of the officers of the association,[85] the chairmen of the various association committees,[86] elected repre-

82. *Daily Telegraph*, 4 February 1965. 83. *Daily Telegraph*, 20 February 1965.
84. Normally known as the divisional council in county constituencies.
85. i.e. president, chairman, three or four vice-chairmen, and treasurer. The vice-chairmen will normally represent the Young Conservatives' divisional committee, the women's divisional committee, the council of trade unionists, and one other.
86. Young Conservatives, trade unionists, political education, local government, teachers, and so on.

sentatives from wards, branches or polling districts, elected representatives from the Young Conservatives, trade unionists, and any local Conservative clubs, together with a specified number of co-opted members. The Central Office agent for the area in which the constituency lies may attend meetings of the council, the chairman of the association is usually chairman of the council and the local agent usually acts as its secretary.[87] Table 2(4) illustrates the extent to which the size of the council may vary from area to area.

Table 2(4): Membership of the Executive Councils in selected Conservative associations, 1958–65

Borough constituencies	Date	Members	County constituencies	Date	Members
Bournemouth East			Petersfield	1960	250
and Christchurch	1958	58	Caithness and		
Richmond	1958	56	Sutherland	1961	129
Sheffield (Hallam)	1958	85	Rother Valley	1963	56
Southend West	1959	70*	Stratford-on-Avon	1963	88
Rotherham	1962	28	Salisbury	1964	90
Glasgow (Cathcart)	1963	39	East Grinstead	1964	400
Woodford	1963	91	Farnham	1965	75
Erith and Crayford	1964	44	S. Worcestershire	1965	182

* Approximate figure.

Generally speaking, associations in county constituencies tend to have larger councils than those in borough constituencies. This is largely a reflection of the size of the former, since the existence of a large number of small but scattered units may demand a larger number of representatives than the geographically smaller and more compact borough constituencies, regardless of the actual membership. Although the executive council is the governing body of the association, the day to day administration of the latter is in the hands of the officers, especially the chairman and the agent,[88] and a smaller body drawn from and elected by the council. This is the finance and general purposes committee[89] (sometimes known as the executive committee or the finance

87. A full description is given in the Model Rules, pp. 6–8.
88. Normally a full-time organizer who acts as secretary of the association.
89. Consisting of the officers, agent, representatives of the divisional committees, and a number of co-opted members. In large county constituencies many of the powers of the executive council may be delegated to the finance and general purposes committee. See Model Rules, Chapter 2, p. 17.

committee), usually numbering some twenty members of the council. The importance of the finance and general purposes committee in the selection of candidates varies: in the event of a by-election it often constitutes the actual selection committee,[90] as it may in other cases;[91] or it may appoint or elect the selection committee, either from among its own members or from the wider body of the council[92] or the association;[93] but often the committee plays a relatively unimportant role, merely making a recommendation to the executive council that selection procedure should begin and leaving it to the council to appoint the selection committee.

The considerable variation in the size of the executive councils shown in Table 2(4), even *among* borough or county constituencies, is due to the freedom[94] with which a local association may adapt the basic framework outlined in the Model Rules to its own desires and needs. The council may therefore be a relatively small body of less than forty persons or it may be over a hundred strong, depending as much on its constitution as on the size of its membership. No matter what its size, however, the executive council plays a crucial role in selection, although it will, in the early stages of the selection, play a role subordinate to that of the selection committee, and possibly to that of the finance and general purposes committee.

Furthermore, it is not a matter for surprise to find that the size of the selection committee varies as much from association to association as the executive council.

Table 2(5) illustrates the extent to which selection committees can vary in size, although the forty-strong committee appointed at Salisbury in December 1964 is exceptionally large. As the table shows, the membership is normally under thirty, and often little more than a dozen. Examination of eight of the associations shown in the table more closely reveals that three of the selection committees were the finance and general purposes committee,[95] two were appointed by the latter,[96] two were appointed by the executive council[97] and one was

90. ibid., p. 14, Rule 21(1)(b), e.g. Stratford-upon-Avon, August 1963.
91. e.g. South Worcestershire, January 1965.
92. e.g. Worthing, December 1963.
93. e.g. Woodford, May 1963.
94. Model Rules, p. 1, Introduction: 'These Model Rules are intended for the guidance of Constituency Associations. . . . The Rules will need to be modified to suit the requirements of individual constituencies.'
95. Sheffield (Hallam), September 1958, Stratford-upon-Avon, and South Worcestershire.
96. Woodford and Worthing.
97. Croydon North-East, September 1963, and Glasgow (Cathcart), January 1964.

Table 2(5): Membership of Selection Committees in selected Conservative associations, 1958–65

Constituency	Type‡	Date	Members
Chichester	C	1958	23
Sheffield (Hallam)	B	1958	21*
Richmond (Surrey)	B	1958	11
Glasgow (Cathcart)	B	1963	15
Woodford	B	1963	9
Dagenham	B	1963	7
Stratford-on-Avon	C	1963	12†
Croydon North-East	B	1963	13
Worthing	B	1963	10
Bromley	B	1964	18
Erith and Crayford	B	1964	7
East Grinstead	C	1964	10
Salisbury	C	1964	40
Farnham	C	1965	14
South Worcestershire	C	1965	27*

* Finance and general purposes committee, though *not* a by-election.
† Two selection committees were used, this being the larger. In this instance a by-election was pending and the larger of the two committees was the finance and general purposes committee.
‡ County (C) and Borough (B) constituencies.

appointed by the officers of the association.[98] The composition of the selection committees also varied: for instance, the six officers of the Richmond Conservative Association formed a sub-committee and then co-opted four members of the association, who, together with the agent, constituted the selection committee of eleven; the Cathcart division of Glasgow, however, appointed a selection committee of fifteen, consisting of the association's officers, the agent and all the branch chairmen, through its executive council. Moreover, it does not necessarily follow that an association will use the same means to establish a selection committee every time a new candidate is selected. At a selection at East Grinstead, for instance, the acting chairman of the association proposed a selection committee consisting of the eight officers of the association, but in response to pressure from the executive council two non-office-holders were added to the committee. Over ten years before, however, when the last selection had occurred, there

98. Richmond (Surrey), 1958.

were only three officers on the selection committee.[99] Occasionally, as at East Grinstead, there is dissatisfaction within the council or the association with the composition or appointment of the selection committee, but such cases are rare, whatever its composition and however it has been appointed.

In practice, the selection committee usually consists of a small group of prominent members of the association: the officers of the association together with the leading members of the council, and the agent, who acts as secretary of the committee. The position of the latter varies: in all cases his advice will be sought and considered, but in most cases the agent has no voting powers on the selection committee. The chairman of the association is normally chairman of the selection committee, unless he himself wishes to be considered for the vacancy.[100]

The task of the selection committee is to reduce the number of applications for the vacancy to a short-list of persons whom it recommends should appear before the executive council. The numerical choice with which the committee is faced is often large.

The figures shown in Table 2(6) are a vivid illustration of the extent to which selection varies from constituency to constituency in the Conservative party. This variation applies not only to Conservative as opposed to Labour-held constituencies, where some differences might be expected, but also to seats *within* both categories. Among the Conservative seats, for instance, the safe seat at Richmond attracted 135 applicants in 1958, yet the impregnable seat at Woodford attracted only eighty-five in 1963, whilst for the relatively less secure seat at Croydon North-East there were ninety-nine applicants. Similarly, the comfortable Labour seat at Erith and Crayford interested seventy would-be candidates, the equally comfortable St Pancras North approximately fifty, and the impregnable Rother Valley none. Furthermore, Erith and Crayford attracted more applicants than the safe and comfortable Conservative seats at Runcorn and Salisbury respectively.

The average number of applicants in a total of twenty-one Conservative-held seats between 1955 and 1965 was 96. In the nine cases where the association was selecting a candidate for a by-election, the average was 92·5, compared with an average of 98·6 applicants for those associations selecting a candidate to replace a retiring member. The difference is almost certainly due to the greater speed at which candi-

---

99. *Daily Telegraph*, 11 December 1964.
100. e.g. East Grinstead, December 1964.

Table 2(6): Number of applicants, number interviewed and number placed on the short-list in selected constituencies, 1955–65

Constituency	Date	Number of applicants	Number of interviews	Number on short-list
St Pancras North*	1955	40–50	20	4
Torrington	1955	190	24	3
Richmond (Surrey)	1958	135	23	6
Sheffield (Hallam)	1958	140	12	3
Chichester†	1958	71	9	3
Rother Valley*	1962	–	1	1
Glasgow (Cathcart)	1963	10	4	1
Woodford	1963	85	24	3
Stratford-on-Avon†	1963	132	7	3
Croydon North-East	1963	99	16	4
Worthing	1963	130	18	3
Runcorn	1964	59	5	3
Bromley	1964	110	5	3
Erith and Crayford*	1964	70	12	3
Salisbury†	1964	50	6	6
East Grinstead†	1964	100	10	3
Farnham	1965	90	8	3
South Worcestershire	1965	85	12	4

* Labour-held constituency.   † By-election.

dates for by-elections must be selected, together with the inability of some aspirants to undertake an election campaign at short notice.

The corresponding figure for six Labour-held constituencies between 1955 and 1963 was 23·3. Only one of these, Ebbw Vale, concerned a by-election, when there were five applicants. A further two cases, Rotherham and the Rother Valley, had no applications for the vacancy and in each case a local candidate was secured by invitation rather than selection. If these three cases are excluded, the average number of applicants becomes 45, rather less than half the average for Conservative seats. None of the six constituencies offered any real chance of success to the Conservative candidate, although the Labour hold on Erith and Crayford, Paddington North, and St Pancras North is less secure than that on the remaining three. It is also curious that the most vulnerable of the six, the marginal Paddington North, should attract fewer applications than Erith and Crayford. The explanation of these differences probably lies partly in the geographical position of these constituencies and partly in the prevailing electoral atmosphere at the time of selection. The three seats which attracted a fairly large number of applicants are all situated in or near London which, whatever their electoral prospects, renders them more rather than less attractive to many candidates. Not all aspiring candidates wish to be elected, whilst others seek electoral experience before competing for a potentially successful constituency; and in such cases London constituencies have the added attraction of being especially accessible to a large number of candidates.[101] The electoral prospects of the party may also play an important part in the number of applications received for a vacancy. Paddington North selected a candidate at a time when the opinion polls were showing a substantial Labour lead; the Conservatives had lost two seats to Labour in the 'little election' of November 1962; and in two out of three of the most recent by-elections the Conservative candidate had been bottom of the poll. Thus, marginal as Paddington North was (2·7 per cent), there was every indication that Labour would retain it at the following general election. To the genuinely ambitious candidate, Paddington North was not an attractive vehicle for electoral experience, for a defeat in a marginal seat is often too close to be considered an honourable contest. For the candidate unable to secure selection for a safe seat held by his own party, constituencies like Erith and Crayford have many advantages, especially when the election is close at hand. Not only can the candidate claim an honourable defeat in which victory is publicly forecast, but privately conceded, but what greater devotion to the party cause than this to point to when, *after* the election, he seeks a candidature in a more hopeful seat? There is, furthermore, in the more fluid politics of urban London, probably a greater chance of making an inroad into the opposing majority than there is in the staunchly Labour areas of the industrial West Riding and South Wales.

Whether a constituency is Conservative-, Liberal-, or Labour-held, however, it is likely that there will be a fairly large number of applicants for any vacancy: generally a substantially higher figure than a Constituency Labour party will receive in terms of nominations.[102] Does this therefore mean that there are more people interested in becoming Conservative candidates? Does it mean that through no action on its part a local Conservative association will normally have a wider choice than its Labour counterpart?

101. See *Daily Telegraph*, 14 January 1965.   102. See Table 5(5), page 156 below.

It is impossible to make a precise comparison in either case, although some assessment of the position is possible. In absolute terms the list of approved candidates maintained by the Conservatives is much larger than the similar lists circulated by Transport House: some 700 names against 300. On the other hand, the Conservative list is weighted by the inclusion of a sizeable proportion of candidates whose availability is limited.[103] Unfortunately no data is available to estimate the extent to which Labour's lists are weighted in this way. Nevertheless, it does not seem unreasonable to suggest that there are more people interested in becoming Conservative than Labour candidates, if only because the Conservative party draws a substantial section of its support from those who have the leisure to take an active interest in politics, not to mention the necessary financial support to utilize their leisure. It is surely no accident that the two leading occupational groups among Conservative and Labour M.P.s respectively are lawyers and teachers, members of professions which provide a degree of financial security and leisure compatible with active politics.

There can, moreover, be little doubt that a local Conservative association will enjoy a much wider choice of candidates in the initial stages of selection, at least in purely numerical terms. Of course, the fact that the Labour party uses a system of nomination rather than application makes comparison difficult, but it is extremely doubtful whether the total number of persons *considered for nomination* by the affiliated and party organizations of a local Labour party is ever equal, in comparable constituencies, to the number of applications a Conservative association is likely to receive for a vacancy.[104] What is much more difficult to judge is how significant this wider numerical choice is, since the system of application inevitably allows prima facie consideration of any individual at his own request and not as the nominee of a party group. The extent to which local associations receive capricious or eccentric applications is unknown, though they certainly occur, but the figures shown in Table 2(1),[105] (which gives examples of the number of applications normally received via Central Office) suggest that such applications are very few, since Central Office is unlikely to forward those which are totally unacceptable. It may be assumed that the majority of applications forwarded by Central Office are worthy

103. See page 21 above.
104. See Part Three, Chapter 5, pages 154–7 below. Constituency Labour parties, such as Kettering, which received fifty nominations before the General Election of 1964, are exceptional.
105. See page 22 above.

of consideration by the local association, and, to this extent, the wider numerical choice is significant in that it increases rather than decreases the chances that the association will be able to select a 'suitable' candidate, by whatever criteria this is to be judged.

The majority of applications will in fact be received via Central Office, though the proportion varies considerably, as Table 2(1) illustrates. Most direct applications come from local aspirants, some of whom may not be on the list of approved candidates. The names forwarded by Central Office will come from a variety of sources: there will be those who have applied for the vacancy through Central Office; those who have asked to be considered for any, for example, Conservative-held constituency; those who have asked to be considered for constituencies in a particular area; and those whose qualifications are in accord with the type of candidate sought by the local association. This process is not entirely left to the Central Office, however: normally there will have been some discussion at constituency level, in the executive council, in the selection committee, or among the officers, of the sort of candidate they would like, and the chairman of the association, the agent, and the area agent usually go to Central Office to peruse the approved list and consult the vice-chairman. The latter, drawing upon his knowledge of the approved list, suggests the names of those he considers suitable according to the criteria laid down by the constituency representatives, but he does no more than suggest: the vice-chairman seldom, if ever, urges the consideration of a particular individual and acts in an entirely advisory capacity. The decision of whether or not to include a particular individual is left to the constituency representatives and, in fact, in recent years, far from urging the claims of persons who might be especially suitable, the vice-chairman has urged constituency representatives to adopt as few preconceived criteria as possible and to give the widest possible consideration to those on the approved list.

The criteria applied by the constituency representatives may be fairly strict: there may be a defined age range, conditions concerning marital status, electoral experience, and so on, but any really strict application of such criteria is more likely to occur at selection committee level rather than the initial consideration of the approved list. The initial stage of selection is therefore not especially arbitrary nor particularly exclusive in character: any individual can insist on being considered by means of a direct application and thereby overcome exclusion at this stage. Much will depend on the location and electoral status of the constituency: in 1958 Richmond, a safe seat near London, attracted a total of 135 applications, of which no less than 131 came via Central Office and only four direct applications were received; in the same year the much safer Hallam division of Sheffield attracted more applications, but fewer via Central Office – 140 applications were received, of which sixty were direct, though not necessarily local. Two factors were probably involved: first, safe seats near London are always in great demand for obvious reasons and Central Office has a long list of candidates hopeful of such a seat; second, the constituency representatives of Hallam may well have applied more strict criteria than those of Richmond when going through the approved list. In fact, Woodford is probably more typical in respect of direct applications, receiving nineteen out of a total of eighty-five applications: this is one of many illustrations that selection is a highly individual process, owing much to the location and circumstances in which it takes place.

The task before most selection committees is formidable: on average roughly a hundred names must be considered for a Conservative-held constituency, and half this number for Labour seats. The methods by which selection committees reduce the original number of applications to a short-list are not subject to any party rules, other than those which apply to the selection as a whole. This process is therefore subject to considerable diversity, especially in the finer points of detail.

The first meeting of the selection committee is usually devoted to procedural matters and the discussion of the criteria which are to be applied in reducing the list of applicants. In some cases the executive council will lay down extensive criteria, sometimes for the guidance, sometimes for the adherence of the selection committee. For instance, the executive council of a Midlands Conservative association agreed that the candidate should, if possible, meet six qualifications. These were: that he should undertake to live in or near the constituency; that he should be prepared to study the problems of horticulture; that he should be prepared to spend a considerable amount of time in the constituency; that he should not be too young or too old; that he should preferably be married; and that he should be either a Christian or a Jew. It was also agreed that no condition demanding the refusal of any future government or party appointment should be imposed on the candidate. Such extensive qualifications are rare, however, and, although age limits are common,[106] it is not unusual to find the selection com-

106. e.g. at Salisbury, December 1964, age limits of 35–50 were imposed – *The Times*, 19 January 1965.

mittee ignoring its own criteria to some extent, whilst many committees ignore arbitrary considerations. For instance, Richmond Conservatives expressed some preference for a candidate over forty years of age, with some parliamentary experience, but in the event chose a man of thirty-one with no parliamentary experience; whilst Hallam, in Sheffield, made no attempt to select on this basis at all. In most cases the committee will have had some discussion as to the sort of candidate required and it is likely that age and, possibly, local considerations in some constituencies, will have played the most important role at this stage.

In the many cases where the selection is occasioned by the impending retirement of the sitting Member, or in the less frequent instances where his retirement is enforced by constituency pressure,[107] the incentive to select a young candidate is strong. Similarly, in some areas, such as Birmingham and Glasgow, local pressures are considerable, whilst it is not unusual to find a candidate of ministerial stature succeeded by a local candidate.[108]

The process of drawing up a short-list normally falls into two stages: the first conducted entirely on paper in which a preliminary short-list is compiled; the second by means of interviews in which those on the preliminary short-list are seen by the selection committee, followed by the compilation of the short-list proper.

Since the first of these two stages is conducted entirely on paper, it is important to convey some idea of the information usually available to the selection committee and on which its decisions are based. The following is typical of the candidates' biographies supplied to selection committees, usually based on information supplied by Central Office:

ROBERT CHARLES SMITH, M.A. Born 1924, Married, 3 children (address)
Educated at Marlborough, New College (Oxford).
1949 First Class Honours in History at Oxford; 1951 called to the Bar.
1955 Joined . . . Ltd, Legal Department; now Company Secretary and legal advisor in . . . group of the company.
1957–61 Vice-Chairman of . . . Conservative Association.
1959–61 Chairman . . . Area P.E.C.[109] Speakers' Panel, Bow Group.

107. e.g. Glasgow (Cathcart). The sitting Member, J. Henderson, retired after nineteen members of the association had presented a motion calling for the adoption of a new candidate. Mr Henderson was seventy-five at the time.
108. e.g. Bromley, January 1964: Harold Macmillan was succeeded by J. Hunt, Mayor of Bromley; Birmingham (Hall Green), April 1965: Aubrey Jones was succeeded by R. Eyre, a local solicitor.
109. Political Education Committee.

1958–61 Member ... County Council.
Has specialized knowledge of Common Market, company law and taxation affairs.
Adopted for ... 1961.[110]

There may also be reports from the chairman of the constituency association to which the applicant belongs, from M.P.s acquainted with the applicant, from the officers of any constituency in which he may have fought local or parliamentary elections and so on. The total information available about each applicant will therefore vary, but the paragraph shown above illustrates the minimum. There is no evidence that selection committees regard the information on which they base their decisions as inadequate, and given the normal criteria on which they base their decisions, it is probably sufficient.

The method by which the selection committee deals with the applications is again subject to variation: some committees adopt a fairly rigid and formal procedure based on a systematic analysis of each applicant's qualifications; others follow the less formal procedure of going through the list on an *ad hoc* basis. A number of applicants are invariably eliminated by predetermined criteria of the type mentioned earlier. Discussion is usually extensive and the committee may be involved in a session of several hours before a short-list of those to be interviewed is drawn up.

The number of applicants likely to be interviewed is shown in Table 2(6). Apart from exceptional cases, such as Rother Valley, where selection is by invitation rather than application, the number may be as low as four or five, or it may be as high as twenty or thirty. In nineteen Conservative-held seats which selected candidates between 1955 and 1965, the average number of persons interviewed was 12·2. The figure for by-elections was lower, however, with 7·8 applicants against 13·7 for other selections. Unfortunately figures for only two Labour seats are available: St Pancras North, which interviewed twenty applicants, and Erith and Crayford, which interviewed twelve.

110. It is not uncommon for a Conservative candidate already adopted for a Labour-held seat to seek selection for a more promising constituency, e.g. the following were selected whilst already adopted for other constituencies:
  E. M. King (adopted Southampton (Itchen)) for South Dorset.
  D. B. Mitchell (adopted St Pancras North) for Basingstoke.
  C. P. Jenkin (adopted for Enfield East) for Woodford.
  J. Hunt (adopted for South Lewisham) for Bromley.
and the following *sought* selection in other constituencies:
  M. St Clair (then M.P. for Bristol South-East) short-listed for Cheltenham.
  T. Stacey (adopted Hammersmith North) short-listed for Woodford.
  D. B. Mitchell (adopted St Pancras North) short-listed for Worthing.

In percentage terms this means that, over the same period, on average 12·3 per cent of the applicants were interviewed, 10 per cent in by-elections and 13·2 per cent in other selections. The highest was Wood-ford, with 28·8 per cent of the applicants interviewed, and the lowest Bromley, with 4·5 per cent. The corresponding figures for St Pancras North and Erith and Crayford were 44·5 and 17·1 per cent. The pro-portion of applicants interviewed will, of course, depend partly on the number of applications received since the committee's capacity to interview is inevitably limited, and quite often the number interviewed is accidental in so far as the process of elimination leaves the com-mittee with five, eight, fifteen, or twenty names as the case may be. There may be some agreement to interview not more than thirty and not less than eight, for instance, but seldom is any single, rigid figure established.

This brings the committee to the second stage of its task: it must now interview the reduced number of applicants and decide upon a short-list. Again, the size of the short-list can vary, as shown in Table 2(6), and in the case of the short-list there is often a decision to limit it to a definite number, or at least to establish a maximum number. Although a number of selection committees do follow the advice of Central Office where one applicant is felt to be outstanding and recom-mend the selection of a particular individual,[111] many committees feel obliged to present the executive council with a genuine choice, how-ever strongly they may feel about a particular applicant. The short-list of one is fairly common in non-Conservative constituencies,[112] especially following an election, when the unsuccessful candidate may be re-selected.[113] It is less common in Conservative-held seats, although it is not unknown.[114]

The average short-list in forty-five constituencies which selected candidates between 1955 and 1965 was 3, but for the thirty-three Conservative-held seats it was 3·4, and for the twelve non-Conservative seats 1·9. If the two non-Conservative constituencies which recom-mended the re-adoption of defeated candidates in the 1964 General Election are excluded, the figure for non-Conservative seats is 2·1. The

111. Selection pamphlet, p. 6: '... additional names should not be submitted as a formality.' See also Final Report, Maxwell Fyfe Committee, p. 55.
112. e.g. Rotherham and the Rother Valley Constituencies, Leicester North-East and the Colne Valley, all in 1962; Paddington North, 1963.
113. e.g. Camberwell (Dulwich) and Orpington following the General Election of 1964.
114. e.g. Rutherglen, Glasgow (Cathcart) and Kidderminster, 1964, and Birmingham (Hall Green), 1965.

largest short-lists were those at Richmond in 1958, Harrow West in 1960, Chippenham in 1962, and Salisbury in 1964, all numbering six applicants. These were, however, exceptional: the agent at Richmond regarded the short-list as unusually large; the executive council at Harrow West and at Chippenham added two names to the selection committee's recommended list of four; and the selection committee at Salisbury did not regard itself as justified in distinguishing between the six applicants it had interviewed.[115]

The difference between by-elections and other selections is again reflected in the figures for short-lists: for by-elections the average short-list in by-elections, discounting any additions made by executive councils, was 3·3, against 3·2 for other selections. This is a reversal of the trend shown in the other figures, which showed that there are likely to be more applicants, a greater proportion of whom are likely to be interviewed, where the selection does not concern a by-election. The earlier figures would suggest that the speed with which a candidate often has to be selected for a by-election probably reduces the number of applicants, partly because of the inability of some aspirants to undertake immediate full-time political activity, and partly because of the shorter period during which applications may be submitted. Furthermore, the selection committee will probably have far less time in which to draw up a short-list and, therefore, less time in which to interview applicants. Nevertheless, on average, short-lists for by-elections are slightly larger than those for other selections. It may well be that the reduced time-lapse between the vacancy and the final selection and the reduced number of applicants and interviews, renders the selection committee more vulnerable to the criticism that it has omitted a worthy applicant from the short-list, or that it is seeking to promote the candidature of a particular applicant, with the result that the committee is inclined to favour a larger and more comprehensive short-list.

The interviews before the selection committee are also notable for their diversity, ranging from the formal examining board to the informal discussion group. In most cases the interview consists of a speech from the applicant, questions from the chairman of the committee, followed by further questions from the members, though not necessarily in that order. In some instances the speech is omitted, in others it occupies at least half the interview. In the more formal type of interview the chairman will ask each applicant the same questions,

115. These included three former M.P.s, two of whom were former junior Ministers, and two local men, for whom there was strong support.

usually in the same order, and the members of the committee will award marks on a predetermined basis. If a dozen or more applicants have to be interviewed, the selection committee may take as long as a week to complete the second stage of its task. When all the applicants have been seen, the committee will draw up its final short-list, although some preliminary discussion may follow each interviewing session. The actual selection of the short-list is usually made by a combination of discussion and voting. Sometimes, however, a 'natural' short-list evolves with little discussion and only a vote of endorsement.

It is at this stage in particular that either the chairman of the association, or the agent, or both, can have a profound effect on the course of the selection. According to Central Office it is the chairman's 'duty to take the initiative in securing the best possible parliamentary candidate for the Constituency',[116] and his position as *chairman of the selection committee* is conducive to the fulfilment of that duty. Potentially the chairman is very powerful, holding, as he does, the full executive authority of the association. He is, moreover, highly respected in both character and judgement. Given favourable circumstances, therefore, and the will and disposition to do so, the chairman may dominate the proceedings of the selection committee by force of character. Indeed, whether he dominates the proceedings or not, the chairman is a pivotal figure in selection, for the committee normally being a small body is especially subject to the domination of one or more of its members, and it lies within the powers of the chairman to assert his own dominant position or allow others to impose their views on the committee.

The agent is in a less powerful position since he does not hold the advantage of the chair, but he represents a continuity of experience which many of the other members of the committee will lack, which places him at some advantage. His advice and influence may be considerable and he may occasionally have a decisive influence. Much will depend, however, on the attitude adopted by other members of the committee towards the agent: in some constituencies the agent is regarded strictly as an employee, albeit loyal and dedicated, but an employee none the less, and therefore someone rather less than an equal. This is partly reflected in the non-voting capacity usually accorded to the agent as a member of the selection committee. Occasionally, the agent is treated as a full member of the committee, although this does not necessarily indicate any substantial influence on the part of the agent, for, as with the chairman, much depends on his character.

116. Organization Series, *Duties of Officers* (revised February 1958), p. 3.

The meetings of the selection committee are also attended by a third person of considerable potential influence and, for that matter, often the subject of considerable misunderstanding. This is the Central Office agent for the area in which the constituency lies. In spite of the fact that his role is almost entirely procedural and only occasionally advisory, the area agent is often the subject of speculation: 'The interest taken by Central Office in the choice of candidate was indicated by the presence ... of ... [the] Central Office area political agent.'[117] In fact, the area agent seldom takes any active part in the deliberations of the selection committee, and then only to advise on procedural matters, such as the timetable for the selection, the powers of the selection committee and so on. He also ensures that the 'simple Party rules' are observed, though it is doubtful whether his presence is necessary for this purpose. Very occasionally his advice and views on a particular applicant will be asked, but the area agent usually limits his comments to factual matters and refuses to offer any advice.

Once the short-list has been compiled the selection committee's task is finished and the executive council becomes the focal point of the selection. The executive council, if it wishes, alters the short-list recommended by the selection committee. The council has the right to reject the short-list entirely[118] or it may amend it, usually by the addition of further names. Outright rejection of the short-list is very rare and there has been no instance in recent years. Additions to the short-list are more common, however, and there have been at least three cases of this happening since 1960. In September 1960 the executive council of Harrow West Conservative Association added two names, one of whom was a vice-chairman of the association, to the recommended short-list of four.[119] Similarly, in August 1962, the executive council of Chippenham Conservative Association added two names to the short-list, one a former mayor of Chippenham and the other a member of a well-known county family.[120] Finally, in January 1965, the executive council of the Kemp Town division of Brighton overruled its selection committee and added the names of two former M.P.s for the seat to the short-list.[121] Each of the three cases is marked by a common factor in that the additions to the short-list always involved local applicants or applicants with local connections. As will be seen in due course, the presence of one or more local applicants is a

117. *Daily Telegraph*, 11 December 1964.   118. Selection pamphlet, p. 9.
119. *The Times*, 15 September 1960.   120. *Sunday Times*, 19 August 1962.
121. *Daily Telegraph*, 30 January 1965.

factor common to the majority of disputes in local associations over the selection of a candidate.

The short-list having been agreed, however, all that remains is for the executive council to make a final choice of candidate, subject only to the approval of a general meeting of the association. The manner in which the executive council makes this choice is probably the stage of Conservative selection procedure which is subject to least variation. Each applicant on the short-list is invited to address the executive council for a specified period, and this is followed by questions from the council. This same procedure applies whether the short-list consists of one or several applicants, and any variations within this general practice concern the length of time each applicant is allowed and the subject-matter of his address. The total period allowed to each candidate is rarely less than twenty minutes, and thirty minutes is the most common period. The division of this period between the applicant's speech and questions from the council does vary, however. In some cases the applicants are strictly limited to a specified period, followed by a similarly limited period of questions; in other cases only the total period granted to each applicant is strictly limited. As far as the subject-matter of the speeches is concerned, practice again varies: in some cases each applicant must speak on a predetermined subject, in others each applicant may speak on a subject of his own choice. Similarly with questions: the chairman may ask each applicant a series of predetermined questions, followed by further questions from the floor, or all the questions may come from the floor.

Most speeches are political in content, with a leaven of personal references, and the same may be said of questions, although the latter are subject to considerable variation, of course.

A most important feature of Conservative selection procedure, a feature peculiar to the Conservative party, is the attention paid to the wives of aspiring candidates and, where applicable, to the husbands of women applicants. It is customary for the wives of applicants to be invited to attend the meeting of the executive council and to be present with their husbands on the platform. Furthermore, it is also customary for the wives of applicants to be invited to attend the interview before the selection committee. In neither instance is this simply a gesture of courtesy on the part of the association, for, although a wife is seldom invited to address either the selection committee or the council, she may be asked questions. It should be stressed that this is a feature which is not found in the Labour party, with the possible exception of the formal adoption meeting, when the candidate's wife is often invited out of courtesy. The importance of this feature of Conservative selection will be dealt with in the ensuing chapters.

The members of the council will have before them the same information concerning each applicant as the selection committee. This information is invariably circulated beforehand to enable the members of the council to make some preliminary assessment of the applicants. It is intended, of course, that the final assessment should be made of the performance of the applicants when they appear before the council.

Inevitably there is often a certain amount of pre-judgement of the issue, and some members may attend the council having previously determined to support a particular applicant, or, at least, not to support another. Occasionally this may take the form of active canvassing for or against a particular applicant, but canvassing is unusual and is largely obviated by the non-federative basis of local associations. There is one exception to this and that is where a strongly supported local applicant is involved and it is doubtful whether any change in procedure could prevent this.

Once all the applicants have appeared before the council, one of two courses is followed: the council may move immediately to the vote, or there may be some discussion of the relative merits of the applicants. Occasionally members of the council will attempt to elicit support for or against particular applicants by asking the chairman leading questions, such as: 'Would the Chairman confirm that Mr X will be in a position to devote enough time to the constituency in view of his business commitments?' or, 'Would the chairman confirm that Mr Y was not at his best this evening?' The chairman may simply parry such questions or he may throw open the meeting to a further discussion. If there is any discussion it is likely to be wide-ranging and sometimes lengthy.

Apart from those cases where there is only one applicant on the short-list, in which case the vote is simply a matter of granting or withholding approval, or where there are only two applicants, an exhaustive ballot is held. In the event of a tie the chairman has a casting vote.[122] Following the emergence of an applicant with an absolute majority, a further, preferably unanimous vote is taken as a sign of the council's approval of the selection and support for the candidate. It is, of course, unusual for this vote to be anything other than unanimous.

There is no endorsement of the selection at national level and the

122. cf. Labour party procedure, Part Three, Chapter 5, page 160 below.

candidate merely receives the usual letter of support from the party leader during the actual election campaign. The selection procedure is not completed with the decision of the executive council, however, since 'any person recommended as prospective Candidate by the Executive Council must be presented to a General Meeting of the Association for Adoption'.[123] In the case of by-elections there is only one general meeting, but in other selections there are two, the first shortly after the council meeting and the second at the beginning of the actual election campaign.

In the majority of selections, the general meeting is a formality, a local party rally of the faithful and a semi-public[124] demonstration of support. The extent to which the general meeting may *normally* be regarded as a formality is demonstrated by the adoption meeting of Stratford-upon-Avon Conservative Association in August 1963, at which the recommended candidate, Angus Maude, used the phrase 'If you adopt me . . .' no less than ten times, although at the end of the meeting members were handed printed posters urging electors to 'Vote for Maude'. There was a greater element of formality in the adoption of R. G. Cooke by Bristol West Conservative Association in February 1957: the candidate was actually adopted in his absence by the general meeting.[125] These were, of course, by-elections, and the meetings were held on the eve of the campaign and any indication of lack or partial lack of confidence by the local association would have been at best an embarrassment, at worst a disaster. This would also apply, however, though possibly to a lesser degree, to a selection which did not involve a by-election. Nevertheless, though normally a formality, the general meeting gives the members of the association the ultimate power over selection, the power, moreover, not only of rejection but of substitution. In other words, the general meeting possesses more than the negative power of veto, for it may elect a candidate other than the person recommended by the executive council, and, though opposition to the latter's choice is infrequent, there have been several cases during the past decade or so. Just as opposition at the general meeting to the council's choice is unusual, however, so *successful opposition* to that choice is correspondingly rare.

In eight constituencies between 1952 and 1963 in which there was

---

123. Model Rules 21(1)(c). The candidate will then be known as *prospective* Conservative candidate. The term 'prospective' is assumed in order to avoid legal election expenses between the time of adoption and the beginning of the election campaign.
124. The press are often invited to attend these meetings.
125. *The Times*, 16 February 1967. The candidate was ill at the time.

opposition at the general meeting to the recommendation of the council, only two resulted in any change of candidate. The first, at Southport in 1952, resulted in the selection of one local man for another,[126] and the second, at Birmingham (Edgbaston) in 1953, resulted in the rejection of a non-local and the substitution of a local candidate.[127] Both cases involved local candidates, and the same is true of the six unsuccessful attempts to oppose the council's choice.[128] The view that the majority of disputes within a local association over the selection of a candidate concern the claims of one or more local candidates is further supported not only by the three cases mentioned above in which local applicants were added to the short-list, but in a number of disputes which have involved the threat of an Independent Conservative candidate at the ensuing election, or the resignation of members of the selection committee or executive council. For instance, at Newcastle North in 1951[129] and Crosby in 1953[130] the local associations were faced with the threat of Independent Conservative candidates; whilst at Southend West in 1959, a member of the selection committee resigned over the selection of Paul Channon, whose family had supplied the division's M.P. since 1912, and at Warrington, in 1963, three members of the executive council resigned in protest over the failure to select a local candidate.[131]

In the normal course of events, however, the successful applicant will be formally adopted by the association at the general meeting, subject only, if it is not a by-election, to a further adoption meeting at the outset of the election campaign. If he is defeated in the election, his candidature is automatically cancelled, although his re-adoption may be recommended.[132] If he is elected he will normally remain M.P. until defeat, death, retirement, or resignation intervenes, subject to a formal re-adoption before each general election. In practice, however, his position as M.P. is somewhat more vulnerable: constituency pressure may informally urge the retirement of the Member or persuade him to

126. See *The Times*, 15 January 1952.

127. See *The Times*, 10, 11, 12, and 13 June 1953.

128. These were: Beckenham, March 1957; Newcastle North, March 1957; Chichester, October 1958; Caithness and Sutherland, April 1961; Cheltenham, February 1962; Solihull, August 1963.

129. Richards, op. cit., p. 21. The Independent Conservative lost his deposit at the General Election of 1951.

130. *The Times*, 15 October 1953. The Independent Conservative later withdrew.

131. *Daily Telegraph*, 12 January 1959 and 6 November 1963. Some constituencies always seem to have disputed selections, e.g. Newcastle North, 1951 and 1957; Caithness and Sutherland, 1948 and 1961.

132. e.g. Camberwell (Dulwich), November 1964; Orpington, December 1964.

submit his resignation, or, failing this, formal pressure may be brought to bear in the direct form of a demand for his resignation or in the indirect form of open criticism or lack of confidence. The ultimate power possessed by the association is, of course, the refusal to re-adopt. Although disputes between M.P.s and their associations and threats to their candidature are by no means uncommon, the use of this power is limited in practice. Even the Suez cases did not result in more than four M.P.s resigning or losing their seats, although at least ten were involved in disputes with the associations over their anti-Suez attitudes.[133] Since 1960 there have been only two cases in which constituency pressure resulted in the rejection of the M.P. These were at Glasgow (Cathcart), where the sitting M.P. withdrew after the association's executive had passed a resolution demanding his retirement, and Carlisle, where the association refused to re-adopt the M.P. after he had criticized the then Prime Minister, Harold Macmillan. These disputes were two among many – at least a dozen since 1960, the majority of which have been settled without recourse to this ultimate power. The disputes ranged over such a variety of issues – Patrick Wolrige-Gordon and his association with M.R.A.; Anthony Fell and his attitude towards the Common Market; Charles Fletcher-Cooke's involvement in a court case; S. Knox Cunningham's alleged neglect of his constituency; and Iain Macleod's refusal to serve under Sir Alec Douglas-Home, to name but a few – that they have little in common. There is no indication that the bitter and prolonged dispute at Bournemouth East and Christchurch has reduced the number of disputes, though it may have done something to temper the militancy of local associations in their determination to press their view to the point of a final break with the M.P.

The results of the disputes are less important than the fact that they occur in the form of threats to disown the M.P. and, though the result may depend on the circumstances peculiar to the M.P., the association, and the constituency, thereby demonstrate the power which the local association has over selection. Not only are local associations constitutionally independent of the Central Office and the National Union, but they are liable to exert their independence whenever the opportunity presents itself and the selection of candidates is a sphere which lends itself admirably to this. The rules or guide-lines which Central Office lays down for the selection of candidates are honoured by local associations not because they are enforceable, but because they are

133. See Epstein, op. cit., pp. 377–80.

acceptable. Ostensibly, selection is an open process, subject to only a few 'simple Party rules': anyone may apply to be considered for a vacancy;[134] a large number of applications are likely to be received and the association's numerical choice is likely to be wide; the method of selection is exhaustive and each stage except the last is subject to endorsement by a higher body. The whole process of selection is designed to ensure that an association makes 'its choice of candidate on merit alone and from the widest possible field',[135] but much depends in practice on the attitude of the selectors on whom the working of the machinery depends.

In most cases the selectors will work within the framework already outlined, but occasionally a constituency association will introduce an important variant. Such a case was the Kemptown division of Brighton, which left the final choice from the short-list to a general meeting of the association, the executive council having previously approved the report of the selection committee, though adding two names to the short-list. This meant that the choice from the short-list was made by 1,000 members of the association instead of the fifty-one members of the executive council. Variations of this sort are largely an indication of the freedom which the local association may adopt towards selecting a candidate, however, and do not usually produce any radical effect on the selection. The machinery of selection establishes the framework within which the selectors work, within which their attitudes become crucial as factors which may not only influence but also determine the selection.

134. There are no membership qualifications – vide the selection of Jimmy Edwards for Paddington North – *Daily Telegraph*, 12 March 1963.
135. Selection pamphlet, p. 2.

CHAPTER THREE

The Factors which Influence Selection

Introduction

The selection of Conservative parliamentary candidates is affected by a large number and considerable variety of factors. Each selection tends to be unique in certain respects and to that extent unpredictable: not all selections are affected by the same factors, whilst what is important in one selection may be insignificant in another. It is possible, however, to suggest the sort of considerations the selectors are likely to take into account and to posit a contextual framework within which selection takes place.

Before dealing with the factors which influence selection, however, a brief description of the time normally devoted to the selection of a candidate is necessary. As with many aspects of Conservative selection this varies widely from association to association. Where the vacancy has been caused by an impending by-election the process can be as short as a month, or even less in the case of a sudden general election. Where there is less urgency, however, selection may be extended over six to eight weeks. In a few instances it may even be a period of three or more months, especially where a general election is unlikely for three or four years and there is no pressure to select immediately. A fairly extended selection process is usually facilitated by the fact that Conservative M.P.s usually give their associations ample notice of their intention to retire. Following the General Election of 1964, for instance, when the close result suggested that a second election might follow within eighteen months, a number of older Conservative M.P.s announced that they would retire at the end of the current Parliament.[1]

1. e.g. Sir G. Nicholson (Farnham), December 1964; Sir H. Studholme (Tavistock), January 1965; R. Spier (Hexham), January 1965; Sir J. Maitland (Horncastle), March 1965.

These announcements were quickly followed by the selection of new candidates.

Most associations, therefore, have a good deal of time in which to select a candidate, and although the work of the selection committee itself is likely to be intensive, often involving a number of long meetings over several weeks, the process as a whole is fairly leisurely. Generally speaking, careful consideration will be given to the type of candidate required and every effort will be made to ensure that an effective candidate is eventually chosen.

Opinions differ, of course, as to what constitutes an effective candidate: clearly, speaking ability, political knowledge and experience, possibly expertise in other fields, ability to identify with the locality, ambition, to name but a few, will to varying degrees be requisites of selection. The selectors will be presented with a combination of personality and ability, neither of which is easy to define. Psychologically it is possible to define various types of personality, but few selectors think in psychological terms: personality is seen as the ability on the part of the applicant to present a favourable and attractive public image; it is spoken of in terms such as 'warm', 'human', or 'sympathetic', 'forceful', 'dominant', or 'imaginative'. In the early stages of selection, when the paper qualifications of applicants are considered, personality cannot be taken into consideration, except where an applicant is already known to the selectors, but it may be crucial in the later stages.

Inevitably ability is also treated in an impressionistic fashion, at least in part. Educational qualifications obviously play an important role since they act as a prima facie indication of ability. Well over two thirds of the candidates selected by incumbent associations between 1950 and 1966, and over half of those selected by non-incumbent associations, were university graduates. Conversely, less than 2 per cent of the former and less than 4 per cent of the latter had had only an elementary education. Beyond this, however, ability is almost impossible to define when applied to the selection of candidates: assessments of ability of various applicants are obviously highly subjective and often inextricably linked with equally subjective assessments of personality. It is therefore difficult to show that ability is a prime consideration in selection – in practice it cannot be entirely ignored since the selectors must judge the capacity of the applicants to fulfil the role envisaged for them, whether it be that of candidate or of M.P. The fact that the selectors will apply criteria other than ability means that the matter becomes a question of *suitability*; and it is the factors which render an applicant suitable for selection as a Parliamentary candidate that must now be discussed.

Probably the most fundamental factor in the selection of Conservative candidates is the dichotomy between incumbent and non-incumbent associations. The two-party system in Britain is dependent upon the mass organizations of the two major parties and upon the capacity of those organizations to mount sustained campaigns against one another. An integral part of this process is the parliamentary candidate: in the seats held by the party he is defending an established or inherited position; in those held by its rival he seeks to challenge such a position. The first is normally a long-term relationship, the second normally short-term. The factors which determine the selection of the potential M.P. and those which determine the selection of a candidate are based upon these assumptions. P. W. Buck has calculated that between 1918 and 1955 the Conservative and Labour parties were responsible for 4,302 candidatures, of which 2,443 involved candidates who were *never successful*.[2] Some of these candidates may have aspired to a political career, but the majority were the parties' 'standard-bearers', whose success was at best unlikely, at worst unattainable. That these candidates should differ from their more successful colleagues is not therefore surprising.

Only 20 per cent of the candidates selected by non-incumbent associations in the General Election of 1951 were subsequently elected between then and 1966, *including* all the Conservative gains in the period 1951–9. The personal characteristics of these candidates were, in fact, closer to those of the candidates selected by incumbent associations over the same period: they showed a *higher* incidence in the proportions of public school men, graduates in general and Oxbridge graduates in particular, and a *lower* incidence in the proportions with local government experience and local connections. Table 3(1) illustrates the contrast between those selected by incumbent and non-incumbent associations.

The contrast between incumbent and non-incumbent associations shown in Table 3(1) is sharp, and is not confined to the fact that the vast majority of those selected by non-incumbent associations were defeated. It is true that there still exists among the non-Conservative constituencies a preference for graduates and those with a public school education, but neither preference is overwhelming and the Oxbridge and Clarendon candidates are now a distinct minority. Furthermore,

2. Buck, op. cit., pp. 84–5.

Table 3(1): *Comparison of the characteristics of candidates selected by incumbent and non-incumbent Conservative associations, 1950–66**

Characteristic	Incumbent associations	Non-incumbent associations
Previous electoral experience	64·2	41·3
Under forty	44·3	54·9
Public school education	78·0	53·9
Clarendon schools	37·6	15·1
University graduates	69·9	52·1
Oxbridge graduates	54·6	28·9
Local connections	62·8	79·4
Local government experience	34·1	37·3

NOTE: For definitions of the above characteristics, see Appendix A.
   * Expressed as percentages of the total number of candidates.

local connections and local government experience are much more in evidence than among the successful candidates. These trends point to the factors which influence the selection of candidates in non-Conservative constituencies. Only in those marginal seats which the party can legitimately hope to win at the next election can the selectors act on the assumption that they may be selecting an M.P. In all other non-Conservative constituencies the selectors know that they are selecting a 'standard-bearer' and their decisions are governed by this fact. It is therefore necessary to examine separately the factors which influence selection by incumbent associations on the one hand, and non-incumbent associations on the other.

Selection by the Incumbent Association: the Selection of the Potential M.P.

It is quite clear that associations in Conservative-held constituencies select their candidates on the assumption that they are choosing an M.P.: the speeches of all the participants in selection meetings, officers, members, and applicants, act on this assumption. In the case of marginal seats they may be wrong, but only a third of the seats are marginal or semi-marginal and two thirds of the associations in Conservative seats can normally be certain that the person they select will become an M.P. This fact does not normally alter the selection procedure, but it has a profound effect on the factors which determine the association's choice of candidate. Various factors affect or are thought to affect that choice: female or anti-female prejudice, religion, previous electoral experience, age, local connections, local government service, occupation, education, whether the selection is for a general or by-election, and, perhaps above all, the type of constituency concerned. It is proposed that each of these should be examined in turn, finally examining the links between the characteristics of the candidates and those of the constituencies which select them.

Women and Selection

It is well known that the Conservative party depends heavily on women for its voluntary workers,[3] and it is equally well known that the number of women Conservative candidates is very small. Of the 282 candidates selected by incumbent associations between 1950 and 1966, only eleven (3·9 per cent) were women. The position was only a little better among the non-incumbent associations: only eighty-eight (5·6 per cent) out of a total of 1,568 were women.[4] This raises two questions: first, to what extent is there a *general* prejudice against women? And second, to what extent is this the result of an anti-female prejudice among women members of Conservative associations?

To take the second question first, Table 3(2) shows that, in each of the selected constituencies, women constituted at least half the membership of the association. In the case of the executive councils, however, only four of the nine associations possessed councils with 50 per cent or more women members, whilst in the case of selection committees, only one, Salisbury, had as many as 50 per cent women members. Similarly, an investigation of the sex of office-holders provides further evidence of male dominance of positions of importance: the more important the office the more likely it is to be held by a man. In 1964 nine of the fifteen branches of Exeter Conservative Association, for example, had male chairmen, against five female chairmen, with one post vacant. The post of branch secretary, however, is more likely to be held by a woman: with two vacant posts, eight of Exeter's branches had female secretaries, five had male secretaries. Association offices are even less likely to be held by women: in 1950 all twelve members of the finance and general purposes committee of Banbury Conservative Association

3. See Selwyn Lloyd Report, p. 4.
4. The corresponding figures for Labour were six (3·2 per cent) out of 187 candidates selected by incumbent constituency Labour parties; and 113 (6·6 per cent) out of 1,723 candidates selected by non-incumbent constituency Labour parties.

Table 3(2): *Proportion of women members in selected Conservative associations and on bodies concerned with selection*

Constituency	In association %	Number/proportion of women On Executive Council	On selection committee
Croydon North-East	50	13 out of 36	3 out of 9
Erith and Crayford	50	22 out of 44	3 out of 7
Richmond	50	28 out of 56	2 out of 11
Stratford-upon-Avon	55	32 out of 88	2 out of 12
Worthing	60–65	29 out of 60	4 out of 9
Woodford	50	22 out of 77	3 out of 9
Salisbury	60	45 out of 90	20 out of 40
Sheffield (Hallam)	66	28 out of 85	10 out of 21
South Worcestershire	55	100 out of 182	12 out of 28

were men;[5] and of a random group of twenty-four associations five had female secretaries, and only two female chairmen. Given that the associations cited are fairly typical there is every reason to believe that women do not assert the dominance, nor the influence, to which their numerical strength invariably entitles them.

The reason is not difficult to find and may, indirectly, have some bearing on the general Conservative attitude towards women candidates. As one agent put it:

... generally speaking, the men tend to take control in matters of importance within the Association with the full concurrence of the women. ... The women play a most important part in the Association – in fact we could not possibly get on without them, but they are a little *reluctant in most cases to take decisions of vital importance*.[6]

In numerical terms at least it is in the selection committee that female applicants are least likely to encounter opposition from members of their own sex. In fact, the same is probably true in other respects: the female members of selection committees attended by the author were not notable for any special degree of influence in determining the course of the selections. The women tended to take little part in the delibera-

5. M. Stacey, *Tradition and Change, a Study of Banbury*, London, 1960, p. 44.
6. Letter from a constituency agent. (Author's italics.)

tions of the committees and the preference for men owed far more to the influence of the male members of the committees. Most if not all the constituencies listed in Table 3(2) received applications from women and yet in only one case, Croydon North-East, did any of these applications survive the selection committee stage and result in a woman being placed on the short-list. At executive council level, therefore, where female influence is likely to be proportionately larger than on the selection committee, more often than not the women members of the council have no opportunity to express any anti-female attitude they may possess, simply because there is no woman on the short-list.

It is significant that one of the recommendations of the Selwyn Lloyd Report was that one of the women applicants for any vacancy should be placed on the short-list.[7] This recommendation could only have resulted from the observation not only that relatively few women were selected, but that most short-lists ignored women applicants, the responsibility for which must be laid at the feet of selection committees. There is, moreover, no reason to believe that this is due to female rather than male influence. Nevertheless, the tiny proportion of women selected, especially among successful candidates, would suggest that prejudice against women exists and, furthermore, that this prejudice is general and not especially confined to women members of Conservative associations.

The extent of this prejudice can be gauged by a comparison of the proportion of women on the list of approved candidates and the proportion of women selected. According to the vice-chairman of the party, approximately 10 per cent of the persons who apply to be placed on the list of approved candidates are women, and that approximately 10 per cent of those placed on the list are women.[8] These figures suggest that there is little or no prejudice against women at national level and that it is largely a question of supply. This means that in the General Elections of 1964 and 1966 less than half the available proportion of women candidates were selected: excluding sitting Members, in both elections less than 4 per cent of the Conservative candidates were women.

7. Selwyn Lloyd Report, p. 34.
8. This is confirmed by a newspaper report, following the reconstruction of the approved list, which stated that women formed 'less than ten per cent of the current total' – *Daily Telegraph*, 14 January 1965. See also the appeal for more women M.P.s and candidates by Geoffrey Johnson Smith (vice-chairman of the Party Organization) – Central Office Press Release 9801, 10 December 1965.

The failure of the Conservative party to select more women candidates appears to be the result of two factors: the adherence to the rather vague notion that being an M.P. or candidate, especially the former, is a man's job; and a general preference for married men. This first factor is seldom openly expressed and it is never laid down as a preliminary condition of selection, but it certainly exists. The feeling that success in some sphere other than politics is an important qualification is strong, and this militates against women in general and married women in particular. A successful career in business or one of the professions is invariably a precondition of selection and marriage and housewifery do not fall into this category. This is reflected in the number of single women selected for Conservative-held constituencies: of the eleven women selected seven were single at the time of their selection.[9] Single women are far more likely to fulfil the condition of a successful career, and, moreover, do not have the family commitments of married women.

At selection meetings the married woman is always confronted with enquiries concerning the amount of time she can devote to a political career, whereas men and single women are regarded as free agents. This is emphasized in the difference between female successful and unsuccessful candidates: of the sixteen unsuccessful women candidates in 1959 only five were unmarried – an almost complete reversal of the position among successful candidates. The reason is clear enough: Conservative-held seats are fully conscious of the fact that they are selecting at best an M.P., at worst a potential M.P., whereas associations in non-Conservative seats are selecting at best a potential M.P., at worst a candidate. In the former the selection process is usually the beginning of a fairly long association between selectors and selected, between candidate and association, and between M.P. and constituency; but in the latter it is essentially a short-term relationship in all but the most favourable of seats. Where the candidate is little more than a standard-bearer for the party colours the question of availability does not arise, since *all* candidates must be and are available during the actual election campaign, but the M.P. must be generally available so long as he or she remains an M.P. and in this respect married women are often at a disadvantage.

If Conservative politics is a man's world, however, it is largely a married man's world, for no less than 81·2 per cent (220) of the male candidates selected by incumbents between 1950 and 1966 were

9. One, Miss M. B. H. Anderson, subsequently married.

married and only 18·8 per cent (51) were single or divorced at the time of their selection. This figure of 81·2 per cent is slightly higher than the proportion of married men found in Social Classes I and II (from which the majority of Conservative M.P.s are drawn), where the figure was 79·9 per cent.[10] Generally speaking, of course, married men tend to be older than single men, but this does not mean that there is a bias against younger candidates: to be married is normally an advantage in Conservative selections, but to be single and of *marriageable age* is no disadvantage. More than two thirds of the single candidates were under the age of forty, against little more than two fifths of the married candidates. Conversely, only a twelfth of the single candidates were over fifty, but over a fifth of the married candidates. The young single candidate may well be asked whether he is contemplating marriage and, whilst such inquiries are normally made in the privacy of the selection committee, the author knows of at least two cases where such a question was put to the candidate at the executive council meeting. It may not be a coincidence that approximately half the single candidates selected over the period subsequently married. If the previous figures are adjusted to allow for this factor – the subsequent marriage of single candidates – it means that just over 10 per cent of the candidates selected by incumbent associations remained unmarried.

In the eyes of Conservative selectors the advantage that the married man has over his single rival is simply that he has a wife: in the words of the chairman of Accrington Conservative Association, 'We mean to win, and we feel a *husband-and-wife team* is needed. . . .'[11] The M.P.'s wife is expected to be an asset to the association and to the constituency. She must support her husband on the platform, at the bazaar, grace the coffee morning and the soirée by her presence and, those functions which he cannot or will not attend, she must:

> The M.P.'s wife is the opener. The pillar of local society, the miraculous provider of clothes for refugees, seaside holidays for handicapped children and comforts for hospital patients . . . the M.P.'s wife moves in four different orbits: in the constituency, in the home, in the House, and in the public eye.[12]

In many respects the role of the M.P.'s wife is comparable to that of the mayoress in local government, who may act as a substitute for her

10. Based on the One Per Cent Sample Tables of the 1951 Census.
11. Quoted *Daily Express*, 26 May 1965. (Author's italics.)
12. Lucille Iremonger, *And His Charming Lady*, London, 1961, p. 12. See also Jean Mann, *Woman in Parliament*, London, 1962, p. 47.

husband in many of the social functions attached to his office. Conservative associations are essentially social as well as political entities, especially during inter-election periods, when the M.P.'s wife can perform the not unimportant role of social and public relations officer between her husband and the association.[13] As it was aptly, though perhaps cruelly put, by one association chairman: 'All you have to do is to tell them how much your husband loves them!'

The married woman is at a distinct disadvantage in these circumstances since it is extremely doubtful whether her husband is either suitable or willing to fulfil the part normally played by the M.P.'s wife. Single candidates, whether men or women, are somewhat less at a disadvantage: they do not have the advantage of a wife, but they do not have the disadvantage of a husband. Not only, therefore, will the selection committee wish to know whether an applicant is married or not, but it will usually wish to interview the wives of applicants. Similarly, the wives of those on the short-list are normally invited to attend the executive council meeting. The selectors are not interested in the political views of applicant's wives (it is assumed that they agree with their husbands) and political questions are never directed at them. The questions at both selection committee and executive council level are functional: is the applicant's wife willing to help with canvassing? Is she willing to accompany her husband to constituency and association functions? Will she attend coffee mornings? Will she take an active interest in the women's branches . . . the Young Conservatives and so on? Will her family commitments enable her to fulfil these demands? These are all typical questions and a wife can affect her husband's chances of selection if she fails to satisfy the selectors.

No applicant is chosen solely because, or even substantially because, he has an attractive wife capable of meeting constituency demands, but the choice between two otherwise equally divided applicants may centre on their respective wives. One matter is quite certain: always at selection committee level, and occasionally at the executive council, the merits of applicants' wives are openly discussed, often at length. The short-list may, therefore, be radically affected by this factor and it may occasionally impinge on the final choice of candidate.[14]

13. This applies equally to Scotland: 'All candidates for interview should be given details of what they are expected to do e.g. *bring wives* . . .' – *Notes for Guidance in the Selection of Candidates,* Unionist Party, Office of the Chairman, January 1965. (Author's italics.)

14. See Chapter Four below.

To be married is normally an advantage; to be divorced is almost certainly a disadvantage. This may, in part, be a reflection of the preference for married men, but its origin is basically religious. The majority of associations tacitly or specifically stipulate that the candidate should be a Christian, although occasional concessions are made to members of the Jewish faith. The term Christian does not necessarily preclude the selection of a divorcee, but it does signify a potential source of opposition towards anyone who has been in any way involved in a divorce. This opposition is likely to be greatest among the women members of the association: if any attempt is made to raise the question of divorce among one or more of the applicants, it is almost always by a woman. It is doubtful, however, whether an applicant would be rejected on the grounds of divorce alone: as with applicants' wives it is one of many factors which may affect his chances of selection, although it could be vital in the final stages of short-listing or in the final choice of candidate.

Some impression of the importance of divorce in selection can be gained from an examination of the incidence of divorce among the Conservative candidates elected between 1950 and 1966. As far as can be ascertained eight candidates were divorced and a further two had married divorcees *before* their selection. Compared with this, at least fourteen Conservative M.P.s secured divorces over the same period and another married a divorcee; and it is some indication of the attitude of many local associations towards divorce that probably half of these Members were under some pressure to resign as a result of their divorces. In 1965, for instance, the Accrington Conservative Association refused to re-select Victor Montague,[15] its defeated candidate of 1964, 'because we feel the *split in marriage* could give the other side ammunition at the next election'.[16] Similarly, the author knows of one case where the family of an applicant's divorced wife were asked whether they objected to him being short-listed. In the event they did not, but consultation did occur because the local association thought it in the best interests of all concerned. Placed in context divorce is probably one of a number of weapons (and one of the most unpleasant) used by an active minority to exclude a particular applicant, which as a factor in selection is far less important than either sex or marriage.

15. Formerly the Earl of Sandwich and Viscount Hinchinbrooke, M.P. for South Dorset, 1941–62.
16. The chairman of the Accrington Conservative Association, quoted *Daily Express*, 26 May 1965.

The Influence of Religion

The Central Office pamphlet on the selection of candidates contains the following small paragraph on religion:

> The candidate's religion is not stated on the biography supplied by Central Office. This information can, however, be obtained by application by the Constituency Chairman or Chairman of the Selection Committee, if required. *Religious prejudices should in no circumstances be allowed to sway the judgement of the Selection Committee.*[17]

It may be taken, of course, that this stricture also applies to the executive council and to the selection procedure in general. Conclusive evidence of religious prejudice is always difficult to find. No Scottish constituency has ever selected a Catholic Conservative candidate: is this the result of direct prejudice on the part of Unionist associations? Or is it a case of indirect prejudice resulting from a disinclination on the part of Scottish Catholics to seek selection for a Protestant constituency? The same may apply to Northern Ireland: how many Scottish Unionists or Ulster Unionists are Catholics?

Table 3(3) shows that there is a rough correspondence between the distribution of the Catholic population and the distribution of Catholic Conservative M.P.s, with, of course, the notable exceptions of Scotland and Northern Ireland. The extent to which these figures are significant, however, is difficult to say: it is doubtful, for instance, whether the selection of Catholic candidates in the Midlands, the north-east, and eastern England can be attributed to specific Catholic influence, but the same is not necessarily true of the north-west and southern England. In 1963 the north-west had only two Catholic M.P.s, but immediately after the 1959 General Election there were four.[18] In 1950 there were no Catholic Conservatives in the north-west, but there was one in 1951, two in 1955, and four in 1959.

Similarly, in the south, there were only two Catholics in 1950 and 1951, but four in 1955 and six in 1959. There is, however, no evidence to show whether this is accidental or the result of a concerted effort by Catholic interests. What is certainly significant is that the overall

17. Selection pamphlet, p. 8. (Author's italics.) According to Humphrey Berkeley, former Conservative M.P. for Lancaster and a Catholic, before 1962 information concerning the religion of applicants was freely circulated by Central Office. This conflicts with the Central Office pamphlet quoted above, which is dated *July 1960*. Berkeley claims that in 1959 he sought to have this information withheld, but without success. See 'Catholics in English Politics', *Wiseman Review* (Spring 1962), p. 307.

18. H. Berkeley (Lancaster), R. Grant-Ferris (Nantwich), P. I. Bell (Bolton East), appointed a recorder in 1960, and J. Watts (Manchester—Moss Side), who died in 1961.

Table 3(3): *Distribution of Catholic M.P.s in the Conservative party compared with distribution of Catholic population, 1963*

Region	Number of M.P.s	Catholic population*
North-west	2	1,180,000
Home counties and south	6†	1,126,000
Scotland	–	790,000
Northern Ireland	–	498,000
Midlands	1	407,000
North-east	2	363,000
Yorkshire (West Riding)	–	250,000
Western	–	139,000
Eastern	1	132,000
Wales	–	128,000

* *Catholic Directory*, 1963.
† Excluding A. G. Brown, formerly Labour M.P. for Tottenham, who took the Conservative whip in 1962.

Catholic representation in the Conservative party has more than doubled and between 1950 and 1959 it almost trebled. In 1950 there were only five Catholic Conservative M.P.s; by 1959 this number had risen to fourteen, falling to twelve by 1962. This may be the result of Catholic pressure, but whether it is or not it clearly represents a weakening of any anti-Catholic prejudice that exists in the Conservative party.

Christopher Hollis, a Catholic and former Conservative M.P., asserts that religious prejudice does exist in the Conservative party, and not only in Scotland and Northern Ireland:

I do know of Catholics of ability who have had to go cap in hand to an inordinately large number of constituencies before they have been able to get one to adopt them. I know of one Jew whose qualifications are quite outstanding but who in spite of this has never been able to get a constituency.[19]

This prejudice works, according to Hollis, in the following way:

... There will perhaps be one obstinate man who will say: 'Of course, no one could accuse me of being a bigot, but we have to face the fact that if we select a Catholic or a Jew, it will lose us a certain number of votes. There-

19. C. Hollis, 'The Conservative Party in History', *Political Quarterly*, 32 (1961), p. 225.

fore we cannot afford not to choose the Protestant.' And, if the Protestant and the Catholic are of roughly equal merit, the others are likely to acquiesce as a matter of least resistance in the selection of the Protestant.[20]

If Hollis is correct (and there is little or no evidence to prove or disprove what he says) then religious prejudice is yet another factor which assumes significant proportions only when applicants are otherwise equally divided. There is, again with the exceptions of Scotland and Northern Ireland, no evidence of an *absolute veto* on Catholic or Jewish candidates, or members of any other denomination. Both Scotland and Northern Ireland are special cases, where religion still plays an important part in politics, especially in the latter. The riots in the Belfast West constituency on the eve of the General Election of 1964 were a cogent demonstration of the religious nature of Ulster politics, whilst Patrick Wolrige-Gordon's association with M.R.A. illustrates the problems associated with any deviation from religious orthodoxy in Scotland.

It is true, of course, that there are at present only two Conservative Orthodox Jews in Parliament[21] and that there have been only a handful of Jewish unsuccessful candidates.[22] Furthermore, the not infrequent preference of local associations for *Christian* candidates is not only a prima facie indication of anti-Jewish prejudice, but is in itself a form of discrimination. On the other hand, the question must be seen in perspective: the Conservative party is not a religious party, but it remains, both in origin and sympathy, the party closest to the Established Church and as such expresses a preference for Christian rather than non-Christian candidates. At only one of a dozen selection meetings attended by the author was any reference made to the religion of any applicant. This occurred at an executive council meeting, when a member wished to know the religious denomination of those appearing before the council. This information is not normally made available and, whilst any enquiry may be regarded as prima facie evidence of prejudice, such enquiries are rare. Such little evidence as exists would suggest that religious prejudice in the Conservative party is general rather than particular, voicing itself less against individual denominations and more as a preference for Christian candidates in the widest sense of the term.

20. ibid., p. 224.
21. Sir Henry d'Avigdor-Goldsmid (Walsall South) and Sir Keith Joseph (Leeds North-East).
22. Probably between six and nine since 1950.

Previous Electoral Experience

Of the 282 Conservative candidates elected by incumbent associations between 1950 and 1966, nearly two-thirds (64·2 per cent) had previously fought a parliamentary election. This would suggest that electoral experience is a factor of some importance and this view has been expressed by several commentators.[23] Too much stress, however, can be laid on the importance of electoral experience: it should be noted that a fifth (36) of those candidates with earlier experience to their credit were former M.P.s and as such fall into a special category. Not only do they have electoral experience, but also *parliamentary* experience. If former M.P.s are excluded, therefore, two fifths (41·1 per cent) of the remaining candidates had had no electoral experience, and three fifths (59·9 per cent) had previously fought one or more constituencies unsuccessfully. Electoral experience is by no means a requisite of selection, although it is an extremely useful asset: a local association will sometimes express a preference for a candidate with electoral experience,[24] but as with most of an applicant's characteristics electoral experience is considered as part of his general experience, and his *overall political experience* in particular. Where a candidate is relatively young electoral experience is a decided asset, which may off-set doubts concerning the wisdom of selecting too youthful a candidate. Excluding former M.P.s, nearly two thirds of the candidates under forty, for example, had fought unsuccessful contests before being selected by incumbent associations; whilst there is some evidence that electoral experience is less likely to be demanded of older candidates, of forty years of age or more.

Electoral experience is probably regarded as a more important asset by the applicant than by the selectors: the applicant sees it as a specific qualification, so much so that, should he fail to secure selection for a safe Conservative seat, he is quite likely to seek selection in a hopeless seat rather than allow a general election to pass without his being a candidate; but few selectors take the view that applicants *must* have had electoral experience – how else is it possible to account for the fact that more than a third of the candidates selected between 1950 and 1966 by incumbent associations had had no electoral experience?

23. e.g. see Ranney, op. cit., pp. 93–4 and p. 276, and Richards, 'A Study in Political Apprenticeship', *Parliamentary Affairs*, vol. XI, No. 3, 1955–6.
24. e.g. Richmond (Surrey), 1958.

The Importance of Age

Electoral experience is seen by the selectors principally within the context of political experience and is not normally treated as an isolated factor, but age is very often treated as a separate or nearly separate consideration. This is partly because age is often used as an arbitrary means of reducing the initial flood of applications and partly because there is often a built-in incentive to select a relatively young man to succeed a retiring Member. To take the second point first, whilst the selection of an applicant over the age of fifty is not unknown, it is the exception rather than the rule. Only three candidates were aged sixty or more on election between 1950 and 1966, and cases such as that of Sir Arthur Salter, who was seventy when he won the Ormskirk by-election in 1951, whilst his predecessor, Sir Ronald Cross, was only fifty-five are rare. Most of the candidates over the age of fifty are former M.P.s, or ex-servicemen, like Vice-Admiral John Hughes-Hallett or Captain J. S. Litchfield, or ex-civil servants, like Sir John Fletcher-Cooke or Sir George Sinclair, who embarked on political careers relatively late in life.

Table 3(4): *Age distribution of candidates selected by incumbent Conservative associations, 1950–66*

Age group	Percentage
Under 30	6·7 (19)
30–39	37·6(106)
40–49	36·5(103)
50–59	18·1 (51)
60 and over	1·1 (3)
	100·0(282)

Table 3(4) shows clearly the marked preference for incumbent associations for candidates under the age of fifty; indeed, the largest single age group is thirty to thirty-nine, closely followed by the forty to forty-nine group, and this accords very closely with the sort of age limits that are often laid down by local associations. There is some evidence that the preference for the under *forty* group is increasing: in 1951, 44·5 per cent of the candidates were under forty, but by 1964, this figure had risen to 52·1 per cent. Candidates under the age of thirty, however, are often thought to lack the necessary experience to become M.P.s, and in particular are invariably regarded as having failed to fulfil the very common Conservative demand that they should have proved themselves in some sphere other than politics before endeavouring to become a Member of Parliament. Conversely, candidates of fifty and over are often regarded as less able to withstand the rigours of political life in general and campaigning in particular, whilst the practice of many Conservative M.P.s of retiring at a fairly early age also militates against the selection of older candidates: few associations relish the idea of frequent selections, and more especially the attendant possibility of frequent by-elections in the constituency.

In response to these views, therefore, local associations frequently lay down age limits for the type of candidate they would like: the borough constituency of Richmond, for example, expressed a preference for a man over forty; Worthing laid down age limits of thirty-seven to forty-eight years of age; whilst Salisbury extended the lower limit to thirty-five and the upper to fifty. These limits are normally used as one of several arbitrary criteria to reduce the initial list of applicants, thus making it all the more likely that the final choice will come from a fairly narrow age range. Of course, selection committees sometimes ignore their own criteria, as in fact happened at Richmond, but it is the practice of applying such limits which is substantially responsible for the age distribution of Conservative candidates.

It is, of course, also a question of supply as well as demand. With the exceptions noted above of the ex-M.P., the ex-serviceman and former civil servant, the majority of aspiring M.P.s are found in the age range thirty to fifty: most of those under thirty who seek a political career in the Conservative party will be among a fortunate minority if they secure a Conservative seat before they are thirty; most of those over fifty will have had their ambition dampened by long years of coming so close yet so far from selection for a Conservative constituency. The demands of political life are such that the young would-be politician must normally establish himself in his career, preferably one which lends itself to the generous giving of both time and money. On the other hand the older man may have both the necessary time and money, but feel that the undoubted uncertainties of political life offer more sobering thoughts than his earlier ambitions.

Local Connections

Approximately three fifths of the candidates selected by incumbent associations between 1950 and 1966 had local connections of varying intensities, ranging from direct to regional associations with their constituencies.[25] There may be pressure for the selection of a candidate with local connections, either in general or in favour of a particular individual. Conversely, there may be opposition to such a candidate, more often against a particular individual, but occasionally in general, on the grounds that a local candidate is always vulnerable because he is too well-known. The advantages and disadvantages of a local candidate are not always clear, but there is no doubt that in the minds of the selectors the question of local connections often looms large.

Section B of Table 3(5) illustrates the various categories of local

Table 3(5): The incidence of local connections among candidates selected by incumbent Conservative associations, 1950–66

A. *Type of local connection*	*Percentage*	
Direct	21·6 (61)	⎫
Area	12·1 (34)	⎬ 62·8(177)
Regional	29·1 (82)	⎭
None known	37·2(105)	
Total	100·0(282)	

B. *Analysis of local connections in selected constituencies*

Nature of local connection	*Number*		*Category*
Officer of local association	8	⎫	
Former officer of local association	6	⎬ 18	Direct
Politically direct (i.e. member of local authority)	4	⎭	
Officer of adjacent association	4	⎫	
Political (i.e. member of adjacent local authority)	2	⎬ 8	Area
Industrial (i.e. associated with local industry)	2	⎭	
Political (i.e. member of local authority in region)	6	⎫	
Industrial (i.e. associated with regional industry)	1	⎬ 7	Regional
Total	33		

25. See Appendix A for definitions.

connections that have been used in this analysis and Section A of the table gives the incidence of local connections among the candidates selected between 1950 and 1966. About a fifth of the candidates had direct connections with their constituencies, a further 12 per cent had area connections, and rather less than a third regional associations. Local connections in the wider sense of the term are, therefore, an extremely useful asset for any applicant to possess, although by no means an essential qualification, since a substantial minority of the candidates had no discernible local connections at all.

Knowledge of the constituency in particular and the area in general gives the local or semi-local candidate an advantage over his less familiar rivals. Almost all applicants who reach the interview stage ensure that they are well-briefed on local conditions and problems. Nevertheless, all applicants are faced with the problem of assessing the extent to which local connections or knowledge should be stressed: too great an emphasis on local affairs may give the applicant a parochial reputation; but to ignore local considerations may label the applicant as superficial. Some knowledge of local affairs is important, if only because the applicant must demonstrate his ability to be a good *constituency* M.P. The presence of a local applicant, however, often leads to problems for the selectors[26] in the form of strong feeling for or against the individual and such selections are often especially recriminatory.

In the majority of Conservative-held constituencies local connections become important only when an applicant with such qualifications is involved, but in certain areas there is a strong desire for local candidates:

... In Birmingham ... the local Tories have ignored the Central Office list and have deliberately chosen local people as parliamentary candidates.[27]

Critchley suggests that 'Birmingham is returning to the caucus politics of the Chamberlains'[28] and that both there and in Liverpool regionalism is an important factor in the selection of local candidates. The figures in Table 3(6) support Critchley's view to the extent that Birmingham and Liverpool constituencies exhibit a strong preference for local candidates. Manchester and Sheffield also appear to favour local candidates, although in the former there is less emphasis on direct

26. See Chapter Two, pp. 50-1 and 54.
27. J. Critchley, 'Candidates: How they Pick Them', *New Statesman*, 5 February 1965, p. 189.
28. ibid., p. 189.

Table 3(6): *Incidence of local connections in large county boroughs,* 1950–66

County borough	Number of selections	Number with local connections	Number with direct connections
Newcastle	2	1	–
Liverpool	3	2	2
Manchester	3	3	1
Bradford	1	1	1
Kingston-upon-Hull	2	1	–
Leeds	1	–	–
Sheffield	2	2	1
Birmingham	5	5	3
Leicester	1	1	–
Nottingham	1	–	–
Bristol	2	1	1
Portsmouth	2	1	1

connections. In general, of course, the figures are too small to allow for firm conclusions, but it does seem that as one moves farther south applicants with *direct* local connections are less likely to be selected. Certainly, local connections are a more important factor in the north: nearly three quarters of the candidates elected for northern constituencies between 1950 and 1966 had some sort of local connections. This seems to be a reflection of two factors: first, regionalism which is often particularly strong in northern cities as cities, as well as parts of wider regions; and second, the strength of constituency party organization, which is supplemented and sometimes overshadowed by the city association. In no case does a city association play any *formal* role, but informally its influence may be great. The city associations have become training grounds for possible candidates and though the term 'caucus' may be too strong in the context of selection, the term '*cadre*' seems especially applicable. Many of these candidates with local connections are prominent members of their *city* associations and where these are strong they are a common source of candidates. A similar situation exists in Glasgow, where six of the eight candidates selected for Conservative-held seats between 1950 and 1966 had direct local connections.

In addition to the types of local connection mentioned above there is a particular type which is peculiar to the Conservative party: this is the *'family seat'*. The concept of the 'pocket borough' predates the Reform Act of 1832, but it remained in a modified form after that date through the influence of socially and politically important families. The longest-standing 'family seat' of this century is Antrim, in Northern Ireland, which was represented by a member of the O'Neill family from 1885 until 1959. The two most famous cases, however, are the Astors' domination of Plymouth and the Guinness's domination of Southend. From 1910, when W. W. Astor became M.P. for Plymouth, until 1959, when J. J. Astor, his son retired as M.P. for the Sutton division of the city, Plymouth has always had an Astor as an M.P. or Conservative candidate,[29] Similarly, since 1912, when Rupert Guinness[30] became M.P. for South-East Essex, Southend has always been represented by a member of the Guinness family.[31] Apart from these seats there are another seven constituencies in which the sitting Member has been succeeded by a member of the same family. Three concerned the succession of father and son, one a father and daughter, and one an uncle and nephew. A further nine constituencies selected candidates, members of whose families had formerly represented the same areas.

Continued domination of a seat by one family is none the less rare: only three of the ten cases of direct succession involved three or more successive M.P.s. Of the remainder, one was in Northern Ireland, where local connections are the rule; and a further two involved widows succeeding their husbands. It is doubtful whether family connections are anything more than a special sort of local connection. The selection of a relative of the previous M.P. is often the subject of criticism: the selection of another member of the Guinness family at Southend West in 1959 resulted in some disagreement within the local party. Nevertheless, the local agent claimed Channon was selected 'purely on his qualifications from over 130 applicants. He is a good speaker and had an overwhelming majority in his favour at his selection before the local executive meeting, which was attended by some seventy members.'[32] A relative of the previous M.P. is often already well-known in the constituency, perhaps well-liked:

29. J. J. Astor was Conservative candidate for Plymouth (Sutton), 1945–51.
30. Second Earl of Iveagh, 1927.
31. The present M.P. for Southend West, Paul Channon, is the grandson of Rupert Guinness (M.P. for South-East Essex 1912–18 and Southend 1918–27) and Lady Gwendolen Guinness (M.P. for Southend 1927–35). Channon's father, Sir Henry, sat for Southend and then Southend West from 1935 to 1959.
32. *The Times*, 14 January 1959.

[Lady Muriel Gammans] shouldered most of the constituency work when her husband became Postmaster-General. Indeed, it is said they preferred to come to her with their problems.[33]

Certainly, it is difficult to find a case in which a candidate was selected because or substantially because he was a relative of the previous Member or a former Member for the constituency. It is possible that in some cases undue consideration may have been given to this factor, but the same is probably true of other factors.

It is important to see local connections as one of a number of factors which may influence the decisions of the selectors. That it is one of several factors is seen by the fact that a marked change of attitude towards local connections has occurred between 1950 and 1966. Lord Kilmuir has asserted that the tendency to select local candidates has increased since the General Elections of 1950 and 1951:

Very few of the new Members who entered the Commons in 1955 and 1959 had achieved a reputation outside Westminster in any field, and far too many of them were *obscure local citizens with obscure local interests*, incapable – and indeed downright reluctant to think on a national or international scale. Perhaps we were spoilt by the quality of the new members in 1950–1.[34]

There is strong statistical evidence to support Lord Kilmuir's view, at least to the extent that the proportion of candidates with *direct* local connections tended to increase sharply after 1951: only one of the eighteen candidates selected for the 1951 General Election had a direct local connection with his constituency, but, by 1959, this had risen to seven candidates out of forty-nine; by 1964 the proportion had risen to a fifth, and by 1966 to nearly a quarter. A similar trend could be detected in by-elections over the period. Beyond this, however, it is a matter of opinion whether these candidates were lacking in ability, and brought with them to Westminster a distinctly parochial outlook, as Lord Kilmuir asserts. As he points out the 1950–1 intake was probably misleading, for whilst there is no doubt that a significant proportion of able candidates were elected then, this was partly due to the high total intake (131 in 1950 and a further forty-one in 1951) reflecting the extensive Conservative gains as well as the high turnover of retiring Members, and partly due to the strong Central Office contingent, represented by men like Edward Heath, Reginald Maudling, Iain Macleod, and Enoch Powell. Moreover, there is a strong tendency for

33. Jean Mann, op. cit., p. 47.
34. Kilmuir, op. cit., p. 158. (Author's italics.)

marginal non-Conservative seats to select candidates with local connections, particularly direct connections, and these were bound to be
reflected in the gains made by the Conservatives between 1951 and
1959. Lord Kilmuir may indeed be right about the quality of many of
those selected after 1951 and it must be acknowledged that the tendency
to select candidates with local connections has increased, but it is
another matter entirely to show that these candidates lacked the ability
of their predecessors. If university education is used as a crude assessment of quality then there is again some evidence to support Lord
Kilmuir's view: over 80 per cent of the candidates selected for the 1951
election were graduates, but by 1959 this figure had dropped dramatically
to 55 per cent, although rising again in 1964 and 1966. In spite of the
fact that these figures are complete populations, it must be remembered
that the totals for each election are small – eighteen in 1951, forty-nine
in 1959, forty-six in 1964, and twenty-one in 1966, so that any conclusions must be tentative.

Closely linked with local connections in many instances is the
question of local government experience: just over a third of the
candidates selected between 1950 and 1966 had had local government
experience.

Local government experience often forms the basis of a candidate's
local connections, especially where these connections are direct, but it is
more important as a general factor. Clearly, the very fact that only a
third of the successful Conservative candidates had had local government experience means that it is not normally regarded as an essential
qualification. Furthermore, such experience is generally typical of
certain types of candidate: more non-graduates than graduates, more
non-public school than public school candidates, more Redbrick than
Oxbridge graduates have had local government experience. It may be
that local government experience is regarded as a partial substitute for
the social background which these candidates lack. Certainly, it is
regarded as a useful experience, as a measure of political ability and
involvement, and something generally in the candidate's favour.
Occasionally, however, it is viewed as a limiting factor, as an indication
of the applicant's parochial outlook and lack of wider experience.

Over and above the general factors already discussed, there are a
number of *regional* differences. Many of these differences are related to
the distribution of various types of constituency within the regions.
For instance, there are over twice as many borough as county constituencies in the northern region, with the result that northern con-

stituencies tend to show a preference for older candidates with a greater degree of local connection and local government experience. Similarly, the distribution of marginal and semi-marginal seats in the north results in the selection of a greater proportion of businessmen. Beyond this, however, there is some evidence that in *general* the northern constituencies are more likely to select candidates who are older and have some sort of local connections. Conversely, constituencies in the home counties and the south are more inclined to select younger candidates, with fewer local connections. The regions which show especially individual trends, however, are Wales, Scotland and Northern Ireland. In all three regions there is an overwhelming preference for native candidates.[35] Furthermore, in Northern Ireland the electoral situation peculiar to that region results in an almost complete absence of electoral experience among the candidates. Although Englishmen occasionally seek selection for Conservative-held constituencies in Wales, they rarely do in either Scotland or Ulster. Apart from the preference of the constituencies concerned this is probably the result of the separate party organizations for each country, which, though in close contact with Central Office in London, are completely autonomous and maintain their own selection machinery.[36]

Occupation

An applicant's occupation may affect his chances of selection in two ways: first as a general qualification, and second as an indication of his future availability. Conservative selectors normally expect applicants to have had a successful, non-political career before seeking a candidature. In other words an applicant's occupation is taken as a measure of his ability together with various other factors and of his suitability for the particular candidacy.

The second consideration is often the more important of the two. Views on the extent to which politics should be a full-time career differ and, whilst many Conservative associations would not wish their Member to be a full-time politician, they all wish to satisfy themselves that his occupation will not interfere unduly with his duties as an M.P. Clearly some occupations lend themselves to a political career, and the legal profession, journalism, and company directorships are obvious examples. On the other hand some occupations, such as teaching, some

35. W. H. Baker, M.P. for Banff, is an Englishman, but he has farmed in Banffshire for many years.
36. See Appendix B, 'The Scottish Conservative and Unionist and the Ulster Unionist Parties'.

careers in business and administration, are incompatible with a political career and the candidate can avoid becoming a full-time M.P. only by finding some alternative, part-time occupation.

These two considerations may conflict: the experience which the applicant has as a result of his occupation may render him especially suitable for the candidacy in question, but it may also be the case that he must give up his career even on a part-time basis since it may clash with his commitments as an M.P.; and neither position may concur with the view of the local association. The continued association of an M.P. with non-political affairs through his occupation is usually welcomed by local associations, but the latter always seeks to reassure itself that this will not limit his political activities.

Table 3(7): *Occupational* breakdown of candidates selected by incumbent Conservative associations, 1950–66*

Occupation	Percentage
Workers	1·1(3)
Professions	29·4(83)
Business	50·0(141)
Miscellaneous	19·5(55)
Total	100·0(282)

* For definitions see Appendix A.

Within these general considerations Table 3(7) shows that Conservative selectors have a clear preference for applicants with a business background, followed by less strong preferences for members of the professions and those in miscellaneous occupations, such as journalists or party research workers. Only a tiny minority of the candidates were workers. This is, of course, almost certainly related in part to supply as well as demand: it is not surprising to find that the occupational category which is most commonly linked with the Conservative party in general provides the largest single group of its candidates. Similarly although there is an important working-class Conservative vote, as an occupational group workers are less active in the Conservative party and proportionately less likely to supply a significant number of would-be candidates, quite apart from the preferences of the selectors. The professions occupy an intermediate position: the professions are, of course, more diverse, and although some, like the legal profession, are an important source of Conservative candidates, others, such as medicine and university teaching, supply rather fewer candidates.

In most selections an applicant's occupation is one of several factors which may influence the selectors' choice. Generally speaking, its influence is of an indirect nature, providing some indication of the applicant's ability and experience and, possibly, of his future availability; but occasionally occupation may have a direct bearing on selection. In 1958, for example, the *Sheffield Telegraph* suggested that the Hallam Division of Sheffield ought to select a local man who was conversant with the needs and problems of the steel industry. A more frequent occurrence is a preference among county constituencies for farmer-candidates: between 1950 and 1964 fourteen farmer-M.P.s were elected to the Conservative benches, of whom only three sat for boroughs. It is not unusual, therefore, to find the selectors discussing an applicant's occupation within the context of the type of constituency for which they are selecting a candidate.

Education and Social Background

It is clear from Table 3(8) that only a very small minority of the candidates had had only an elementary education or some sort of post-

Table 3(8): *The educational* breakdown of candidates selected by incumbent Conservative associations, 1950–66*

Education	Percentage
Elementary	1·8 (5)
Elementary/secondary plus	2·8 (8)
Secondary	25·5 (72)
University	69·9 (197)
Total	100·0 (282)

* For definitions, see Appendix A.

secondary full-time education other than at a university. The majority, well over two thirds, in fact, had had a university or equivalent education, and the remaining quarter ceased full-time education at secondary level. It is not necessarily the case, however, that selectors apply educational criteria in any direct sense, but the educational characteris-

Table 3(9): *Educational* background of candidates selected by incumbent Conservative associations, 1950–66*

Educational background	Percentage
A. *Public school education*	
Public school education	78·0(220)
Non-public school education	21·6 (61)
Not known	0·4 (1)
Total	100·0(282)
B. *Type of public school*	
Clarendon schools	48·2(106)
Other public schools	51·8(114)
Total	100·0(220)
C. *University education*	
University graduates	69·9(197)
Non-graduates	30·1 (85)
Total	100·0(282)
D. *Choice of university*	
Oxbridge	78·2(154)
Other universities	21·8 (43)
Total	100·0(197)

* For definitions, see Appendix A.

tics of Conservative candidates are in general indicative of a particular social background, as Table 3(9) illustrates.

Not only do Conservative selectors appear to have an overwhelming preference for university graduates, but an even more overwhelming preference for Oxbridge graduates, who provided nearly four fifths of the university-educated candidates selected between 1950 and 1966. There also appears to be an equally strong inclination to select those from a public school background, and more particularly for those educated at the nine Clarendon schools.[37] Although slightly more

37. Eton, Harrow, Winchester, Charterhouse, Shrewsbury, Rugby, Westminster, St Paul's, and Merchant Taylors', as defined by the Royal Commission on Public Schools, 1864, of which Lord Clarendon was chairman.

candidates were in fact educated at non-Clarendon schools, it should be remembered that there are 265 schools affiliated to the Headmasters' Conference and that a *disproportionate* number of candidates are therefore drawn from the Clarendon schools.

In his study *The British Political Elite*, W. L. Guttsman suggests that social influences are of considerable importance in the composition of the polity:

If we ascend the political hierarchy, from the voters upwards, we find that at each level – the membership of the political parties, party activists, local political leaders, M.P.s National Leaders – the social character of the group is slightly less 'representative' and slightly more tilted in favour of those who belong to the middle and upper levels of our society.[38]

Furthermore, in reference to the Conservative party in particular Guttsman argues that:

... In the selection of men for Parliament the basic character of the Conservative Party leadership is generally perpetuated. Local selection committees, composed of the leaders of the local organization, men and women of worth and status and generally of advanced years, are inevitably and perhaps almost unconsciously prejudiced in favour of men who in their *social background* are like themselves or above them.[39]

The very fact that the preferences shown in Tables 3(8) and 3(9) are so marked suggest not only that social background is a factor in the selection of Conservative candidates, but that it is an extremely important factor. It remains open to question, however, whether it is a conscious factor in the minds of the selectors. One matter is certain: social background is not normally the subject of open discussion among the selectors; to that extent it is unconscious. Nevertheless, to presume that social and therefore class influences play no part in selection is probably unjustified, since all studies of *electoral* behaviour in Great Britain support the view that social class is the most important *single determinant*.[40] If this is the case then it is a natural corollary that social class should affect attitudes *within* British political parties. The whole question is complicated by the twin problems of subjective and objective analysis of class structure[41] and conscious and unconscious class

38. W. L. Guttsman, op. cit., p. 27.
39. ibid., p. 289. (Author's italics.)
40. See M. Benney, A. P. Grey, and R. H. Pear, *How People Vote*, London, 1956, p. 113; R. S. Milne and H. C. Mackenzie, *Straight Fight*, London, 1954, p. 50; J. Bonham, *The Middle Class Vote*, London, 1954, pp. 194–5; R. R. Alford, *Party and Society*, London, 1964, Ch. 6.
41. See Alford, op. cit., pp. 20–31.

influence: some selectors may overtly assess their class position in the form of status and allow this to influence their decisions in selection; others may be influenced by various values consistent with an unacknowledged class position. To distinguish between the two is beyond the scope of the present study, but in either case any class influence is *individual* rather than *collective* and there is no evidence of any *concerted* action by Conservative selectors to bring factors of social class into their decisions: to this extent the influence of social class is covert. It remains as the background, the context within which selection takes place rather than a particular cross-pressure to which selectors are subjected.

By-Elections and General Elections

Whether a candidate is being selected for an impending by-election or for a general election, which may be some time away, might be thought to be of some importance – the fact that by-elections tend to concentrate national attention on one or two constituencies in particular, the alleged interest of the national party organization in the selection, the pressure to select a former M.P. or leading party member, or alternatively similar pressure in favour of a prominent local aspirant, are all factors which may apply especially to by-elections. That national attention is usually focused on a constituency in which a by-election is being held is undoubted, and this alone is justification for the active interest of the national party organization, but its power to interfere is limited: if the local association does select a former M.P., an ex-minister or a leading party member, it does so not at the insistence of Central Office, nor, necessarily, at the latter's behest, but because it is willing to do so. In fact in only one respect do candidates selected for by-elections differ markedly from those selected for general elections, and this is in the matter of local connections: associations faced with a by-election are more likely to select a local candidate. Only 16·4 per cent of the candidates selected for general elections had *direct* connections with their constituencies, but no less than 29·8 per cent of those selected for by-elections had *direct* connections. There is also some evidence that associations selecting for a by-election are more likely to select a fairly young candidate and there are probably two reasons for this: first, by-election campaigns are generally more exacting than general election campaigns and a young candidate often presents a more vigorous image; second, many by-elections are caused by the death or retirement of M.P.s over the age of fifty, and even in the case of resignation for other reasons, the M.P. is seldom under forty.[42] In such circumstances the local association is likely to favour a young and fresh candidate. This is not, however, a particularly strong tendency and by no means as important as the question of local connections.

The Type of Constituency

With the exception of the factor just discussed, whether the contest concerned is a by-election or a general election, all the factors dealt with so far have concerned the characteristics of the candidates. There is also evidence, however, that these characteristics will be seen in the light of the *type of constituency* for which the candidate is being selected. In particular the relative safeness or marginality of a seat and the extent to which it is rural or urban both play an important part in the selection of candidates by incumbent Conservative associations.

There is some evidence, for example, that associations in safe and impregnable constituencies are more willing to select applicants under thirty and of fifty years of age or more, with rather less concentration on the middle group of forty to forty-nine than in marginal and semi-marginal seats. More particularly, however, there is a very marked contrast in the educational backgrounds of candidates chosen by marginal and semi-marginal seats on the one hand, and safe and impregnable seats on the other, as Table 3(10) shows.

The figures in Table 3(10) are not simply a reiteration of the preference of Conservative-held constituencies for candidates with a particular educational and, therefore, social background, but are clear evidence of an express preference for such candidates among safe and impregnable constituencies. In other words the general preference for candidates with a public school education, with particular emphasis on those who attended the Clarendon schools, and for university graduates, with particular emphasis on Oxbridge graduates, is reinforced in these constituencies.

There are also other differences: marginal and semi-marginal seats are more likely to select members of the professions than safe and impregnable constituencies; conversely, the latter are more likely to favour those in miscellaneous occupations than marginal or semi-marginal constituencies; whilst neither seem more inclined than the other to choose those from a business background beyond the fact that

42. The cases of D. K. Freeth (Basingstoke 1955–64), who announced his retirement at the age of thirty-nine, and B. Z. de Ferranti (Morecambe and Lonsdale 1958–64), who resigned at the age of thirty-four, are exceptional.

Table 3(10): *Educational background of candidates selected by incumbent Conservative associations in marginal and semi-marginal constituencies compared with safe and impregnable constituencies, 1950–66*

Educational background	Marginal and semi-marginal	Safe and impregnable
A. *Public school education*		
Public school education	63·2(43)	80·5(136)
Non-public school education	36·8(25)	18·9 (32)
Not known		0·6 (1)
Total	100·0(68)	100·0(169)
B. *Type of public school*		
Clarendon	37·2(16)	55·2 (75)
Other public schools	62·8(27)	44·8 (61)
Total	100·0(43)	100·0(136)
C. *University education*		
University graduates	58·9(40)	73·9(125)
Non-graduates	41·1(28)	26·1 (44)
Total	100·0(68)	100·0(169)
D. *Choice of university*		
Oxbridge	62·5(25)	80·8(101)
Other universities	37·5(15)	19·2 (24)
Total	100·0(40)	100·0(125)

the latter is the largest single occupational group. There is also evidence that safe and impregnable seats are more likely to select applicants with local connections, especially direct connections, although the same constituencies appear to regard local government experience as relatively unimportant.

A similar though by no means identical pattern emerges if the extent to which constituencies are rural[43] or urban[44] is taken into account. For example, the educational pattern which arises from the electoral

43. i.e. constituencies with a rural population of more than 50 per cent.
44. i.e. constituencies with an urban population of 50 per cent or more.

analysis described above is partially repeated among rural and urban constituencies. There seems little difference between the two in their respective preferences for graduates, but when the analysis is extended to include public school education and choice of university the pattern described above reasserts itself:

Table 3(11): Educational background of candidates selected by incumbent Conservative associations in rural constituencies compared with urban constituencies, 1950–66

Educational background	Rural	Urban
A. *Public school education*		
Public school education	84·4(108)	72·7(112)
Non-public school education	15·6 (20)	26·7 (41)
Not known	– –	0·6 (1)
Total	100·0(128)	100·0(154)
B *Type of public school*		
Clarendon	50·0 (54)	46·4 (52)
Other public schools	50·0 (54)	53·6 (60)
Total	100·0(108)	100·0(112)
C. *University education*		
University graduates	69·5 (89)	70·2(108)
Non-graduates	30·5 (39)	29·8 (46)
Total	100·0(128)	100·0(154)
D. *Choice of university*		
Oxbridge	82·0 (73)	75·0 (81)
Other universities	18·0 (16)	25·0 (27)
Total	100·0 (89)	100·0 (108)

The figures in Table 3(11) show that the respective preferences of rural and urban seats are less marked than the similar preferences shown in the electoral analysis, but they are nevertheless important. There is, of course, some correlation between the extent to which constituencies are safe and rural and the extent to which they are marginal and urban, but it is far from being a complete correlation: it is true that less than a fifth of the rural seats which selected candidates between 1950 and 1966 were marginal or semi-marginal, compared with more than a quarter of the urban seats which selected candidates over the same period; but a similar proportion of both rural and urban seats, three fifths, in fact, were either safe or impregnable. This means that within the *general* preference for candidates of a particular educational and social background additional pressures may exist which make it even more likely that such candidates will be selected in particular constituencies. It also means, of course, that cross-pressures may be introduced: selectors in a safe constituency which is also urban are less inclined to select candidates with a public school background than their colleagues in safe rural seats.

This question of cross-pressures, however, is further complicated by the fact that there are other differences between rural and urban constituencies. Selectors in rural seats, for instance, are less insistent on previous electoral experience than those in urban seats: excluding former M.P.s rather more than half (54 per cent) of the candidates selected for rural constituencies had had previous electoral experience, compared with more than three fifths (62·9 per cent) of the candidates selected for urban constituencies. An even stronger preference exists among rural seats for candidates under the age of forty: exactly half the candidates selected for rural seats were under forty compared with less than two fifths (37·6 per cent) of those selected for urban seats.

The reason why rural constituencies should prefer younger candidates is not difficult to discern, particularly when the size of most rural constituencies is taken into account: the physical task of conducting an election campaign in a large constituency tends to favour the selection of a younger candidate. Certainly, this point was stressed at the selection of Sir Gerald Nabarro by the South Worcestershire Conservative Association. Sir Gerald had the advantage of being a local resident, well-known and generally well-liked, a good speaker, experienced in elections and in the Commons itself, and conversant with local problems. Furthermore, there was clearly a strong feeling in his favour, but prior to the General Election of 1964 he had announced his retirement as Member for Kidderminster on grounds of ill-health: he had now to persuade South Worcestershire that he was fully fit and again capable of undertaking the arduous duties of an M.P. Several members of the association's executive council expressed concern about this and stressed the *size of the constituency*. In the event Sir Gerald was selected, but not without some discussion regarding his *age and health*.

There is also more stress in urban seats on local connections in general: two thirds (66·2 per cent) of the candidates selected for urban constituencies had local connections of some sort, compared with just under three fifths (58·6 per cent) of those selected for rural seats. On the other hand, there does not appear to be any significant difference between rural and urban constituencies as far as occupational categories are concerned, nor in the extent to which candidates with local government experience might be preferred.

Thus a series of reinforcing pressures on the one hand and cross-pressures on the other may be established: the fact that a constituency is marginal may lead the selectors to favour a particular type of candidate, but the fact that it is also rural may introduce countervailing factors. It is, in fact, possible to suggest which types of constituency are likely to favour which types of candidate.

Very few of the candidates selected by incumbent Conservative associations between 1950 and 1966 could be described as working class, but neither is the Conservative party in this sense a party of the middle class: the candidates are not representative of the middle class as a whole, and whilst potential Conservative M.P.s are not drawn *exclusively*, they are drawn *substantially* from the upper echelons of the middle class. A former Conservative M.P. has added a slightly different view of this social distinction:

> Traditional seats were, until 1962, at least, the preserve of the 'gentlemen' of the party. The first 'player' to succeed in becoming adopted for a *county* seat was Mr John Biffen.[45] Other 'players' such as Mr Iain Macleod[46] and Mr Heath[47] sit for suburban seats.[48]

This distinction between the 'amateur' and the 'professional' may be something of a caricature, but there does appear to be some substance in the view that the more traditional type of Conservative constituency prefers the more traditional type of Conservative candidate, and this view is supported by preferences shown in Table 3(12). It should be pointed out, of course, there are really two types of traditional Conservative seat: the strongly held county constituency based on a predominantly rural interest; and the equally strongly held borough constituency based on middle and upper middle class residential areas. It is especially these constituencies which prefer candidates with the

45. M.P. for Oswestry since 1961.
46. M.P. for Enfield West since 1950 and a former Conservative Minister.
47. M.P. for Bexley since 1950 and Leader of the Conservative party since 1965.
48. Critchley, op. cit., p. 189. (Author's italics.)

Table 3(12): *Types of candidates compared with types of constituency,*
1950–66

Rural: marginal and semi-marginal constituencies	*Urban: marginal and semi-marginal constituencies*
Previous electoral experience – *preferred*	Previous electoral experience – *fairly strong*
Aged 30–49 – *very strong*	Aged under 50 – *strong*
Public school education – *fairly strong*	Public school education – *fairly strong*
Clarendon schools – *preferred*	Other public schools – *strong*
Graduates – *preferred*	Graduates – *fairly strong*
Oxbridge graduates – *strong*	Oxbridge graduates – *preferred*
No local connections – *preferred*	Local connections – *strong*
Business occupations – *preferred*	Business occupations – *preferred*
Professional occupations – *above average* (44 per cent)	

Rural: safe and impregnable constituencies	*Urban: safe and impregnable constituencies*
Previous electoral experience – *preferred*	Previous electoral experience – *fairly strong*
Aged under 50 – *very strong*	Aged under 50 – *strong*
Public school education – *very strong*	Public school education – *strong*
Clarendon schools – *preferred*	Clarendon schools – *preferred*
Graduates – *fairly strong*	Graduates – *strong*
Oxbridge graduates – *strong*	Oxbridge graduates – *very strong*
Local connections – *fairly strong*	Local connections – *fairly strong*
Business occupations – *preferred*	Miscellaneous occupations – *above average* (24·4 per cent)

NOTE: (a) very strong = 80 per cent or over; (b) strong = 70–79 per cent; (c) fairly strong = 60–69 per cent; (d) preferred = 50–59 per cent.

public school and Oxbridge background which is associated with a particular social background.

This is not an immutable pattern, however: Guttsman has clearly demonstrated the changes which the Conservative party has undergone since 1932 and, indeed, more recently with a changing occupational pattern.[49] Because it is linked with the social background of the candidates it is a pattern which is changing only slowly, partly under the pressure of social changes themselves, partly because the Conservative party has become a mass party in image if not in fact.

Thus applicants who lack a public school background, those who are Redbrick graduates or non-graduates, those over the age of fifty, or those who lack electoral experience are not necessarily summarily rejected: in fact they form an important minority of the candidates selected by incumbent Conservative associations, but they are less likely to be selected for rural constituencies or for safe and impregnable constituencies. Those who are selected often find themselves fighting urban marginal or semi-marginal seats, and to that very important extent are less favoured than their more socially acceptable rivals.

It is within the context of the characteristics of both applicants and constituencies that the question of ability will be discussed by the selectors, and it is because of this, that over and above the question of ability, the selectors will ask themselves: *is this person the right candidate for this constituency?* It is at this point that the selectors will assess the applicant's ability within the context of his age, his marital status, his occupation, his local connections or lack of them, his local government experience and so on against an unconscious social background, all of which must be measured against the type of constituency for which the candidate is being sought. In the eyes of the *observer* the *ablest* applicant may be rejected, but in the eyes of the *selectors* the *most suitable* applicant will have been selected, for the two do not necessarily coincide: ability may be sufficient to secure a place on the short-list; it is seldom sufficient to secure the nomination.

The 'Standard Bearer': the Selection of Candidates by Non-Incumbent Conservative Associations

Between 1950 and 1966 non-incumbent Conservative associations contested 1,568 constituencies, of which only eighty-two were Conservative gains. The vast majority of the candidates selected to fight these constituencies were 'standard-bearers', and factors which influenced their selection were related to this central fact. The principal criterion was the ability of the applicant to fulfil the demands of an electoral campaign which, in most cases, was likely to be successful only in so far as it reduced the majority of the opposing party. Although most of the factors which influence the selection of candidates by non-incumbent

49. Guttsman, op. cit., Chh. 1, 4, and 10, esp. pp. 296-8.

associations may appear similar to those which affect selections by incumbent associations, they are substantially modified by the nature of the relationship which is being established: the one potentially short-term the other potentially long-term. Furthermore, selection is a process which all but a small minority of non-incumbent associations must repeat at least once between general elections, perhaps more often if a by-election occurs or a candidate withdraws. The *timing* of selection in non-Conservative constituencies is therefore a factor of some importance.

In the case of general elections, the aim of Central Office is to ensure that every constituency has a candidate six months before the possible election date. The latter is not, of course, always in the hands of the Conservative party, but the current political trends will normally enable Central Office to estimate when an election is likely to occur. The possibility of a June or October election in 1965 tended to speed the selection of candidates after October 1964, for example. Thus by the time the date of the 1966 General Election was actually announced, only twenty-three Conservative associations in Labour-held constituencies had not selected their candidates.[50] Similarly, during the party's last period of power, Central Office had to be prepared for an election from at least October 1963 onwards. In practice this meant that in March 1964 the Vice-Chairman could announce that 'practically every constituency has adopted its prospective candidate'.[51] This is one of the principal tasks of each area organizer – to see that each of the constituencies in his charge selects a candidate in good time for the election.

The normal sequence is for marginal and semi-marginal seats to select fairly soon after a general election, whereas hopeless seats often delay choosing a candidate until a relatively short time before the election. For instance, of twenty-three constituencies which selected candidates between November 1964 and August 1965, eight were marginal, ten semi-marginal, two comfortable, three safe, and none impregnable. Conversely, of the twenty-three constituencies which were without candidates on 1 March 1966, none were marginal, four were semi-marginal, one was comfortable, six were safe and twelve were impregnable.

One other problem which is associated with the timing of selection is that of the withdrawal of candidates. Unfortunately, no compre-

50. *The Times*, 1 March 1966.
51. *Huddersfield Examiner*, 14 March 1964.

hensive figures are available to illustrate this problem: such figures as are available, however, suggest that the number of withdrawals among Conservative candidates is small. Between March 1963 and August 1964, ten Conservative candidates resigned for various reasons;[52] over the same period twenty-six Labour candidates resigned. The basic difference between the two parties is that Labour has a much greater problem resulting from withdrawals of candidature,[53] but the extent to which this can be attributed to differences in selection procedure is open to question. It may be that the more exhaustive procedure normally applied by Conservative associations is more likely to produce a candidate whose allegiance to the constituency in general, and the association in particular, will remain strong whatever the prospects of electoral victory. On the other hand, the difference may be a product of acknowledged social divergences among the candidates: Conservatives are probably less likely to be subjected to unacceptable pressures on their time and money, whereas Labour candidates may find that neither their leisure nor their financial resources are sufficient to meet the demands of a prolonged candidature. The twin problems of compatibility and availability may loom much larger among Labour candidates.

It is against the background described above that the characteristics of the candidates selected by non-incumbent Conservative associations and the types of constituency which select them will now be discussed.

Previous Electoral Experience

Between 1950 and 1966 nearly two fifths of the candidates selected by non-incumbent Conservative associations had previously fought one or more parliamentary elections. Closely involved, of course, with previous electoral experience is the tendency to re-select candidates who have fought the constituencies before. Where the inter-election period is short, such as in 1950-1 or 1964-6, the proportion of re-selections tends to be higher, as might be expected. On both of these occasions approximately 30 per cent of the candidates were re-selected. Moreover, when general elections are close together it is the marginal seats which are most likely to re-select their former candidates: thus in 1951 58·7 per cent of the marginal constituencies re-selected their

52. These were two for business reasons, one on health grounds, two because they had been adopted elsewhere, two because of a split in the local association, one to make way for Sir Alec Douglas-Home, and two not known.
53. See Part Two, Chapter Eight, pages 216-18.

candidates, compared with only 20·7 per cent of the impregnable seats; the corresponding figures for 1966 were 41·9 per cent and, again, 20·7 per cent respectively. Obviously, the advantages of selecting a candidate who has recently fought the constituency are considerable, especially where the electoral swing is favourable, as it was in 1951.

Where the inter-election period is much longer, however, the proportion of re-selections falls to between 11 and 20 per cent, and it is the safe and impregnable seats which are more likely to re-select their former candidates. The reason for this is, in fact, a negative one in that, whereas the proportion of marginal and semi-marginal constituencies fluctuates considerably according to the length of the inter-election period the proportion of safe and impregnable seats which re-select their candidates tends to remain fairly constant.

There is an even stronger tendency to re-select a candidate when a by-election occurs, or where a selection *follows* a by-election: thus a third of the candidates who fought by-elections between 1950 and 1966 had fought the same constituency at the *previous* general election; a further third fought the same constituency at the general election *following* the by-election; and another 5 per cent fought the same constituency in both general elections and the by-election. In other words, nearly three quarters of the candidates selected for by-elections eventually fought the same constituencies at least twice.

Despite the tendency to re-select a significant proportion of candidates, there is, none the less, a relatively high turnover of candidates in general. The majority of candidates at any general election, more than four fifths, in fact, will either be fighting their first elections or have fought only once before, either at the previous general election or at a subsequent by-election. There is, in other words, an 80 per cent turnover of candidates every two general elections. This means that even if a non-incumbent association does re-select a former candidate it cannot normally hope to retain his services for more than two elections, including by-elections. For the great majority of associations, election day terminates its relationship with the candidate and the process of selection must begin again.

Previous electoral experience is, of course, a valuable asset to any applicant and many associations do seek candidates who have fought other constituencies, but the majority find themselves with a candidate who is fighting his first parliamentary election: less than 10 per cent of the candidates selected by non-incumbent associations between 1950 and 1966 had unsuccessfully contested more than one election.

Age

Between 1950 and 1966 non-incumbent associations have tended to select more and more candidates under forty years of age: in 1951, 46·5 per cent of the candidates were under forty; by 1964 this figure had risen to 60·6 per cent, dropping slightly in 1966 to 58·7 per cent. Constituencies faced with by-elections tended to select an even higher proportion: 69·2 per cent. As might be expected, the proportion of candidates of fifty years of age or more has declined almost as sharply from 19·8 per cent in 1951 to 13·3 in 1966, whilst only 5 per cent of the by-election candidates were aged between fifty and fifty-nine and none was sixty or over.

The whole age structure of candidates selected by non-incumbent associations is weighted in favour of those under fifty in general, and under forty in particular. Youth, for this is what it is in political terms, is seen by the selectors as an electoral advantage: in most cases the candidate chosen by the non-incumbent association will be opposing a sitting Member who will normally be older, often considerably older than he is. The candidate can be presented as a youthful and vigorous alternative, however hopeless the seat might be. Furthermore, a young candidate may be expected to conduct a more vigorous election campaign than many of the older applicants. Finally, there is the question of supply: many young applicants, especially those under thirty, feel that an unsuccessful contest is a necessary qualification for selection for a Conservative-held seat, and this feeling may be reinforced as a general election draws near and the safe seat continues to prove elusive; better a well-fought contest in a hopeless constituency than embarrassing questions at some subsequent selection as to what the applicant was doing at the last general election. This view is supported by the fact that well over a third of the candidates under thirty selected by non-incumbent associations were found in impregnable constituencies, and it is the latter which are normally selecting their candidates as a general election draws near.

Educational Background

It has been shown that incumbent Conservative associations have very strong preferences for candidates with a public school background, particularly those who attended the nine Clarendon schools, and for graduates, especially those from the two senior universities. These preferences may also be found among non-incumbent associations, but to a much lesser degree. Rather more than half of the candidates selected by non-incumbent associations had been to public school, and of these less than a third attended any of the Clarendon schools. Similarly, just over half the candidates were graduates, of whom rather more than half went to either Oxford or Cambridge.

That these preferences are genuine is clear when it is remembered that the majority of the population have not been to a public school, let alone to one of the Clarendon schools, nor are they graduates, let alone Oxbridge graduates. Although the preferences are less strong than among incumbent associations, they nevertheless remain, and as such are evidence of *social* factors in the selection of Conservative candidates.

Occupation

If further evidence is required that social factors are important, it is only necessary to look at the occupational breakdown of the candidates selected by non-incumbent associations, which was very similar to the occupational breakdown of the candidates selected by *incumbent* associations. In both cases the order of preference was businessmen, professional men, those in miscellaneous occupations, and, a long way behind, workers. Again half the candidates came from a business background, nearly a third from the professions (a slight increase), a seventh from miscellaneous occupations (a slight decrease), and less than 4 per cent were workers (a small increase). Moreover, the majority of the working class candidates in general and the trade unionists in particular are found in the northern half of the country and in strong union areas in particular. In fact the number of trade unionists (and working class candidates) has tended to fall over the period: in 1955 ten candidates were members of trade unions, in 1959 nine, but by 1966 the number had fallen to six. The selection of unionists illustrates one of the basic features of the selection of candidates by non-incumbent associations, that of the importance of local connections.

Local Connections

Nearly four fifths (79·4 per cent) of the candidates selected by non-incumbent associations had local connections, compared with just over three fifths (62·8 per cent) of those selected by incumbent associations. This is a reflection of the tendency among non-Conservative seats to select candidates who are readily available during the long period of 'nursing' the constituency which may precede the actual election campaign. The potentially successful candidate who has inherited a

Conservative majority can be expected to make himself available either by taking up residence in or near the constituency or by paying regular visits to it. The potentially unsuccessful candidate cannot be expected to purchase or rent property in the constituency in order to make himself available for a task which normally ends with the termination of the election campaign. The simplest answer is often the selection of a candidate who lives within reasonable proximity of the constituency, to whom the regular journeys between the latter and his own home are little hardship.

Local government experience is quite often the basis of a local government connection, but it usually means more than this to the selectors in non-incumbent associations: it normally represents a degree of *electoral* experience and a knowledge of the *nature* of local problems. Nearly two fifths of the candidates had been or were members of local authorities at the time of their selection, a slightly higher proportion than among the candidates selected by incumbent associations.

The Type of Constituency

The factors discussed so far have been seen within the context of the *general* problem facing non-incumbent associations: the problem of finding a candidate who can fulfil what are basically *electoral* demands in terms of campaigning, 'nursing' the constituency, promoting and representing the party image, forcing the incumbent party to commit its electoral forces, and so on. In a minority of the constituencies, however, there is always the possibility that a favourable electoral swing will cause the seat to change hands so that the non-incumbent party becomes the incumbent party. Between 1950 and 1966, 16·1 per cent of the non-incumbent seats fought by the Conservative party were marginal, and a further 18·6 per cent were semi-marginal. Concentrating on the marginal seats, however, and comparing the candidates chosen by these with the candidates selected by impregnable constituencies, it is possible to see to what extent the knowledge that the seat could be gained has on the type of candidate chosen.

The figures in Table 3(13) illustrate the extent to which the candidates selected by *marginal non-Conservative* constituencies have, in a number of respects, more in common with the candidates selected for *marginal Conservative-held* seats, than with those selected for *non-Conservative impregnable* constituencies. This is the case with electoral experience, age structure, public school education, and local government experience,

Table 3(13): Comparison of the characteristics of candidates selected by incumbent and non-incumbent Conservative associations with the electoral status of constituencies, 1950–66

	Incumbent associations		Non-incumbent associations	
	All	*Marginal*	*Marginal*	*Impregnable*
Characteristic	*(per cent)*	*(per cent)*	*(per cent)*	*(per cent)*
Previous electoral experience	64·2	63·0	68·6	26·0
Age under 40	44·3	48·2	42·9	67·7
Public school education	78·0	62·9	63·1	49·4
Clarendon schools	37·6	29·6	22·6	14·3
Graduates	69·9	63·0	53·6	48·6
Oxbridge graduates	54·6	44·4	35·3	27·3
Local connections	62·8	62·0	81·7	78·2
Local government experience	34·1	43·4	41·6	31·2

NOTE: The total figures for incumbent associations are included for comparative purposes, since the marginal seats constitute a small population.

and to a lesser extent with university education. Local connections are an important exception and demonstrate the extent to which selectors in marginal non-Conservative constituencies are aware that they *may* be selecting an M.P.: in almost every other respect the marginal seats seek candidates whose characteristics mirror those of the 'potential M.P.', but the local or semi-local candidate represents those few extra votes which may further reduce or even eradicate the opposing majority. The task of making a local candidate known to the electorate is usually less formidable than that of promoting a stranger, whilst the very fact that he is a local candidate may reinforce the electoral swing. So runs the theory: its justification is unimportant since the selectors invariably act as though it were the case.

Thus the initial factor in determining the course of selection in non-Conservative constituencies is electoral status: the more marginal the seat the greater the likelihood that the selectors will be influenced by questions of electoral experience, age, local connections, and local government experience. Within the context of these considerations the selectors will judge the applicants on their ability and this becomes a question of *suitability* as with the candidates selected by incumbent associations. The most able applicant may be rejected in favour of another who is considered more suited to the needs of the particular constituency.

The Selection of Conservative Candidates

Compared with the problem of selecting a potential M.P., that of selecting a 'standard-bearer' is less complicated. The selectors can afford to make a mistake which is easily rectified after the election following the candidate's defeat, but if he is once elected, the local association can rid itself of its Member only at the risk of internal dissension and possibly the loss of the seat. The factors which govern the selection of potentially successful candidates are therefore greater in number and complexity: the selectors are less interested in the period which precedes election day and very much more interested in that which follows. The selectors in the non-Conservative seat are intent on maintaining the party challenge and even in the most marginal of seats this must be their first consideration. In both cases, selections are conducted with *basically similar machinery* and, what is more important, depend upon *basically similar factors*, but the *manner* in which these factors affect selections in Conservative and non-Conservative constituencies differs considerably.

One of the most interesting features of Conservative selection is the general absence of political considerations. Finer, Berrington, and Bartholomew have pointed out that, as far as M.P.s are concerned, 'the terms "Left" and "Right" are misleading and dangerous',[54] and that 'the division of the Conservative party into Left and Right, progressive and reactionary, moderate and diehard, finds no warrant in Conservative history'.[55] There is no reason to believe that the political spectrum which applies to Conservative M.P.s in particular does not apply to Conservative candidates in general. It is doubtful, therefore, that any applicant for a candidacy is selected or rejected because he is regarded in a general sense as left wing or right wing. Particular issues may, however, have some bearing, but these are usually non-political or quasi-political matters which are basically social in origin. Outright political questions affect selection only when there is a clear dichotomy within the Conservative party as a whole, such as the bitter differences over the party's Suez policies in 1956–7. Thus Nigel Nicolson's successor had to be a pro-Suez man.

54. S. E. Finer, H. B. Berrington, and D. J. Bartholomew, *Backbench Opinion in the House of Commons, 1955–59*, London, 1961, p. 104.
55. ibid., p. 105.

The other type of political question which may affect selection is a leadership crisis. One of the side-effects of the Suez affair was a leadership crisis, of course, and selections which took place during this period were certainly influenced by it: candidates were expected to maintain party solidarity, whether it was a matter of following Eden or Macmillan. Similarly, in June 1963, during the challenge to Macmillan's leadership at the time of the Profumo affair, applicants short-listed for one Conservative seat were asked how they would have voted in the censure debate which had occurred shortly before the meeting. Only one of the three applicants said he would have abstained and this met with disapproval among the members of the executive council: he was not selected. The leadership crisis of October 1963 ensured that applicants for candidacies in the ensuing months were often closely questioned about their support for Sir Alec Douglas-Home. The tradition of party solidarity is strong among the Conservatives, especially over the leadership: differences within the party over policy are acceptable, but differences over the leadership are anathema. Iain Macleod at Enfield West[56] and Donald Johnson at Carlisle[57] were challenged by their local associations less over their objections to certain policies than over their criticism of the party leadership.

With the exception of these particular forms of political disagreement the selection or rejection of an applicant because of his views is normally limited to non-political matters such as support for or against blood sports, or quasi-political matters, such as the abolition of capital punishment.

Nigel Nicolson asserts that his own selection for Bournemouth East and Christchurch in 1952 was 'determined by considerations which were transitory'.[58] This is, of course, true in the sense that the course of a particular selection is influenced by the immediate political situation, by the problems which are affecting the constituency at the time, by the views and prejudices of the selectors – all factors which may be quite different the *next* time the constituency association selects a candidate. It is this which makes every selection a separate entity, influenced as it is by factors peculiar to itself and the timing of the selection. There are, however, common factors which, though they may not play an equal part in every selection, are none the less present. If there is one word which sums up Conservative selection it is *personality*.

56. See *Daily Telegraph*, 29 January 1964.
57. See *Daily Telegraph*, 16 October 1963.
58. Nicolson, op. cit., p. 41.

Within this one word is summarized the variety of factors upon which Conservative selections depend: of considerable importance before the selection committee and paramount before the executive council, the personality of the applicants will determine the course of the selection. An applicant's education, his social background, his occupation, his local government experience or lack of it, his ability, will all contribute to the personality he presents to the selectors and it is in this that the weakness of Conservative selection lies.

The members of a selection committee are less likely to be swayed by an applicant's ability to project his personality, partly because they may reject the applicant for arbitrary reasons, such as age or political experience, and partly because they are normally able to examine the applicant at close range, probe his faults and assess his advantages and disadvantages fairly accurately. The members of the executive council, however, are less well-acquainted with the applicant and must make their decision on the basis of brief biographical details, a short speech and a few questions. Where one applicant is clearly outstanding this presents no problem, but the 'executive council must be careful not to be swept off their feet by sheer oratory'.[59] Nicolson has argued that his own selection was determined by considerations which were *superficial*. It is interesting to note that two would-be candidates, one just after the end of the Second World War[60] and the other after the general election of 1964,[61] should both attribute their failure at previous selections to poor addresses to the executive council. Another Conservative M.P. recalls that, at one selection meeting he addressed, he sensed that the council had not taken to him and he had not taken to the council.[62]

The executive council is always vulnerable to the applicant whose personality can outshine his ability, and whilst it may be possible to suggest that in such cases the '*most suitable*' applicant has been chosen, the whole purpose of the selection of parliamentary candidates becomes open to question.

59. Selection pamphlet, p. 8.
60. M. Astor, *Tribal Feeling*, London, 1963, pp. 175–7.
61. A former junior Minister short-listed in a Conservative seat.
62. Private communication.

CHAPTER FOUR

Four Case-Studies

A Routine Selection

This first case-study concerns the selection of a candidate for a Conservative-held constituency in Greater London prior to the General Election of 1964. The constituency is one of three Conservative seats in a divided borough, and at the General Election of 1959 had a majority of 19·4 per cent, making it a safe constituency for the Conservatives.

The selection took place, however, at a time when Conservative fortunes were at a relatively low ebb. The Orpington by-election of 1962 had left the Conservatives in this basically commuter constituency somewhat uneasy. They felt that they, too, might be vulnerable to a Liberal challenge, and that the substantial majority of 1959 was an indication of past and not future security.

The retiring Member had first been elected in the mid 1950s, and although still comparatively young for an M.P. at the age of sixty-one, he felt that he ought not to embark on a further parliamentary term, which could mean another four or five years, and that he should make way for a younger man. Certainly it was the hope of his association that he would remain for a further term and the news of his impending retirement was received with regret. There was no especial hurry to select a successor, although there were the usual rumours of an autumn election, nor was there any question of a by-election.

Following the announcement of the M.P.'s retirement, the executive council appointed a selection committee, which consisted of the chairman of the association (who was also chairman of the selection committee), the association's four vice-chairmen (who included representatives of the Young Conservatives' and women's sections), the association treasurer, the chairmen of the association's five branches, a co-opted member, and the secretary/agent of the association, a total of thirteen. The secretary/agent was allowed to take a full part in the discussions, but had no vote. The co-opted member was a prominent member of the local business community with which the association had strong connections. Three members of the committee were women. Three members were retired, and the occupations of the remainder were as follows: solicitor, silversmith, sales representative, building director, housewife, student, broker, and a banker. Although this represented a wide degree of experience and a variety of occupations, the selection committee was solidly middle class. The youngest member was the student, who was chairman of the Young Conservatives, and the other members were all over forty. Only one member of the committee was a borough councillor.

In the meantime the chairman of the association had had a meeting with the vice-chairman of the party organization and had secured a list of possible candidates. A few direct applications were received, but the majority of the ninety-nine names eventually considered came from or via Central Office. The chairman and the agent each made an independent examination of all the applications and each drew up his own short-list for further consideration. These two preliminary examinations were based on the biographical details supplied by Central Office and, in a few cases, by the applicants themselves. Two or three of the applicants were already known to either the agent or the chairman. One applicant, for instance, was an acquaintance of the latter, and another was a local councillor. Both applied similar criteria: the successful applicant should be between thirty and fifty years of age and should have had a successful career in a field other than politics. In the opinion of the agent in particular, a local candidate was desirable only if he were outstanding, since he felt there was a danger in a local candidate being too well-known.

After their separate considerations of the applications, the chairman and agent compared their respective short-lists. These coincided fairly closely, and between them they drew up a joint list of twenty-two applicants, which was presented to the selection committee.

The selection committee was given the opportunity of examining every application, in addition to the twenty-two recommended by the chairman and agent. In fact the committee's views were similar, and sixteen of the twenty-two were selected for interview. This completed that part of the selection based, with the exceptions noted, entirely on the paper qualifications of the applicants.

One of the sixteen applicants invited for interview subsequently withdrew, leaving fifteen to be seen by the committee over a series of four meetings. This process took just over a week: three applicants were seen on one evening and four on each of the other three. Each applicant was interviewed for a period of half an hour, and, broadly speaking, each interview took the same course. Where applicable, the wife of each applicant was invited to attend the interview. The chairman would ask the applicant to address the committee on a subject of his own choice, and this was followed by questions from the members of the committee. Finally, the applicant was given the opportunity to ask the committee any questions. Apart from the overall limit of thirty minutes, no restriction was placed on the length of applicants' speeches.

Before each applicant was interviewed, the chairman gave the committee any additional information at his disposal. For instance, one applicant had been recommended by an M.P.; another was the wife of an M.P., and the chairman had made a point of contacting the latter; a third was a prospective candidate in a Labour-held seat; and so on.

Most of the applicants made basically political speeches, but with some personal references included, and few spoke for longer than twenty minutes. It is difficult to assess the importance of these speeches, but as a basic aptitude test they served their purpose, since the committee could judge which applicants were likely to be effective on a public platform and which were not. This particular aspect apart, the questions were probably the more testing part of the interview.

Generally speaking there was a considerable diversity of questions, although one member of the committee persisted in asking every applicant about the rating system in local government. The interesting facet of the questioning of applicants was the roles played by the various members of the committee. For example, at one of the four meetings, at which four applicants were interviewed, a total of thirty-one questions were asked, spread more or less equally among the applicants. Nearly half the questions (fourteen) were put by the chairman, although this was not part of a set procedure by which each applicant was asked the same questions through the chair. Only one question was put by a female member of the committee, and only one by the Young Conservative. Apart from the chairman, no other member of the committee was especially active in questions, including the agent, who asked none.

No formal discussion of the relative merits of the applicants occurred until the last of the four meetings. At this meeting the discussion which led to the final short-list was held after the last of the interviews. At the suggestion of the Central Office area agent, who attended the meetings of the selection committee in an advisory capacity, an immediate vote was taken to reduce the fifteen to a more manageable number. This resulted in a short-list of six names, one of which was included on the casting vote of the chairman.

The area agent again intervened and advised the committee that their main consideration should be to select a short-list of persons whom they felt were *best suited to the constituency and not those who had impressed them most*. He went on to point out that 'a mistake was made at Orpington' where the selected candidate would have made an excellent M.P. but *'was not the right man for the constituency'*.

The committee agreed to bear in mind the area agent's remarks, and decided that a short-list of not more than four and not less than three should be their aim. A further vote was therefore held with the result that one of the six names was eliminated. The area agent suggested that discussion should be limited to the two applicants who had received the smallest number of votes, with a view to eliminating one of them and leaving a short-list of four; but the chairman urged that views on all five should be expressed, and this was accepted by the committee.

The five were Mr Black, a member of the Central Office Staff; Mr Brown, an economist; Mrs Gray, the wife of an M.P.;[1] Mr Green, a barrister and local councillor; and Mr White, a company director. The discussion lasted over an hour and was opened by one of the female members of the committee, who pointed out the close resemblance that Mr Green bore to the retiring Member. There was general agreement that this was so, but there was some suggestion that a candidate with a more forceful personality than that of the retiring Member was desirable.

At this point the chairman produced the written comments of one member of the committee who had not been able to attend this final meeting. The committee member had based his comments on the following criteria: integrity, resilience, success in the applicant's career, personality (this included an assessment of the applicant's wife and family circumstances), leadership and enthusiasm, ability to understand and put over policies, and personal service to the community. The party line, he stressed, was unimportant. The application of these criteria led him to favour the selection of Black or White.

Another member felt that Black was the most brilliant of the five,

1. There were two women among the fifteen applicants interviewed.

but one of his colleagues feared that Black might prove a difficult candidate and Member to handle, since he had shown himself to be not only independent of mind, but somewhat unamenable to criticism. The chairman reminded the committee that Black had acted as adviser to the Prime Minister, and this comment drew expressions of further support for Black from the Young Conservative and another member of the committee.

Discussion now turned to Brown, whom another member favoured together with White, although he felt that the latter was less experienced. The area agent intervened to point out that this remark was unfair to White and that there was little to choose between the two in this respect. Some doubt was expressed concerning the forcefulness of Brown's personality, but this was rebutted and some emphasis was laid on his possible appeal to the younger elements of the electorate. Moreover, it was felt that Brown would stand up well to a hostile audience and that his training as an economist would be invaluable in the Commons.

The discussion reverted briefly to White and Black, and then back to Green. One member said that there were too many lawyers in Parliament and doubts were raised about his availability. The Young Conservative terminated this part of the discussion by saying he had not been impressed by Green.

For the first time mention was made of Mrs Gray. Feelings were much divided: the chairman was clearly opposed to her inclusion and argued that, although her contribution to local government had been considerable, she lacked the ability for national politics; but a woman member reminded her colleagues that the Selwyn Lloyd Report[2] had urged the inclusion of at least one woman applicant on the short-list. The chairman suggested that a short-list of three was more desirable, otherwise the council meeting would be prolonged. This brought a proposal from another member that the short-list should be Black, Brown, and White, but the chairman, in response to the earlier suggestion, questioned whether Mrs Gray should be added out of deference to the Selwyn Lloyd Report.

An attempt was made to elicit the advice of the area agent, but he would only say that, although Mrs Gray was a most capable woman, any decision to include her must be their own.

The committee then voted on the five names before it, with the result that Green was eliminated, Black, Brown, and White were

2. Published earlier that year.

placed on the short-list by a unanimous vote, and Mrs Gray by the casting vote of the chairman. The three female members of the committee expressed satisfaction at the placing of Mrs Gray on the short-list and thought that this would at least satisfy the women members of the association, even if she were not eventually selected.

Arrangements were made to convene a meeting of the executive council in three weeks' time and the meeting closed some four hours after it had started.

The process by which the short-list was compiled was illuminating: no mention was made of the political views of the applicants and the discussion was primarily concerned with the abilities and personalities of the applicants relative to the needs of the constituency and the House of Commons. The initial vote had found Black and Mrs Gray to be the least favoured among the five, but in the final analysis it was Green who was excluded. As far as the male members of the committee were concerned, discussion was evenly distributed, but only two of the three women spoke prior to the actual vote; the Young Conservative's contribution was limited to two comments and the constituency agent made only one contribution. Conversely, the chairman was fairly active, particularly in opposition to Mrs Gray and her inclusion on the short-list on his casting vote was almost certainly a tactical move rather than a change of heart. Her inclusion would appease the women members of the association and pay lip-service to the Selwyn Lloyd Report, neither of which could do any harm, since the chairman anticipated Mrs Gray's rejection at the council meeting.

The part played by the two party professionals, the area agent and the constituency agent, were not especially important. Only where he gave *procedural* advice did the area agent urge a particular course upon the committee, and his comments on the applicants were either noncommittal or designed to ensure that justice was being done to a particular individual. There was no indication that he was attempting to secure the selection, or prevent the rejection, of one or more of the applicants. Nor, during the short break that occurred, did the area agent attempt to exert any informal or indirect pressure.

The constituency agent merely acted as the committee's secretary, and the one comment he made was brusquely rejected by the chairman, who tended to treat the agent not as an equal but as an employee of the association.

Once the preliminary short-list of five had been agreed, it rapidly became clear that there was general support for Black and White, fairly strong support for Brown, and rather less for Green, whilst no immediate support for Mrs Gray was forthcoming. Green's support waned under pressure and a short-list of three seemed to be emerging. Then pressure was brought to bear on behalf of Mrs Gray and with the success of this pressure the short-list became one of four and not three. It is possible that had the chairman limited discussion to each of the five in turn a different result would have emerged. Instead, he allowed the discussion more or less to take its own course. No attempt, for instance, was made to discuss what type of candidate was desired as a separate consideration and this question was raised only incidentally to other comments. The form which the discussion took gives credence to the view that a forceful exposition on behalf of or against a particular applicant by one member of the committee was sufficient to sway the committee as a whole. For example, Black only just escaped exclusion from the preliminary short-list, but a powerful plea early in the discussion raised his status in the eyes of the committee to that of a leading contender. Conversely, Green owed his exclusion to the discussion, whilst Mrs Gray owed her inclusion to the recent publication of the Selwyn Lloyd Report.

The executive council of the association, before which the four short-listed applicants now had to appear, consisted of thirty-six members, thirteen of whom were women. The council comprised the officers of the association (seven), ward representatives (twenty-five), and representatives of the Young Conservatives (three) and the Conservative Club (one). The meeting was attended by twenty-eight members of the council. In opening the meeting the chairman said that the council's task was 'to choose a new M.P. for this constituency'. He submitted a verbal report from the selection committee, outlining the procedure which it had followed and the criteria on which it had based its decisions. These were 'integrity, personal and mental alertness, success of life to date, enthusiasm, co-operation with his or her own association, the ability to criticize, service to the party and country, and contemporary outlook'. He hoped that the council would judge the four applicants on a similar basis. Almost as an afterthought the chairman added, 'There are *no divorces among the four*.'

Each applicant would appear before the council for thirty minutes, and would speak for ten to fifteen minutes, followed by questions from the floor. The wives of the three men would attend, as would Mrs Gray's husband. It was in order to ask them questions. Each member of the council was supplied with biographical details of the applicants.

These were in fact reproductions of the Central Office biographies of each candidate.[3]

Although all four applicants chose to open their remarks with personal references, the content of the four speeches varied considerably. Apart from Mrs Gray, whose speech lasted over twenty minutes,

Table 4(1): *Details of speeches given by applicants*

Gray	Brown	White	Black
Personal	Personal	Personal	Personal
Female politicians	Role of M.P.	Business experience	Education
Local government experience	Electoral experience	Economy	Economy
Local government reform	Personal	Defence	Defence
Trade unions	Wife	Nationalization	Education
Personal	Government record	Personal	
Attack opponents	Defence		
	Economy		
	Attack opponents		

the applicants kept their speeches to the requested length. All except White used notes, and this was reflected in the latter's speech, which lacked the expertise and detailed content of his rivals' addresses. Brown and Black impressed with their ability, whereas the strength of Mrs Gray and White lay in their personalities.

Table 4(2): *Questions asked by council members per applicant*

Applicant	Number of questions
Gray	6
Brown	6
White	5
Black	6

Because she overran her time on her speech, Mrs Gray was given an extra ten minutes for questions. This meant that she received the same number of questions as the other applicants.

3. See Chapter Two, page 45 above.

Table 4(3): Subjects of the questions asked by council members

Subject	Number of questions
Foreign affairs and defence	4
Home affairs	15
Local problems	–
Personal	3
Miscellaneous	1

Apart from the question classed as miscellaneous, which referred to Private Members' Bills, and the three personal questions, all the questions put to the applicants concerned current political problems in so far as they were related either to matters of immediate interest, such as Britain's application to join the Common Market or the 'brain drain', or problems of perennial concern to the party, such as the Welfare State or the nuclear deterrent. Despite the preoccupation of the Conservative party with the latter, there was only one question on the subject of nuclear weapons. In fact, foreign affairs and defence matters were outnumbered by nearly four to one by questions on home affairs. Even the Common Market was the subject of only one question. The variety of questions was considerable and topics ranged from national assistance and rating reform to technology and industrial expansion in home affairs, but only one question, rating reform, was put to more than one applicant.

In the case of Black, questioning was extended to his wife, and to her husband in the case of Mrs Gray, but neither Mrs Brown nor Mrs White was questioned. The questions to Mrs Black and Mr Gray were put by the chairman. Mrs Black was asked what her interests were and whether she would help her husband in his constituency work. Mr Gray was asked to what extent he could give his wife active support and what her commitments were to his own constituency. Both replied that they would be glad to assist in whatever way they could, and Mr Gray stressed that his wife had only minimal commitments to his constituency. It would appear that neither Mrs Brown nor Mrs White were asked similar questions because their husbands had supplied the answers earlier, the one in his speech and the other in answer to questions. What was quite clear was that the council was interested in the applicants' spouses and that the chairman made it his business to ensure that the necessary information was forthcoming.

The problem of assessing the performance of the applicants is formidable but important, for it is basically upon their performance that the council must make its choice. The biographical data provides useful background material, but is hardly sufficient to enable a reasoned choice to be made, and certainly insufficient to justify such a choice. To what extent should the council member make allowance for what might be tactics on the part of the applicant? Mrs Gray laid great stress on her political experience and, of course, on being a woman; Brown sought to emphasize the advantage of being an economist; White urged himself upon the council as a non-specialist, an amateur not a professional; finally, Black stressed the variety of his experience coupled with specialist knowledge. To what extent should allowance be made for the stress of the occasion? Was it this that made Mrs Gray loquacious, Brown nervous, White vague, and Black hesitant? One thing was clear (at least in the view of the author): there was little to choose between the three men, all of whom were superior to Mrs Gray in performance.

This was the background to the discussion which preceded the council's vote, and it was no surprise to find that the chairman opened the discussion by suggesting that Mrs Gray should be eliminated from further consideration. No support for Mrs Gray was forthcoming and the council agreed to confine their discussion to the three men.

The discussion which followed was similar to that which had occurred in the selection committee: the chairman allowed it to follow its own course, intervening only occasionally with a personal comment.

Opinion in the council was sharply divided on both Brown and Black. Brown was variously described as sincere and efficient, aggressive and ambitious, as a candidate who showed a mastery of his subject and who would appeal to youth; and as being 'too clever' and a 'cold fish'. No mention was made of Mrs Brown.

Black was regarded as a potentially tough candidate, with wide experience who would also appeal to youth and as the *'best man for the constituency'*; and also as a poor public speaker, 'disappointing' in performance, who was *'better-suited to a rural constituency'*.[4] Mrs Black was described as 'unimpressive'.

There was little criticism of White, although it was generally acknowledged that he was less able than his two rivals and one member described him as 'charming but a waffler'. Comment on White centred around his *personality*: he had 'a good personality', 'the best persona-

4. Six months later, Black was in fact selected for a rural constituency.

lity', the 'personality *for the constituency*'; he was confident, would appeal to small businessmen, and would be 'easy to present to the electorate'. As for Mrs White, she was described as '*the best wife*'.

The only general comment was that the council should not select a specialist, though this was probably aimed at Brown as much as anybody. At one stage during the proceedings a council member wished to know whether the area agent's advice could be sought, but the latter declined to comment.

At the end of the discussion the chairman summed up. Brown, he said, was an able candidate, whose particular talents would be useful in the Commons. His ambition was something in his favour, and his principal fault was a tendency to be 'lengthy and prosy'. Mrs Brown was obviously attractive and able. White, the chairman agreed, had a most attractive personality and showed great sincerity. His wife was undoubtedly attractive, but did White have a special contribution to make to the party in the Commons? Black clearly suffered from having travelled from Eastern Europe that day and he had been outstanding before the selection committee. He was 'the sort of man the House wanted', but he had been disappointing that evening. His wife was less attractive than Mrs White, but 'was this paramount?'

Table 4(4): *Result of balloting*

Applicant	1st ballot	2nd ballot
White	13	18
Black	8	10
Brown	7	–
Total	28	28

After the first ballot, the chairman ascertained that the council was prepared to accept either White or Black. The result of the balloting was clearly in line with the trend of the discussion: council members generally found it difficult to choose between Black and Brown, whereas there was rather less criticism of White. As far as the chairman was concerned, however, the choice lay between Black and White, and his personal preference, though he did not vote, was probably Black.

It is quite clear that much depended on the performance of the applicants, and the fact that Black did not live up to expectations told against him, even though there were mitigating factors. Furthermore, the personality of the applicants was much in the minds of the council members and White scored heavily in this respect, despite the open acknowledgement that he was less able than his rivals. Finally, the wives of the applicants were obviously regarded as relevant to the choice of candidate, a fact which was an asset to White and a handicap to Black. Nevertheless, the constantly recurring factors were those of *personality* and selecting the '*best man for the constituency*', and it is difficult to avoid the view that ability took second place to personality.

If this was a typical selection, and the constituency agent believed that it was, then three conclusions emerge: first, any woman applicant must be really outstanding to overcome the handicap of her sex; second, the test before the selection committee is primarily one of ability, whereas the test before the executive council is primarily one of personality; third, performance before the council counts heavily in the latter's deliberations. To sum up in the words of the constituency agent: the association 'was mainly concerned with the *type of M.P. they would like for* ——. There were some candidates who were *not suitable for this constituency*, but Mr White seemed the *most suitable one*.'[5]

How much does the wife count?

The second case-study also deals with the selection of a candidate in a Conservative-held constituency, but with the much more substantial majority in 1959 of 51·6 per cent. Situated in southern England the constituency represents a particular type of Conservative stronghold *par excellence*, being based very largely on an elderly, retired, middle class population. A substantial proportion of the population of this borough constituency are old age pensioners, and more than half are over fifty years of age, and some indication of the importance of this to the Conservative Association in particular is found in the decision to hold the adoption meeting on a Saturday afternoon in order to accommodate the many elderly people whom it hoped would attend.

This constituency is one of the safest Conservative seats in Great Britain, and the local association had little to fear, therefore, from a Liberal challenge, or an anti-Conservative swing, or both: the members of the Conservative Association actively involved in the selection knew that they were selecting an M.P. and acted accordingly.

5. Private communication. (Author's italics.) The council's decision was, of course, subject to the approval of a general meeting of the association, but in this case it proved to be a formality.

The retiring Member had represented the constituency for nearly twenty years. His original reason for announcing his impending retirement was that of ill-health, but it was subsequently revealed that his wife was suing him for divorce, a situation which the local association found embarrassing and unpalatable. Since he had already announced his intention to retire, there was no question of the association attempting to force his retirement, although it is quite likely that some pressure would have been exerted by the latter had this not been the case. The news of the impending divorce proceedings had two results: it speeded up the selection process should a by-election prove necessary, and it ensured that the question of divorce played a part, albeit a minor part, in the selection.

As soon as the chairman of the association was informed by the sitting Member that he intended to retire, he called a meeting of the executive committee at which a selection committee of nine, plus an observer, was appointed. Three of the nine members were women, and the committee consisted of two of the association's elected officers, the president and chairman, one representative each from the Young Conservatives, Women's Advisory Committee, the Political Committee, and the local Borough Council, two representatives from the branch committees and the constituency agent. The observer was a vice-president of the association. Apart from the Young Conservative, all the members of the committee were middle-aged or older, and three of the nine were retired. Their occupations were as follows: company secretary, investment consultant, company director, chief engineer, solicitor, bank official, secretary, and one widow and one unmarried woman neither of whom worked. The selection committee was therefore solidly middle class and probably fairly representative of the constituency association. One way in which the committee differed from most Conservative selection committees was in the freedom accorded to the agent, who was a full member with normal voting rights. This was both unusual and, as it happened, important.

The committee's first meeting was devoted to the discussion of 'the type of candidate likely to be *best suited for the constituency*.'[6] Five basic criteria were agreed:

(1) A married man was preferable to a single man.
(2) A single woman was preferable to a married woman.
(3) The age group for men should be 37–48, and for women 34–40.

6. Report of the Selection Committee to the Central Council. (Author's italics.)

(4) The candidate should be willing to reside within fifteen to twenty miles of the constituency, although not in it.

(5) The candidate should be a practising Christian, although not of any particular denomination.

None of these stipulations should be regarded as unusual or peculiar to this selection: although these, or similar conditions, are not always formalized by the selection committee, they are invariably in the minds of its members.

A total of 127 applications for the vacancy were received. As in the first case-study, only a small number of direct applications were received, the remainder coming via Central Office. No preliminary examination of the applications was undertaken by the chairman or agent or by any other member of the committee, and the latter devoted the remainder of its first and two subsequent meetings to the initial task of reducing the applications to a more manageable number. The following extract from the selection committee's report to the executive committee describes this process:

The process of elimination was carried through in accordance with the prearranged stipulations as to the candidate's necessary qualifications, but to this were added factors, such as *personal knowledge and ability, experience, both political and industrial, environment,* and so on. The final complete list thereupon contained some twenty-eight names. This was felt to be over-weighted, and if all the candidates were to be interviewed, there would be insufficient time for each of them to be examined thoroughly.

The committee thereupon re-examined the qualifications of all the twenty-eight candidates most comprehensively and finally agreed to a reduction of fifteen. This was subsequently raised to eighteen on the receipt of further applications.[7]

At its first meeting the committee had also drawn up a series of questions which were to be put to each of the applicants interviewed. The view of the committee was that an address by each applicant served no useful purpose and that a wide range of questions, with well-prepared supplementaries, would provide a far more searching test. A total of twenty questions and eighteen supplementaries was therefore prepared on a wide range of subjects. Nearly half were concerned with current political problems and party policies, a further quarter with the national and local electoral situation, and the remainder with personal matters. Not unnaturally, the questions of the party leadership and the

7. ibid. (Author's italics.)

recent Common Market negotiations figured prominently, whilst there was a skilful use of supplementary questions. Apart from the predictable enquiry concerning the support of the applicant's wife, there were two questions of particular interest. Each applicant was asked whether he or his wife had been married before, and whether he would be financially dependent on his parliamentary salary. The first question was a reflection of the background to this selection in particular, and, although not normally put so directly, of the Conservative distaste for divorce in general. The second question was an ironical reversal of the pre-Maxwell Fyfe situation, for the committee was concerned not with the applicant's ability to make a major contribution to constituency funds, but with his ability to maintain himself as an M.P.

> In compiling the list of questions the committee sought to examine exhaustively the candidate's views on matters both international and local, and his approach to Conservatism generally, and personal views on more controversial aspects of policy.
> At the interviews each member of the committee had before them the biographical notes of each of the candidates, the list of set questions with spaces for comment, and a marking sheet which covered such items as *personality*, *appearance*, and so on.
> On each of three evenings the candidates were all invited to be present for refreshments. Each candidate was given some 35–45 minutes with the selection committee and whilst the remainder were waiting they were entertained by the wives of the chairman, the secretary and Councillor ———.
> At the end of each evening the committee invited comments from these three ladies on the *social* as opposed to the political abilities of the candidates and *their wives*.
> The ability of the various candidates was discussed by the committee at the conclusion of each session and those who did not warrant further consideration were eliminated.[8]

The interviewing technique used by this selection committee was undoubtedly more exhaustive than that of the first case-study, but its aims were basically similar: the committee sought to test the *knowledge*, *ability, and personality* of the applicants with a view to determining their *suitability*, not just as potential M.P.s, *but as M.P. for* ———. That this involved an assessment of their social attributes and their wives is demonstrated by the special arrangements made to entertain the applicants and report back to the committee. The practice of eliminat-

8. ibid. (Author's italics.)

ing unsuitable applicants at the end of each session was an advance on the method of the first case-study, since it avoided the danger of confused memories and impressions.

At the end of the third and final session the committee had narrowed its short-list to six, but further discussion swiftly reduced this to five: Mr Black and Mr Brown,[9] Mr Jones,[10] a wine merchant, Mr Smith, on the staff of Central Office; and Mr Wood, a public relations consultant.

The discussion began with an exchange of views on the type of candidate the committee wanted and discussion turned to the wives of the applicants. At this point the agent, possibly suspecting too much emphasis might be placed on this issue, reminded his colleagues that they were selecting a candidate, not his wife – '*she could only tip the balance*'. It was generally agreed that the choice lay between a good constituency Member and the potential Cabinet Minister, and that of the five, Black and Smith were politicians and potential Ministers, that Jones and Wood would be good constituency men, and that Brown was a border-line case. Although no objection was raised against the prospect of selecting a potential Cabinet Minister, it was soon clear that there was strong opposition to both Black and Smith, nor was the committee impressed by their respective wives. It was felt that Black would secure the selection if he were short-listed, and to this the agent protested strongly, arguing that he would find Black difficult to work with. At the same time it was agreed that the short-list should consist only of those applicants whom the selection committee was prepared to see as the Member for ——, and if there were objections to Black he should be excluded.

There then followed some discussion about the length of the short-list, and it was agreed that three rather than four would be ideal, since the council meeting should not be unnecessarily prolonged. The committee did not feel obliged to present a variety of applicants to the council, however, and this opened the way to the exclusion of Black and Smith. It rapidly became clear, before any vote was taken, that the majority opinion was in favour of Brown. Although the committee felt justified in offering a lead to the council by the *composition* of the short-list, it did not feel justified on tactical and procedural grounds to recommend the selection of a particular individual. Moreover, the fact that both Black and Smith were Central Office employees tended to mitigate against them since the committee wished to avoid any

9. Both short-listed in the first case-study.
10. Interviewed, but not short-listed in the first case-study.

impression, however ill-founded, of Central Office pressure or influence.

Finally a vote was taken in which Black and Smith came at the bottom of the ballot, and after some further discussion a short-list of the remaining three was agreed.

It was apparent from the discussion that both Black and Smith, although acknowledged as able men, had not impressed the committee on other grounds. Neither had, as far as the committee was concerned, the right type of personality, nor had their wives. The matter of Central Office connections was largely an afterthought. In fact, there was little doubt that, had the committee been responsible for the final selection, Brown would have been chosen. There are strong grounds, therefore, for arguing that Jones and Wood were placed on the short-list almost by default, out of procedural and tactical necessity, with the proviso that all three were acceptable as the final choice.

The executive or central council, as it is known in this constituency, with whom the final choice lay, comprises sixty persons representing over 11,000 members of the association. Just under half (twenty-nine) of the council members are women, and it is in this respect that the council is least representative, since the agent estimated that the proportion of women to men in the association was at least 60:40, possibly 65:35 in favour of women. The full council was present at the selection meeting.

The chairman of the association opened the meeting by presenting the selection committee's report. There were two questions arising from the report concerning the committee's stipulation that the candidate should be prepared to live near the constituency, but the chairman stressed that, although all three applicants had accepted this condition, too much emphasis should not be laid on it. The applicants would be seen in alphabetical order and each would speak for a quarter of an hour and answer questions for a similar period. Each applicant had been asked to prepare an address on 'Restoring the Conservative Image'. Any questions, political or personal, were in order from any member of the council.

The decision to stipulate the topic of the applicants' speeches meant, of course, that they were all basically similar. The topic was sufficiently broad, however, to allow for individual contributions and was not especially limiting. For instance, Brown simply adapted the speech that he had given to two previous selection meetings. All three applicants chose to refer to local problems, in particular the question of retired

Table 4(5): *Details of the applicants' speeches*

Wood	Brown	Jones
General election	Personal	Personal
Attack on Liberals	Government record	Local problems
Attack on Labour	Local problems	Foreign affairs
Leadership	Personal	Home affairs
Government record	Government's difficulties	Leadership
Foreign affairs	Foreign affairs	Personal
Economy	Economy	
Local problems	Attack on Labour	
General election	Attack on Liberals	

people in the constituency. At the same time the speeches were wide-ranging: all three mentioned home and foreign affairs, two mentioned the party leadership, two the government record, two the economy, two attacked their opponents, and only Wood refrained from any

Table 4(6): *Number of questions asked by council members per applicant*

Applicant	Number of questions
Wood	9
Brown	7
Jones	8

personal references. In fact, Wood rather clumsily attempted to emphasize a family connection with the constituency as he was leaving the meeting.

The number of questions put to each applicant did not vary widely, although Brown was inclined to give lengthy answers.

Table 4(7): *Subjects of the questions asked by council members*

Subject	Number of questions
Foreign affairs and defence	2
Home affairs	11
Local problems	1
Personal	3
Miscellaneous	7

There was less emphasis than in the first case-study on policy questions, although the dichotomy between foreign and home affairs was similar, with the stress on the latter. The three personal questions were all put to Wood, one concerning his wife and the other two his industrial and political experience. The higher incidence of miscellaneous questions was probably the result of the set topic, since they related to such matters as electoral reform, recent by-election results and the party image. The wife of each applicant was asked the same question: to what extent would she support her husband?

It was clear that the council was impressed with all three applicants and that the choice was not easy. The performance of the applicants was especially interesting in the light of subsequent events, which emphasized the crucial importance of the applicant's performance before the council. In the view of the author, the order of the applicants in terms of performance was Wood, Brown, and Jones.

Before allowing any questions or discussion, the chairman made it clear that there had been no pressure from Central Office and that the 'selection was a completely free decision by the constituency'. He reminded the council that the applicants had been understandably nervous and that among the many points they should bear in mind was that they '*must select a pair: the wife of the candidate would have a very important role to play*', and this should not be forgotten. In this connection it should be remembered that although Mrs Jones was expecting a baby, this should not be taken into consideration. Finally, the selection committee was willing to give its views should the council wish.

There were five questions from the floor and one further comment from the chairman. Only two were of interest: one member wished to know the ages of Wood's and Jones's families, and another the candidates' religions. In reply to the first, the chairman said he did not think that either Mrs Wood or Mrs Jones would be unable to fulfil the obligations of a candidate's wife; and to the second that 'all are practising Christians'. The chairman then commented that all three had strong recommendations from the Central Office and from their own local associations. He then asked if there was any desire for discussion, but the majority feeling was that a vote should be taken at once.

The three ballots which proved necessary were ultimately inconclusive, since the two leading contenders, Wood and Brown, both had thirty votes. Jones was eliminated on the first ballot, in which Wood led Brown by a single vote. The second ballot would normally have

Table 4(8): *Result of balloting*

Applicant	First ballot	Second ballot	Third ballot
Wood	24	31	30
Brown	23	29	30
Jones	12	–	–
Spoilt papers	–	2	–
Total:	59	62	60

been decisive despite the close result, but the scrutineers decided that a further ballot was necessary on two grounds. First, the two spoilt papers were marked in such a way that they could have been meant for Brown; and second, the total number of votes cast was three more than in the first ballot. The situation was complicated by the presence of a number of members of the association as observers, who were not members of the council, but may have thought themselves entitled to vote.

The decision of the scrutineers was conveyed to the chairman, who told the council that there would have to be another vote, but *before saying why* he said: 'Remember, you are picking *a pair and the wife does count.*' The observers were asked to leave the body of the meeting and a count was taken of those entitled to vote, the total number being sixty. Ironically, however, the third ballot was a tie.

Two solutions were offered to this dilemma: the presentation of the two applicants to a general meeting of the association, a suggestion which was promptly rejected; and a proposal that the chairman should exercise his casting vote. The latter agreed to do so provided the council gave its approval, which it did.

Before announcing his decision, the chairman made it clear that his choice was the result of careful consideration of the interests of the national party and the association: one of the two applicants had been more strongly recommended by Central Office, and considering the wives of the two men as well, he felt bound to cast his vote in favour of Brown. A motion was then carried giving unanimous support to his decision. The latter was, of course, subject to final approval by a general meeting of the association, but as in the first case-study this was a formality.

The council meeting demonstrated very forcibly how much selection depends upon the brief appearance of the applicants. The council was much more impressed with Wood than the selection committee had been. The latter had assumed that the short-list gave a clear run to Brown, but on the night his performance did not match that of Wood and he almost paid the penalty, saved only by the chairman's casting vote. Indeed, the fate of the three short-listed applicants is an interesting commentary on Conservative selection: Brown was, of course, adopted as candidate for this constituency and became its M.P. in October 1964; Jones was selected for a safe Conservative seat three days after his rejection in this constituency; and Wood failed to secure selection at all, after coming so close.

The selection committee in this second case-study had not felt procedurally justified in recommending only one applicant to the central council and had therefore endeavoured to arrange the short-list to favour, as it thought, its own choice. The plan misfired because the favourite's performance was below, and one of his rival's above, expectation. The earlier rejection by the committee of both Black and Smith is an indication of the extent to which the successful candidate must, in the view of the selectors, *suit the constituency*. In theory the selection committee had agreed to accept any one of the three short-listed applicants, but in practice they anticipated the selection of Brown.

The part played by the constituency agent was significant: he later stressed that his full participation in the deliberations of the committee was unusual, a fact clearly shown by the degree of influence he had in the selection. His antipathy towards Black was largely responsible for the latter's exclusion, and it may be suspected that he had similar feelings about Smith. During the balloting at the council meeting, moreover, the agent privately made his lack of enthusiasm for Wood abundantly clear. After the second and abortive ballot he impressed his views upon the chairman, and this may well have had some influence on the latter's subsequent remarks.

The chairman, apart from his actions towards the end of the council meeting, was not especially influential in directing the course of the selection. At the committee he was content to allow the discussion to take its own course, intervening only occasionally and then never in any decisive way. This contrasted with the behaviour of the chairman in the first case-study. The chairman's use of his casting vote and his remarks which preceded both it and the third ballot were of greater significance, however. The situation was unusual, however, both in that a ballot was declared invalid and that a tie resulted in the subsequent ballot. None the less, the chairman need not have expressed any views following the second ballot and before the third, other than to explain why a further ballot was necessary. Yet he chose to do so and, though he mentioned no names, there was little doubt that he favoured the selection of Brown: of all the wives Mrs Wood had been the least impressive and the chairman reminded the council, 'Remember, you are *picking a pair and the wife does count.*'[11] When he came to give his casting vote the chairman specifically mentioned consideration of the wives of the two applicants and emphasized that on this, as well as other counts, he felt bound to vote for Brown.

Can it be said, therefore, that the selection was decided in favour of Brown because he had a more attractive or more suitable wife? There is, of course, strong evidence to suggest that this is the case, but was this the reason for the chairman's decision or his excuse? At the selection committee the agent had pointed out that the wife 'can only tip the balance': did Mrs Brown tip the balance in favour of her husband? In so far as she provided the chairman with a *reason* for giving his casting vote to her husband, Mrs Brown clearly did tip the balance, and had Mrs Brown and not Mrs Wood been the least impressive of the wives, this would not have been possible; but this is not to say that Brown was selected *because* he had the most suitable wife. Brown was their choice in any case, not simply because he had a suitable wife who could fulfil the demands of an M.P's wife, but because they regarded him as superior to Wood in particular and to all the other candidates in general. He was not, as they acknowledged in their discussions, the most able applicant, but he was, in their view, the most *suitable*, and they hoped and expected that the central council would agree with their views. The selection demonstrated beyond all doubt that the applicant's wife has an important bearing on selection, and it suggests that very occasionally this can be a decisive factor: in the case of this constituency, however, this was only *tactically* true, for had Mrs Brown been less suitable doubtless the chairman would have found another reason for giving his casting vote to her husband.

This case also casts some light on the role of women in Conservative selections: over half the members of the local association and nearly half the central council are women, and yet only three women were appointed to the selection committee by the executive committee. At

---

11. In the view of an American observer attending the council meeting (he had *not* attended any of the selection committee meetings), this was clearly a declaration in favour of Brown.

one session of the selection committee the three women members asked only three questions between them, and during the discussion, of eighty-eight comments made, only nine were made by women members. Similarly, only seven of the twenty-four questions put to the applicants at the council meeting and two of the five questions which preceded the balloting came from women. Whatever their numerical strength, women do not dominate selection, nor would it seem that their influence is commensurate with their numbers. This is certainly true of their open part in selection, although it is possible that their influence is discernible in the voting at council meetings. It may well be that women are more likely to favour the applicant with an attractive personality: was this why White was chosen in the first case and Wood came so near in this? Both possessed great charm and personality. In neither case, however, did women form a majority of the council, but it is possible that women formed a nucleus of their support. Certainly in the earlier case several women spoke enthusiastically in favour of White, but the evidence is inconclusive. It has been argued that Sir Anthony Eden attracted women voters in the General Election of 1955:[12] does the personable applicant win the support of Conservative women selectors?

In general, this selection showed that Conservative selection, despite its exhaustive procedure, is inevitably subject to haphazard factors, such as the performance of the applicants, both at the selection committee and the council meeting, but especially at the latter, and the personalities of those on the selecting bodies, especially the selection committee. Powerful advocacy can result in the selection or rejection of one or more of the applicants and to this extent some modification of the conclusions drawn from the earlier case-study are necessary. There is no evidence from this second study, however, to contradict the view that a woman must be outstanding to overcome the handicap of her sex: the one women interviewed in this second study was not outstanding and was not considered for short-listing.

Despite the rejection by the selection committee of two applicants who were acknowledged to be more able than those placed on the short-list ability remained the primary consideration, subject, however, to the overriding consideration of *suitability* for the constituency. To the three conclusions based on the first case-study a fourth must be added: the *overriding consideration of an applicant's suitability for the constituency*.

12. *Sunday Times*, 24 May 1965.

The constituency agent in this second study felt that Brown's selection was 'not entirely typical' in so far as there was a sharp division in the council as to which of two applicants was the most suitable for the constituency, based less on the abilities of the two men concerned and more on a disagreement as to the type of candidate the constituency needed. In general he expressed the view that the most important consideration in Conservative selection is '*the differences which exist in the various constituencies*'.[13]

Selection in two 'hopeless' constituencies

The purpose of the final two studies is to explain not why a particular individual was selected, but to describe the conditions of selection and the considerations in the minds of the selectors in a 'hopeless' constituency.

The first of these two constituencies is an industrial seat in Greater London. Even in 1959, when Labour's electoral fortunes were at a low ebb, the constituency had a majority of 38 per cent, and in such circumstances the selection of a candidate could be little more than an inter-election ritual for the local Conservative Association.

None the less, the local association approached its task with commendable thoroughness. A selection committee consisting of the chairman and six members of the association was appointed and arrangements were made to interview the applicants. Each interview took the same form: a first period of five minutes, during which the chairman asked five previously agreed questions; a second period of ten minutes, during which the applicant gave a speech on a subject of his own choice; and a final period of ten minutes, during which other members of the committee could question the applicant. The five set questions were:

(1) Why did the applicant wish to become an M.P.?
(2) How much time could the applicant devote to 'nursing' the constituency?
(3) Was the applicant willing to undertake personal canvassing?
(4) Was there any value in contact with non-political organizations in the constituency?
(5) Would the applicant's wife or husband be willing to help in the constituency?

---

13. Private communication. (Author's italics.)

In practice these questions were rephrased by the chairman and supplementary questions were put where necessary, but these were the bases of the questions. With the exception of the first question, which was based on the assumption that the applicant had parliamentary ambitions even though this constituency could offer no prospect of fulfilling them, all the questions were concerned with the ability of the applicant to fulfil the role of parliamentary candidate rather than an M.P. Indeed, the supplementary to the first question was: 'Why have you applied to this constituency?' None of the questions sought to test the applicant's knowledge of party policy. Of the questions put to the applicants during the third period, less than half concerned party policy, and only in the speeches of the applicants did the latter predominate.

Each member of the selection committee had a mark sheet for each applicant on which he could record his assessment. The maximum possible score was a hundred: fifty marks for the applicant's responses to the questions; twenty-five for the speech; fifteen for the second period of questions; and ten for personality and appearance. There was no specific provision for awarding marks for the applicant's knowledge or ability, and any assessment of these could be made only under one or the other headings.

In so far as the overall consideration at this selection was finding a *suitable* candidate, the selection differed little from either of the two previous case-studies, and a similar *method* of selection was used. The definition of what constitutes a suitable candidate, however, is very different. Both the Conservative seats were seeking an M.P. and based their actions upon this assumption; the association in the Labour-held seat was seeking a candidate and examined all the applicants purely in electoral terms. The context of the selection in this 'hopeless' constituency was the *election campaign* which had to be fought within the next eighteen months.

The second constituency in this final section is an industrial seat in the West Riding of Yorkshire.[14] The principal sources of employment are steel and coal-mining and the Labour M.P. is sponsored by the Yorkshire Area of the National Union of Mineworkers. The constituency is in fact one of Labour's twenty safest seats, having had a majority in 1959 of 48·2 per cent.

---

14. This constituency was *not* typical, however, in that the local association did not go through the normal procedure of selection committee, executive council, and general meeting.

The local Conservative Association is fairly well-organized, but it faces a more formidable task than its counterpart in the first of these two 'hopeless' seats. The political situation in the latter is probably more fluid than in this West Riding constituency: social mobility is greater and more favourable industrial conditions exist, both of which are likely to render attempts to reduce the Labour majority more successful. In the Greater London seat the Labour vote had dropped by 11,000 between 1950 and 1959; in the Yorkshire seat no substantial impression appears to have been made, despite a favourable national swing to the Conservatives. The sheer solidity of the opposition to the Conservative party in the mining constituencies of Yorkshire makes the prospect of a candidature on behalf of that party singularly un-attractive. Budding politicians in search of electoral experience prefer constituencies where some tangible result can be achieved and mining seats do not normally fall into this category.

The problem of the Yorkshire Conservatives, therefore, was not to select a candidate so much as to find one. No formal machinery was set up to deal with this task: members of the executive council were asked to approach any possible candidates and informal enquiries were made in the surrounding districts. The result of these enquiries was that someone from a nearby constituency let it be known that he wished to be considered. The fifty-six strong executive council interviewed the applicant and decided to recommend his adoption.

This second study is, of course, an extreme case: normally a local association does not have to search for a candidate, since sufficient applicants are normally forthcoming. The constituency does illustrate the problems of selection in a hopeless seat, however: the principal task is to find an individual who is capable of fulfilling the demands of an election campaign. This is what is meant by the term 'suitable': it is much more important that the candidate is acquainted with the mechanics of an election campaign, and is capable of playing his part as its focal point, than for him to be especially able. It may be an exaggeration to say that availability is more important than ability, but in non-Conservative seats the balance between the two is tilted less in favour of the latter: the mining constituency's candidate, inevitably in view of the method used to select him, was a local man; and all the applicants in the Greater London constituency came from the Greater London area. It is less a question of familiarity with the constituency and more one of availability: a candidate and a standard-bearer must be selected.

Part Three
The Labour Party

Part Three

The Labour Party

CHAPTER FIVE

The Machinery of Selection

The procedure for the selection of parliamentary candidates in the Labour party is laid down in two documents: the Labour Party Constitution[1] and the appropriate Constitution and Rules[2] for Constituency Labour Parties (C.L.P.).[3] Under Clause III (2) of the Labour Party Constitution, C.L.P.s 'must . . . adopt the Rules laid down by the Party Conference'.[4] The procedure to be followed is given in considerable detail: one clause of the Party Constitution, concerned specifically with the selection of parliamentary candidates, consists of eight sections, one of which is divided into four sub-sections; whilst one clause of the C.L.P. Constitution, also concerned specifically with selection, consists of ten sections, one of which is divided into seven sub-sections and another into two sub-sections, together with three appendices illustrating the prescribed nomination form and circulars to be used in the selection. There is, of course, a certain amount of duplication of the Party Constitution in the C.L.P. Constitution, but between them these two documents provide a complete, formal selection procedure. The latter is inevitably involved, but, broadly speaking, it is possible to discern two areas of selection procedure, that which is the basic concern of the national party, represented by the National Executive Committee of the Labour party (N.E.C.), and that which is the basic concern of the C.L.P. The first section of Clause IX of the Party Constitution states: 'The National Executive Committee shall

1. As approved by the Annual Party Conference, 1958. To be referred to as the Party Constitution.
2. As approved by the Annual Party Conference, 1930.
3. There are five sets of rules, A–E: A for undivided constituencies; B for county constituencies; C for Local Labour parties in county constituencies; D for Central Labour parties in divided boroughs; and E for Constituency Labour parties in divided boroughs. With the exception of Central Labour parties (Set D) and Local Labour parties (Set C), both of which have the right of *nomination* to the C.L.P., the rules governing selection are the same in each set. Reference will therefore be made only to Set A.
4. Model Rules, Set A, p. 3. To be referred to as the C.L.P. Constitution.

co-operate with the Constituency Labour Party for each constituency in selecting a Labour Candidate for any Parliamentary Election.'[5]

The Role of the National Executive Committee

The powers of the N.E.C. over the selection of candidates are considerable and its role is continuous: from the moment it gives permission for selection procedure to begin to the moment it finally endorses the choice of the C.L.P., the N.E.C. is closely involved and it is very easy to assume that selection is a national rather than a local matter. In fact, it is neither, and whilst it is something of an exaggeration to describe the role of the N.E.C. as purely peripheral, to regard it as passive rather than active would be no injustice: its powers are extensive; their use is limited.

Under Clause XII (1) of the C.L.P. Constitution, 'the desirability of contesting the Constituency shall be considered by the Executive Committee [of the C.L.P.] in consultation with the National Executive Committee or its officers prior to the procedure laid down in this Clause being set in motion'.[6] This clause applies to the selection of a candidate for a by-election[7] as well as normal selections which fall between General Elections. The original purpose of the clause was to ensure that the resources of the party were wisely used, especially when the Labour party was unable to contest every constituency. Thus where a local Labour party was especially weak it was discouraged from contesting elections,[8] whilst it provides the N.E.C. with a safeguard against the action of extremist elements in local parties. During and since the war, however, this power has been used to control the timing of selection. During the war the N.E.C. decided 'to hold in abeyance the machinery of selection'[9] as part of the electoral truce agreed in 1940 between the three major parties. When vacancies did occur in Labour-held constituencies, a modified form of the normal selection procedure was used.[10] After the war, however, with the Labour party contesting nearly all the seats in Parliament, including some in Ulster in co-operation with the Northern Ireland Labour party,[11] the question of securing the N.E.C.'s permission to select a candidate seemed to have become a formality. Following the General Election of 1951, however,

5. Party Constitution, Clause IX(1).
6. C.L.P. Constitution, p. 15.   7. See below, pages 143–9.
8. e.g. Westminster by-election, March 1931 (N.E.C. Report, APCR 1931, p. 21). See also the list of seven by-elections in N.E.C. Report, APCR 1932, pp. 36–9.
9. ibid., APCR 1942, p. 15.   10. ibid., Appendix III, APCR 1942, p. 179.
11. For details of the agreement with the Northern Ireland Labour party, see N.E.C. Report, APCR 1938–9, p. 79.

the position appeared to alter, and in its Report to the Conference in 1952 the N.E.C. said: 'Immediately after the General Election many requests were received from Constituency Labour Parties for permission to proceed with the selection of prospective Parliamentary candidates. Though the *N.E.C. has been anxious to avoid selection taking place with undue haste*, selections have proceeded steadily.'[12] This was the first visible sign of a new departure: for various reasons the N.E.C. wished to delay the selection of candidates[13] and began to use its power to withhold permission to achieve this.

The period immediately following the General Election in 1959 saw an even wider use of this power, and the N.E.C. reported that in response to requests to proceed with selection it *'decided that permission to select* could not be granted'.[14] This, as will be seen later, altered the whole timing of the selection of candidates in Conservative-held constituencies.

In addition to its power over the initiation of selection procedure, the N.E.C. has the right, under Clause XII (3)(d) of the C.L.P. Constitution, to examine the validity of all nominations that the C.L.P receives for the vacancy. All this normally means is that the nominations are examined to ensure that all the conditions laid down in Clause IX (7) of the Party Constitution and Clause XII (3)(c)[15] of the C.L.P. have been fulfilled. For the N.E.C. to invalidate a nomination is a relatively rare occurrence, and then only on technical grounds. Of course, such invalidation often gives rise to criticism since the decision may appear to be based on other than technical grounds. For instance, the nomination of Vernon Thornes, secretary of Sheffield Trades and Labour Council, for a vacancy at Rotherham in 1963, was declared invalid by the N.E.C. on the grounds that he was a full-time employee of the Labour party and therefore ineligible for consideration. This ruling was based on a decision of the Party Conference in 1942 which laid down that *'Constituency Party Agents* whilst retaining their appointments shall not be eligible for nomination as Parliamentary Candidates for any Constituency'.[16] This ruling was reaffirmed in

12. N.E.C. Report, APCR 1952, p. 14. (Author's italics.)
13. See Chapter Eight, pages 212–20 below.
14. N.E.C. Report, APCR 1960, p. 24.
15. (a) Has given his written consent; (b) if a member of the parliamentary panel of an affiliated organization, the consent of the executive committee of that organization has been obtained. See also pages 137–43 below.
16. N.E.C. Report APCR 1942, p. 179; adopted by conference, p. 150. (Author's italics.) There is also a ban on seeking a candidature in the constituency for which the individual was agent for two years following the termination of his employment in that position.

1957 on the recommendation of the N.E.C., but the wording was altered slightly, from '*Constituency Party Agents*' to '*full-time agents*'.[17] There is no evidence that this change in wording was intended or significant, but it was sufficient to render Thornes's case difficult. He was not a constituency agent at the time of his nomination, although he had, from 1949 until 1957, been full-time agent at Rotherham; but this did not invalidate his nomination under the 1942 ruling since more than two years had elapsed since he had relinquished the post. As secretary, however, of Sheffield Trades and Labour Council he was an employee of the Labour party, and it was on these grounds that his nomination was declared invalid. It is difficult to justify the action of the N.E.C. in so far as the ban on full-time agents had been irregularly applied since its inception: in 1954, for example, G. M. Lawson, secretary of Edinburgh Trades Council, was selected for Motherwell,[18] whilst there is no overall ban on Labour party employees at Transport House.[19] The situation was aggravated by the fact that Thornes was regarded as 'favourite' for the vacancy against the strong opposition of the British Iron, Steel and Kindred Trades Association (B.I.S.A.K.T.A.) which had previously held the seat. It may be that the N.E.C., advised by its organization sub-committee, chose to use its power of invalidation to placate B.I.S.A.K.T.A., which, if it lost Rotherham, would have had no representative in Parliament. Moreover, the fact that D. H. Davies, assistant general secretary of B.I.S.A.K.T.A., was at that time also chairman of the N.E.C., made it difficult for Thornes's supporters to believe that the N.E.C. had acted fairly.

None the less, if only because of the danger of such protests, the N.E.C. is reluctant to declare any nomination invalid unless there are genuine grounds for doing so, and its power of validation cannot be regarded as anything more than a means of maintaining overall surveillance of selection, a process which continues throughout the

17. N.E.C. Report, APCR 1957, p. 15; adopted by Conference, p. 126. (Author's italics.)

18. See also F. Longden, Labour and Co-operative M.P. for Birmingham (Deritend), 1929–31 and 1945–50, and Birmingham (Small Heath), 1950–52, who was full-time agent for Deritend, 1931–45; W. J. Irving, Labour and Co-operative M.P. for Tottenham North, 1945–50, and Wood Green, 1950–55, who was full-time agent for Tottenham North, 1927–45; and J. Taylor, Labour M.P. for West Lothian, 1950–62, who was regional organizer for the Eastern Counties, 1935–39, and Scottish Secretary of the Labour party, 1939–50. Following the Thornes case representations were made to the N.E.C. by the National Union of Labour Organizers and Election Agents, and unsuccessful attempts were made to modify the ban on full-time agents at the 1963 and 1964 Annual Conferences.

19. Members of Transport House staff are allowed to seek candidatures after five years' service.

period of selection. On the other hand, the validation of nominations cannot be regarded as signifying the N.E.C.'s approval of the nominees in any other than a technical sense.[20]

As part of its role of overall surveillance of selection, 'the N.E.C. must be represented by an officer, or by a representative appointed for this purpose'[21] at all relevant meetings of the C.L.P. Apart from selections for by-elections, when the national agent or assistant national agent may attend, this function is normally performed by the party's regional organizer.[22] It is, of course, easy to assume that this is evidence of direct control or intervention in selection by the N.E.C.: in practice the regional organizer or other N.E.C. representative usually holds a watching brief over selection meetings, acting as a guide on procedure and a guarantor of the efficacy of the selection; and, as the assistant national organizer pointed out in 1956, 'no officer or representative of the N.E.C. should be allowed to speak on the merits or demerits of the nominee'.[23]

As a final control over selection, the N.E.C. has, under Clause IX (3) of the Party Constitution, the power to veto any selection. This power of endorsement is, like that of validating nominations, a technical matter in so far as the N.E.C. cannot refuse endorsement merely because it does not like a particular candidate or would have preferred an alternative nominee: there must be valid grounds for refusing to approve a candidate's selection. These grounds are very similar to those on which validation can be denied, but in addition to the personal eligibility[24] there are two additional grounds for refusing endorsement. First, under Clause IX (4) of the Party Constitution, the N.E.C. must be satisfied that 'the election expenses of the Candidate are guaranteed'.[25] In effect this means either that an affiliated organization or the C.L.P. has undertaken financial responsibility for the candidature.[26] Second, the N.E.C. must be satisfied that the selection has been carried out in accordance with the party regulations.

The first condition dates back to the inter-war period when the local

20. *Labour Organizer*, January 1956, pp. 13–14.
21. ibid., May 1952, p. 89.
22. ibid., January 1956, p. 13. The regional organizer submits a report to the N.E.C.
23. ibid., January 1956, p. 14. See also ibid., May 1952, p. 89. Ranney, op. cit., pp. 143–4, quotes one regional organizer who claimed that he could, given *favourable circumstances*, secure the *short-listing* of a particular aspirant. Most selections are subject to behind-the-scenes preliminary negotiation (e.g. Leyton and Nuneaton, 1964–5), but the circumstantial limitations on regional organizers are severe.
24. See footnote 15, page 133 above, and pages 137–43 below.
25. Party Constitution, Clause IX(4).
26. See Chapter Eight, pages 228–39 below.

parties were relatively weak and often relied heavily on individuals or affiliated organizations for financial support, and, unless an individual or affiliated organization was prepared to support a candidature, the position was economically impossible. It is therefore unlikely that endorsement could now be refused on these grounds, since, if financial responsibility is not undertaken by an affiliated organization, the C.L.P. will itself assume responsibility. In fact, nowadays the C.L.P. always undertakes to meet all or part, where the candidate is sponsored, of the election expenses by means of a formal motion at the end of its selection conference.

The second condition, however, provides a genuine possibility of a veto by the N.E.C. of a particular selection. At any stage during a selection any nominee, any locally affiliated or party organization, any individual member of the C.L.P., may raise with the N.E.C. the validity of the selection procedure. Such objections may, however, remain unvoiced until after the C.L.P. has made its choice, at which stage the selection is formally challenged in the form of an official complaint to the N.E.C.

Cases in which such a complaint is made are not particularly frequent, and since 1958 there have been only three. The first of these was at Islington North in March 1958, when there was a dispute over the validity of two delegates to the selection conference. It was alleged that the two delegates lived in the Borough of Islington but not in the constituency of North Islington. The question was important because it was alleged that the successful candidate had defeated his nearest rival by only two votes in the final ballot.[27] The N.E.C. investigated the complaint and eventually endorsed the candidature.[28] The second case occurred at Nottingham North in July 1959, when the N.E.C. invalidated the selection of W. C. Whitlock after a complaint by the National Union of Mineworkers (N.U.M.) of irregularities in the voting procedure at the selection conference. A fresh selection was ordered and Whitlock was eventually re-selected.[29] The third case occurred at Newark in July 1963, when the N.E.C. refused to endorse the selection of R. W. Bowes on the grounds that there had been canvassing on his behalf by members of the C.L.P., and a new selection was ordered. In this case the candidate first chosen was not re-selected.

Whatever the motives for the complaints to the N.E.C., it was essential that evidence of irregularity in procedure be produced, and

27. *The Times*, 24 March 1958.   28. *The Times*, 27 March 1958.
29. *The Times*, 17 August 1959.

unless this is done, no matter how much the N.E.C. or any members of the C.L.P. disapprove of the choice of candidate, there is no question of endorsement being refused on grounds other than ineligibility.

The question of eligibility, however, is another matter and provides the N.E.C. with an absolute veto on any candidate under the terms of Clause IX(7) of the Party Constitution. The four sub-sections of this clause stipulate first that the candidate must be an individual member of the Labour party and, if eligible, be a member of a trade union affiliated to the T.U.C. or of a *bona fide* union recognized by the latter;[30] second, that the candidate must not belong to any organization proscribed by the Labour party;[31] third, the candidate must 'accept and conform to the Constitution, Programme, Principles, and Policy of the Party';[32] and finally, the candidate must undertake 'to accept and act in harmony with the Standing Orders of the Parliamentary Labour Party'.[33] Sub-section (c) of this clause in particular provides the N.E.C. with extremely wide powers of discretion, laying down as it does that the candidate must accept party *policy*. Should a particular candidate be politically unacceptable to the N.E.C., this condition renders the rejection of his selection a relatively simple matter: it is not difficult to show that a candidate's views on some aspect of policy are in conflict with the party's declared view, especially if the alleged deviation is to the left rather than the right. It is not without significance that, of the majority of cases in which the N.E.C. refuses endorsement under Clause IX(7) of the Party Constitution, it is on the grounds that the candidate has deviated to the left of party policy.

Before the Second World War there were two grounds on which the N.E.C. was likely to refuse endorsement. The first of these was technical: in 1929 the N.E.C. established an insurance scheme against the loss of deposits at parliamentary elections, the basis of which was a premium of £10 to be paid by the candidate or by the C.L.P.[34] Following the inception of this scheme a number of constituencies failed to meet their commitments under the conference ruling, and in order to enforce the latter in 1932 the N.E.C. withheld endorsement from five constituencies.[35] The other cases were concerned with

30. Party Constitution, Clause IX(7)(a).
31. ibid., Clause IX(7)(b). Generally speaking, Communist or Communist-associated organizations, or extreme right-wing bodies, a list of whom appears in an appendix to the Annual Conference Reports.
32. ibid., Clause IX(7)(c).
33. ibid., Clause IX(7)(d).
34. N.E.C. Report, APCR 1929, pp. 8–9.
35. ibid., APCR 1932, p. 35.

Clause IX(7), however, and were part of the Labour party's disagreement with the Independent Labour party. A number of I.L.P. candidates objected to the ruling of the N.E.C. that they must accept the Standing Orders of the Parliamentary Labour party,[36] although this was not in 1930 part of the Party Constitution. Because of their refusal to accept Standing Orders, therefore,the N.E.C. refused to endorse the candidatures of T. Urwin at East Renfrewshire in 1930 and of D. Hardie at Rutherglen in 1931, following a decision of the N.E.C. to demand a written undertaking from I.L.P. candidates.[37] Previously verbal assurances had been accepted by the N.E.C., but the failure of J. McGovern to conform to Standing Orders after his selection for the Shettleston Division of Glasgow in 1930 led to the demand for a written undertaking, and in 1931 the Annual Party Conference added sub-sections (c) and (d) to Clause IX(7).[38] In 1932 the N.E.C. refused to endorse the selection of E. P. Bell for Wood Green and Southgate, 'because of a qualification on the subject of the Standing Orders of the Parliamentary Labour Party attached to his nomination form'.[39] The N.E.C.'s report added that a number of nominations had been declared invalid on similar grounds.[40]

After the Second World War the N.E.C.'s main difficulty was with candidates who clashed with the party on the question of foreign affairs – a problem which was manifest among Labour M.P.s as well, of course. As far as the latter were concerned, the N.E.C. could withdraw the party whip or, if necessary, expel members of the P.L.P. who disregarded the official policy of the party leadership. Thus strong disciplinary action was taken over the Nenni Telegram, and under the threat of expulsion from the party, fifteen of the thirty-seven signatories claimed that they had not signed the telegram or had since retracted, twenty-one gave assurances of their future conduct, and one, J. Platts-Mills, was expelled from the Labour party.[41] This meant that Platts-Mills's constituency party, Shoreditch and Finsbury, was compelled to seek a new candidate for the next general election. This was not, however, a case of the N.E.C. refusing to endorse a candidate, although it does illustrate the ultimate power possessed by the N.E.C. over M.P.s as well as candidates. The redistribution of parliamentary constituen-

36. Similar difficulties were experienced with the Communist party in the 1920s.
37. N.E.C. Report, APCR 1931, p. 302.
38. ibid., pp. 33 and 176.
39. N.E.C. Report, APCR 1932, p. 35.
40. ibid.
41. N.E.C. Supplementary Report, 17 May 1948, APCR 1948, p. 17.

cies, following the recommendations of the Boundaries Commissions in 1948, presented the N.E.C. with further problems with left-wing M.P.s. The redistribution meant that a number of sitting M.P.s had to seek re-selection, either in entirely new or in partly reconstituted constituencies. This was the case with K. Zilliacus, one of the two M.P.s for Gateshead, and L. J. Solley, M.P. for the Thurrock division of Essex. Both Zilliacus and Solley were accused of openly opposing the Labour government's foreign policy, and when their candidatures came before the N.E.C. for endorsement, not only was it refused, but both M.P.s were expelled from the Labour party.[42]

Since the clashes with left-wing M.P.s in 1948–9 the N.E.C. has refused, *on political grounds*, to endorse at least seven other candidates. The first of these was in 1949, when the N.E.C. rejected the selection of W.G. Fisher at Bridgwater. In 1945, Fisher, it seems, had supported Vernon Bartlett, the Independent Member for Bridgwater since 1938, who had succeeded in retaining his seat against Conservative and Labour opposition. Despite resistance from the Bridgwater C.L.P., the N.E.C. refused to reverse its decision.[43]

In 1953 the N.E.C. refused to endorse the candidature of J. Lawrence at Woodford, but the reasons were not publicly specified,[44] although the fact that Lawrence was, in 1958, expelled from the Labour party for his activities on the St Pancras Borough Council suggest that any deviation from party policy on his part was to the left rather than the right.

A year later the N.E.C. vetoed the selection by Wimbledon C.L.P. of Tom Braddock, former Labour M.P. for Mitcham. As in the case of Fisher, the C.L.P. tried to persuade the N.E.C. to change its mind, but after interviewing Braddock, who was well-known for his left-wing views, the N.E.C. confirmed its decision.[45]

Similarly, in 1958, the N.E.C. refused to endorse the selection of S. Goldberg by Nottingham South C.L.P., 'due to his past political associations and it was felt that insufficient time had elapsed since he had broken those associations.'[46] Goldberg was a member of the Executive Council of the Electrical Trades Union (E.T.U.).

42. N.E.C. Supplementary Report, 27 May 1949, APCR 1949, p. 18. A similar case was that of Lester Hutchison, M.P. for the Rushcliffe division of Manchester, which disappeared in the 1948 redistribution. Hutchison sought nomination for Manchester (Ardwick) early in 1949, but was not short-listed after the N.E.C. had written to the Ardwick C.L.P. See *Manchester Guardian*, 26 February 1949.
43. See Ranney, op. cit., p. 162.
44. Conference proceedings, APCR 1953, p. 196.
45. See Ranney, op. cit., p. 162.
46. Quoted in M. Harrison, *Trade Unions and the Labour Party Since 1945*, London, 1960, footnote p. 285.

Then, in 1961, E. A. Roberts, the left-wing assistant general secretary of the Amalgamated Engineering Union (A.E.U.), was refused endorsement following his selection for Horsham.[47] Within six months the N.E.C. had also refused to endorse the candidature of Illtyd Harrington at Dover. Harrington was an active member of the Campaign for Nuclear Disarmament and Dover was a semi-marginal seat.[48]

The most recent case of the N.E.C. vetoing a selection was its refusal to approve the *re-selection* of John Palmer for Croydon North-West for the General Election of 1966. Palmer was a member of C.N.D. who had been acceptable to the N.E.C. late in 1962, when it had endorsed his first candidature for Croydon North-West. Whether this was an oversight, a reflection of the increasing anxiety that the serious illness of Hugh Gaitskell was causing the Labour party, or whether Palmer's left-wing views were more in evidence during and after the 1964 election, is not clear. What is clear is that the N.E.C. refused to endorse the selection of Palmer in March 1966, after the announcement of the general election, and 'imposed its own candidate'.[49] This last action was presumably under the threat of disaffiliation of the C.L.P. The latter accepted under protest and raised the matter again at the 1966 Annual Conference, but was defeated.[50]

The reasons for withholding of endorsement are not usually announced unless the grounds are technical, such as a failure to follow the proper procedure. The cases cited above are all examples, however, of use of the veto power for political reasons. In the early 1960s, for instance, there is little doubt that the struggle in the party over defence policy was manifested in part in the selection of candidates. At a selection conference in the Small Heath division of Birmingham in 1960, the successful nominee, D. H. Howell, a member of the Campaign for Democratic Socialism, received fifty-six votes against none for the bottom candidate, E. S. D. Bishop, a member of the Campaign for Nuclear Disarmament.[51] The Bolton East by-election of 1960 was punctuated with accusations and counter-accusations over the alleged refusal of Transport House to allow certain M.P.s from the north-west to take part in the campaign;[52] whilst the Labour candidate, R. L. Howarth, was removed from Draughtsmen's and Allied Tech-

47. *The Times*, 14 and 21 December 1961.
48. See A. Howard 'The Dover Road', *New Statesman*, 1 June 1962, p. 782.
49. *Guardian*, 10 March 1966. See also *The Times*, 7 March 1966, and *Guardian*, 8 March 1966.
50. Conference proceedings (private session), APCR 1966, p. 274.
51. *The Times*, 20 December 1960.
52. Report of the Co-operative Congress, 1961, p. 341.

nicians' Association's (D.A.T.A.) parliamentary panel because he refused to support his union's declared policy of unilateral nuclear disarmament. At the 1962 Conference Horsham C.L.P., following the rejection of Roberts, expressed disquiet at 'the number of occasions regarding the withholding of endorsement by the N.E.C.'.[53]Moreover, according to the secretary of C.N.D.'s general election planning group in 1964, the movement expected to have seventy-one supporters of C.N.D. in the House of Commons should the Labour party achieve parity with the Conservatives in the number of seats won at the General Election, and ninety-seven with a majority of a hundred.[54]

Almost all the cases cited so far concern candidates whose attitudes have been too far to the left to be acceptable to a majority of the N.E.C., and it would be misleading to suggest that deviation to the right of party policy is necessarily more acceptable to the N.E.C. None the less there has, over the same period, been only one case in which an individual has deviated to the right and has had disciplinary action of the type mentioned above taken against him. This occurred in the case of Alfred Edwards, M.P. for Middlesborough, who, in 1948, made it clear that he could not accept the party's policy of steel nationalization. As a result Edwards was expelled from the Labour party.[55] This suggests that a deviation too far to either left *or* right of party policy is likely to result in disciplinary action against candidates and M.P.s, but that in the nature of things deviation to the left is a more frequent occurrence in the Labour party. The two other cases of deviation to the right both resulted in the voluntary resignation of the persons concerned, one of his position as M.P., the other of the Labour Whip.[56]

What these cases show is that the N.E.C. does refuse to endorse the selection of some candidates on *political* rather than personal grounds, and that such cases appear to occur more frequently with left-wing candidates. It is difficult to prove, apart from extreme cases like that of Goldberg, where Communist or former Communist associations are evident, that this is due to left-wing attitudes on the part of the candidates concerned and little evidence can be brought to bear. There is one case, however, which suggests that the N.E.C. does consider some selections in a left–right light. This is the case of R. W. Bowes,

53. Conference proceedings (private session), APCR 1962, p. 223.
54. *Guardian*, 28 August 1964.
55. N.E.C. Supplementary Report, 17 May 1948, APCR 1948, p. 17. There is, of course, the more recent expulsion of Desmond Donnelly. (See *Daily Telegraph*, 28 March 1968.)
56. Stanley Evans (Wednesbury), 1956, and A. G. Brown (Tottenham), 1962.

whose selection for Newark in 1963 was invalidated on the grounds that irregularities had occurred in the selection procedure. Officially, no complaint was made against Bowes when the N.E.C. gave its ruling, merely that certain of his supporters had canvassed on his behalf. The decision of the N.E.C. to order a new selection was not unanimous: '*Left-wing* members [of the N.E.C.] opposed this on the ground that the complaints should have been considered by the organisation sub-committee, not just the officers, but mustered few votes.'[57]

As far as the selection procedure is concerned, the endorsement stage is the last point at which the N.E.C. can veto the choice of the C.L.P., although its powers to expel M.P.s and candidates from the party remain. Apart from expulsion, however, there is one other method by which the N.E.C. can signify its disapproval of a candidate: this is for the Leader of the party to withhold his support at the ensuing election. This last occurred when Attlee withheld his letter of support from H. Lawrance, Labour candidate in the Bristol West by-election in 1951. The Leader's support was withheld on the ground that Lawrence had declared that he was unable to support the government's rearmament programme.[58]

Despite the extensive powers possessed by the N.E.C., there is little to suggest that they are used to excess, and although action is taken more frequently against left-wing deviants, this is probably nothing more than an indication of greater left-wing deviance in the Labour party. That the N.E.C. probably divides left–right on these cases can be seen from the Newark affair, and it would be extremely interesting to see what effect a left-wing majority in the N.E.C. would have. It is important to remember that the N.E.C. can only make use of these powers where there are grounds for doing so: if some irregularity in procedure has occurred, if the candidate appears to be ineligible under the party rules, if the candidate has indicated a clear disagreement with party policy, then some action by the N.E.C. is possible, but more often than not the N.E.C. must be made aware that there are grounds for refusing to approve a selection and this normally means an official complaint to the N.E.C. by members of the C.L.P. For instance, shortly before the General Election of 1959, a member of Buckingham C.L.P. objected to the candidature of I. R. Maxwell on the ground that he had only been a member of the Labour party for a year.[59] The

57. *The Times*, 25 July 1963. (Author's italics.)
58. *Keesing's Contemporary Archives*, 1951, p. 11272.
59. *The Times*, 6 February 1961.

N.E.C. rejected the complaint because in 1948 the Annual Conference had passed a resolution laying down that candidates should have 'at least twelve months' membership of the Party'[60] and that Maxwell had fulfilled that condition.

To this extent, therefore, the power of the N.E.C. to interfere in selection is limited, but it is limited further in that it does not wish to give the impression either that it wishes to prevent a C.L.P. from selecting the candidate of its choice, or that it wishes to impose on a C.L.P. a candidate of the N.E.C.'s choice. It is not unusual for local parties to accuse Transport House of attempting to force a candidate upon them: this may sometimes be the case, but it is most unlikely that Transport House would use the formal machinery of selection to achieve this. For one thing, this machinery is largely negative so far as the N.E.C. is concerned: it can declare nominations invalid, it can declare selections invalid, it can refuse to endorse a candidate, but no part of the selection machinery at its disposal is conducive to ensuring the selection of a particular individual. Even if a dangerous rival of the candidate the N.E.C. would like to see selected is eliminated by this machinery, this cannot ensure the selection of the N.E.C.'s protégé. The very suspicion that the N.E.C. has a protégé is often sufficient to ensure the unfortunate nominee's defeat.

All that has been said so far applies to the selection of any candidate for the following general election: it applies only in part to the selection of candidates for by-elections. Under Section (5) of Clause XII of the C.L.P. Constitution, Section (3), which lays down normal procedure, is suspended 'and the National Executive Committee shall co-operate with the Executive Committee of [the C.L.P.] in the nomination of a candidate'.[61] Furthermore, the 'National Executive Committee may, if it deems it necessary in the interests of the Labour Party, *advise* the Executive Committee of [the C.L.P.] *to select a nomination it may submit to it*'.[62] Clearly the operative word is 'advise', and exactly what this means is not always apparent. The general justification for a more positive role by the N.E.C. is clear enough: '*by-elections are not local contests to be fought without reference to the Party as a whole*',[63] as a former national agent has pointed out. There has, it seems, been a change of emphasis in the way in which this power has been used by the N.E.C., a change which was acknowledged by the N.E.C. in 1958,

---

60. Conference proceedings, APCR 1948, p. 209.
61. C.L.P. Constitution, Clause XII(5).
62. ibid., Clause XII(5). (Author's italics.)
63. *Labour Organizer*, June–July 1946. (Original italics.)

when a modified selection procedure for by-elections was introduced. During the inter-war period it was fairly common for the N.E.C. to make use of this advisory power to secure the selection of particular candidates. For instance, in 1923 the N.E.C. decided in consultation with the Newcastle Borough Labour party that the vacancy at Newcastle East should 'be used for securing the return to the House of Commons of the Chief Whip of the Party, Mr Arthur Henderson'.[64] Similarly, in 1929, Craigie Aitchison, the Lord Advocate, was nominated by the N.E.C., although on this occasion his nomination was opposed by the I.L.P. To some extent this was a symptom of the growing independence of the local parties, often led at this time by the I.L.P.[65] Thus, in 1930, when the N.E.C. sought to secure the selection of the newly appointed Solicitor-General, Sir Stafford Cripps,[66] at Bristol East, the local party resisted the action of the N.E.C. There was no question of the N.E.C. attempting to force Cripps's candidature against the wishes of the local party, however, as Eric Estorick's biography of Cripps shows:

A meeting of the Executive Committee and General Council of the East Bristol Labour Party was specially convened on December 13th, 1930. The *National Organizer* of the Party attended. He said '*I urge the local Party, nay I implore you, to accept him.*'

It was not so easy a matter to persuade this working-class party of East Bristol to adopt such a course [and there were objections] to the Executive's method of dumping on to them a rich man, an aristocrat and a knight.[67]

The N.E.C.'s Annual Party Conference of 1931 merely records that the Bristol East D.L.P. was 'advised'[68] to adopt Cripps, although his obituary in the Conference Report of 1952 says he 'was found a safe seat at East Bristol'.[69]

It is well known, of course, that by-elections provide a useful means of securing the return to the House of Commons of defeated Ministers in particular and defeated Members in general. There are, furthermore, a number of cases where a vacancy has been created with the express intention of returning a particular individual. In 1940 Ernest Bevin,

64. N.E.C. Report, APCR 1923, p. 54.
65. ibid., APCR 1930, p. 14.
66. Cripps was appointed Solicitor-General on the resignation of Sir James Melville because of ill-health. Cripps was not a Member of the House of Commons.
67. E. Estorick, *Stafford Cripps*, London 1949, pp. 81–2. (Author's italics.)
68. N.E.C. Report, APCR 1931, p. 19.
69. ibid., APCR 1952, p. 36.

recently appointed Minister of Labour, had no seat in the Commons, whereupon Colonel Harry Nathan M.P. for Wandsworth Central, offered to vacate his seat to make way for Bevin.[70] The offer was accepted and Bevin was duly returned. Similarly, in 1950, Sir Frank Soskice, the Solicitor-General, was without a seat in the Commons, having been defeated at Bebington in the General Election of 1950. Colonel Harry Morris, M.P. for the Neepsend division of Sheffield, 'voluntarily retired in order to give Sir Frank Soskice ... a seat'.[71] The most recent cases are those of Patrick Gordon Walker and Frank Cousins, at Leyton and Nuneaton respectively. In both cases the sitting M.P.s, R. W. Sorenson and Frank Bowles, were offered and accepted peerages. Unlike the earlier cases of Nathan and Morris, who also received peerages, Sorenson and Bowles were given life peerages which *created* the vacancies in Leyton and Nuneaton and made way for Gordon Walker and Cousins. Of this connection there can be no doubt: Bowles was reported as saying that 'when first *approached by the Chief Whip* ten days ago, he was shocked, tremendously worried, and ill'.[72]

Such cases are rare, however, and despite the powers of the N.E.C., must be the subject of great tact and close co-operation between Transport House and the C.L.P. if local resentment is to be avoided. The *creation* of a vacancy emphasizes the role of the N.E.C. and generally arouses local resentment much more than any routine suggestion of Transport House interference. Certainly there are grounds for believing that the two earlier cases were handled somewhat more tactfully by Transport House, if only in the timing of the peerages. Moreover, it would appear that little if any coercion was applied to either Nathan or Morris, whereas it was rumoured that both Sorenson and Bowles were forced out of their seats, and in such matters rumour is often at least as important as fact.

Apart from the cases already cited, the N.E.C. does, from time to time, use casual vacancies to find Ministers or ex-Ministers seats. The post of Solicitor-General for Scotland has presented Labour governments with as much difficulty as the Conservatives and several holders of this post have been without a seat in the Commons. This occurred under the Labour government of 1945–51 with successive appointees: John Wheatley,[73] who held the post from March to October 1947, and

70. *Daily Telegraph*, 4 November 1963.
71. Quoted in correspondence by G. M. Block, *Daily Telegraph*, 7 November 1963.
72. *Daily Telegraph*, 21 November 1964. (Author's italics.)
73. Elected at a by-election at Edinburgh East, November 1947. In the meantime, Wheatley had become Lord Advocate *before* his election.

his successor, Douglas Johnston,[74] who held the post from October 1947 until the resignation of the Labour government in 1951. Apart from the specific case of Sir Frank Soskice, there were three cases following the General Election of 1950 in which by-elections were used to return defeated members of the government.[75] None of these, however, involved senior members of the Attlee administration.

Table 5(1): *Number of by-elections in Labour-held constituencies in which Ministers, former Ministers and ex-M.P.s were returned, 1950–66*

Election	Ministers or former Ministers	Former M.P.s	By-elections in Labour constituencies
1950–1	4	1	8
1951–5	1	6	19
1955–9	1	3*	18
1959–64	–	5	24
1964–6	2	–	5
Total:	8	15	74

* Including two former *Liberal* M.P.s.

The figures given in Table 5(1) do not suggest that the N.E.C. abuses its right to nominate candidates for the consideration of C.L.P.s at by-elections, even assuming that all the former M.P.s included in the table were nominated by the N.E.C., which they were not. It should be noted that although Arthur Creech Jones, former Colonial Secretary under Attlee, was selected at Romford in 1951, following his defeat at Shipley in 1950, this was a *Conservative-held* seat; and furthermore that Creech Jones was rejected by Bristol South-East C.L.P. in favour of Anthony Wedgwood Benn in 1950. Despite the fact that he was a former Cabinet Minister, he did not secure re-election until the Wakefield by-election in October 1954. Similarly, Sir Frank Soskice, who for the second time had the misfortune to lose his constituency as a result of redistribution, was rejected in 1955 by the Gorton division of Manchester in favour of the left-winger, Konni Zilliacus, and did not

74. Elected at a by-election at Paisley, February 1948.
75. (i) T. Steele, parliamentary secretary, Ministry of National Insurance 1949–50, defeated at Lanark, 1950, and re-elected for West Dunbartonshire in April 1950. (ii) L. J. Edwards, parliamentary secretary, Board of Trade, defeated at Blackburn West, 1950, and re-elected for Brighouse and Spenborough in May 1950. (iii) C. P. Mayhew, under-secretary at the Foreign Office, 1946–50, defeated at Norfolk South, 1950, and re-elected for Woolwich East in June 1950.

fight the 1955 General Election at all, eventually being re-elected at Newport in July 1956.

The case of Edith Summerskill in 1955 is similar: both she and W. T. Williams were affected by the 1954 redistribution. Dr Summerskill's constituency of Fulham West was abolished and was divided between the two new constituencies of Barons Court and Fulham. W. T. Williams's constituency, Hammersmith South, was similarly divided between the reconstituted Hammersmith North division and Barons Court. Michael Stewart, the sitting Member for Fulham East, was adopted as candidate for Fulham, leaving Dr Summerskill and Williams rivals for the Barons Court nomination. The position was further complicated by the fact that both were simultaneously short-listed for Warrington, which was also selecting at this time. Since Williams was the favourite at Barons Court and the latter was, in any case, likely to be a very marginal seat, Transport House tried to persuade Barons Court C.L.P. to bring forward the date of the selection conference so that it preceded the Warrington selection and cleared the way for Edith Summerskill. Although it also was subject to extensive boundary revision, it should be noted that Warrington was a much safer seat than Barons Court. In the event Barons Court C.L.P. refused to co-operate, Warrington held its conference first, selected Dr Summerskill, and the next day Williams secured the nomination at Barons Court.[76]

Finally, one other case which is sometimes regarded as an attempt by the N.E.C. to pre-empt a candidature, that of Morgan Phillips at North-East Derbyshire in 1959,[77] requires some comment. Although Phillips was general secretary of the Labour party at the time, this should not be regarded as evidence of N.E.C. interference in the selection: the attempts to secure selection were *personal initiatives* on the part of Phillips and there is no evidence that the N.E.C. actively sought his selection. North-East Derbyshire is a classic case of a belief among certain sections of the local party that Transport House was seeking to usurp their constitutional right of selection because one of the nominees had clear and undoubted connection with party headquarters.

The occasions on which the N.E.C. has actually used its right to nominate at by-elections are few in number, and since the war at least two have been rejected by the C.L.P. concerned. It was a series of these nominations after the 1955 General Election which led to the

76. See Richards, *Honourable Members*, pp. 21–2. It is ironical that Edith Summerskill's successor at Warrington in 1961 was W. T. Williams.
77. See Chapter Six, page 174 below.

change in by-election procedure of 1958. In December 1956 the N.E.C. nominated Lady Megan Lloyd George to be considered 'in conjunction with any other name that may be suggested'.[78] Of the four nominees on the short-list, two withdrew and Lady Megan was successful in a straight ballot with the other.[79] It was a different story in March 1958, however, when the N.E.C. nominated Woodrow Wyatt at Islington North.[80] Although Wyatt was short-listed he was eliminated before the last ballot.[81] The final blow to the N.E.C.'s position came in April 1958, with the refusal of St Helens C.L.P. to place Tom Driberg, then chairman of the N.E.C., on its short-list. Strictly speaking Driberg was not an N.E.C. nominee: he had been nominated by a number of locally affiliated organizations and had informed the Chairmen's Sub-Committee of the N.E.C. that the short-list at St Helens was 'weaker than it should be and said that he was willing to stand himself'.[82] The sub-committee agreed to support Driberg, although Gaitskell, Bevan, and one of the leading trade unionists, Sam Watson of the N.U.M., were absent from the meeting.[83] The St Helens Labour party resented what appeared to be the intrusion of the N.E.C., partly because there was fierce union competition for the seat, and partly because the constituency's last M.P., Sir Hartley Shawcross, had been selected under pressure from Transport House in 1945.[84] The result of the affair was that a trade union member of the N.E.C., which had not met prior to the selection at St Helens, moved a resolution at its next meeting preventing the sub-committee from approving such nominations without the consent of the full N.E.C.: this motion was carried.[85] It also led to a change in by-election procedure.

It was decided that the selection procedure for by-elections should be as close to the normal procedure as possible. In fact, what the N.E.C. did was to recognize what had long been the practice: generally speaking, normal procedure was telescoped and instead of the selection taking two or three months it took two or three weeks. Moreover, the N.E.C. had gradually surrendered its powers of 'advising' the selection of a particular candidate, in practice, if not in theory, and contented itself with the right to nominate an individual who 'should be considered with others sent in by local bodies'.[86] Even the exercise of this right had led to difficulties with local parties, and the N.E.C. decided

78. *The Times*, 1 December 1956. Carmarthen was at this time a Liberal-held seat, of course.
79. *The Times*, 10 December 1956.   80. *The Times*, 3 March 1958.
81. *The Times*, 24 March 1958.   82. *The Times*, 28 April 1958.
83. ibid.   84. ibid.   85. ibid.   86. *Labour Organizer*, June 1958, p. 107.

not to nominate for future by-election vacancies.[87] The cases of Leyton and Nuneaton were marked by a period of pre-selection negotiation and the N.E.C.'s position was far more that of a supplicant making a request than of a dictator making a demand.

By-election procedure now differs from normal procedure in four respects: first, the period of selection is much shorter; second, the N.E.C. may nominate a candidate, in theory at least; third, the short-list has to be approved by the N.E.C.;[88] and finally, the meeting of the General Management Committee, which normally meets before the selection conference to consider the Executive Committee's recommendations for a short-list, is dispensed with.[89]

There is one further role which the N.E.C. plays in selection and this is the maintenance of lists of possible candidates. There are two such lists: the first is known as List 'A' of Available Candidates, which comprises candidates for whom trade unions are willing to accept financial responsibility; and the second is known as List 'B' of Possible Candidates, comprising candidates whose names have been submitted by C.L.P.s and other affiliated organizations, but for whom no financial responsibility is undertaken by the nominating body. Both were established before the Second World War and lists of available sponsored candidates (List 'A') regularly appeared in the N.E.C.'s Report to the Annual Conference. The current lists are published by the party for circulation at the request of C.L.P.s seeking a candidate. In 1960 List 'A' consisted of eighty-five candidates from nineteen unions, and a year later this number was eighty-seven.[90] Not all the unions which sponsor candidates place their nominees on List 'A', two notable exceptions being the N.U.M. and the T.G.W.U. List 'B' is much larger and in 1960 consisted of 152 candidates and a year later of 219 candidates.[91]

Before 1960 both lists were compiled by similar methods. For List 'A' unions submitted nominations to the national agent, who requested nominees to complete an application form. This is placed before the Organization Sub-Committee of the N.E.C., which makes recommendations to the N.E.C.[92] A similar procedure was followed in compiling List 'B' with C.L.P.s making the nominations.[93]

87. Harrison, op. cit., p. 302.
88. The N.E.C. may alter the short-list, e.g. at Middlesbrough East, in 1962, the local executive committee left the B.I.S.A.K.T.A. nominee off the short-list, but the N.E.C. ordered that he should be placed on the short-list. (Ranney, op. cit., pp. 146–7.)
89. *Labour Organizer*, June 1958, pp. 107 and 119.
90. N.E.C. Report, APCR 1961, p. 10.   91. ibid.
92. *Labour Organizer*, April 1960, p. 74.   93. *Labour Organizer*, May 1960, p. 94.

The examination of nominations for both lists was conducted on paper and no nominees were interviewed by the N.E.C. or the sub-committee. Neither list was therefore regarded by the N.E.C. as consisting of *approved* candidates: 'the Lists are only a source of information about members who are available for consideration as candidates'.[94] Indeed, there appeared to be a reluctance to introduce any system of interviews for nominees for either list: 'personal interviews with nominees would be a very long drawn out job, so that it would be a very long time before the panel was completed'.[95] Within six months, however, there was a drastic change of attitude, and in its Report to the Annual Conference of 1960, the N.E.C. said: 'The N.E.C. has now decided that the List 'B' shall consist of members who have been *approved by the N.E.C. as suitable* for consideration by constituency parties seeking a candidate, and who have been nominated by constituency parties and other affiliated organizations'.[96] Furthermore, 'a panel of N.E.C. members is *to interview nominees* for the lists where this is thought necessary'.[97] The object of both changes was to improve the quality of the lists, particularly List 'B'. The panels which interview nominees are drawn from the Organization Sub-Committee, and a year after the institution of the new system 114 candidates had been interviewed.[98] Not all candidates are interviewed, especially those who have previously fought parliamentary elections. There is insufficient evidence at present, however, to judge to what extent this reform was responsible for the recruitment of the many young and able candidates who stood in the General Elections of 1964 and 1966.

As far as the N.E.C.'s control over selection is concerned it has meant that this control has been increased rather than reduced. Replying to a protest that a nominee had been excluded from List 'B', Miss Alice Bacon said that 'the N.E.C. had the responsibility of *approving names* on this list. *When it did not approve a name, it must have the right of excluding it.*'[99] As with all the powers of the N.E.C., in practice, if not in theory, this is a negative control.

94. ibid.   95. ibid.
96. N.E.C. Report, APCR 1960, p. 24. (Author's italics.)
97. ibid. (Author's italics.)
98. ibid., APCR 1961, p. 10.
99. Conference proceedings, APCR 1961, pp. 228–9. (Author's italics.) In 1961, two members of the Brighton Labour party, D. Lesley-Jones and D. H. Hobden, had their applications refused by the N.E.C. Lesley-Jones, a former Mosleyite, was eventually placed on the list after his third attempt, and Hobden, although rejected for a second time in 1961, was eventually placed on the list, and won Brighton (Kemptown) from the Conservatives by seven votes in 1964.

Much that has been said might imply that the N.E.C. and the C.L.P.s are constantly clashing over the question of selection, but this is a false impression. Most selections are conducted in an atmosphere of co-operation between national and local levels: the normal selections often go unnoticed, those which are disputed are news. Despite its powers under the Party and C.L.P. Constitutions, there is little that the N.E.C. can do to *force* a local party to adopt a candidate of the N.E.C.'s choice, though much can be done with persuasion, with due regard to local sensitivities, but such efforts are often fraught with dangers of misrepresentation, resentment and opposition.

The Role of the C.L.P.

Although there are a variety of types of local party each has the same basic organization. Under Clause VI(1) of the C.L.P. Constitution, the management of the local party is in the hands of a general management committee (G.M.C.), comprising delegates of all affiliated organizations, ward committees, women's sections, youth sections, together with the secretaries of the ward committees as *ex officio* members, with voting powers. The basis of representation must be approved by the N.E.C.[100]

Since 1945 the highest average individual membership of C.L.P.s was in 1952, when it was 1,629, although the present figure varies

Table 5(2): Average individual membership of constituency Labour parties, 1945–65*

Year	Average membership	Year	Average membership
1945	775	1956	1,367
1946	1,027	1957	1,477
1947	968	1958	1,438
1948	1,001	1959	1,371
1949	1,190	1960	1,281
1950	1,481	1961	1,213
1951	1,429	1962	1,242
1952	1,655	1963	1,343
1953	1,629	1964	1,343
1954	1,510	1965	1,322
1955	1,364		

* Based on N.E.C. Reports, 1945–66.

100. C.L.P. Constitution, Clause VI(1).

between 1,200 and 1,300. There is, of course, considerable variation among constituencies: the constituency with the largest membership in 1965 was Woolwich West, which had 6,010 members, whilst there were sixty-eight constituencies with memberships of more than 2,000.

The average trade union affiliated membership per constituency is much higher than the average individual membership, however. For instance, in 1950 it was 6,854 per constituency and by 1959 had risen to 8,236. Because trade unions and local party organizations are often affiliated on different bases, these figures are not directly comparable, but they do provide some basis for comparison. Normally the individual membership will, in proportion to their numbers, be over-represented compared with the trade union affiliated membership, though this can, of course, be justified in terms of personal commitment. Generally, the act of individual membership is the result of a personal and positive allegiance to the party, whereas more often than not affiliated membership merely represents the amount the particular organization can afford or is prepared to pay to the C.L.P. funds. There are also important differences between various regions.

Table 5(3) shows that in those regions where there is a high

Table 5(3): Rank order index of regions according to average trade union affiliated membership compared with average individual membership of regions, 1950 and 1959

Region	Rank order (T.U. membership)*	Average Ind. membership†
Wales	2	Below
Northern	5	Below
Lancs. and Cheshire	5	Average
East Midlands	8	Below
Yorkshire	10	Below
Scotland	13	Below
West Midlands	13	Below
London	18	Above
South-Western	18	Average
Southern	19	Above
Eastern	21	Above

* Based on the average trade union affiliated membership per constituency in each region in rank order, 1950 and 1959. Each figure is the sum of the two ranked orders, so that the lowest possible score is 2 and the highest 22.

† Based on the average individual membership per constituency in each region between 1950 and 1959.

trade union affiliation a low individual membership is likely. This would suggest that in some constituencies the local party may be subject to greater trade union influence than others, whilst in others, not only is trade union influence less, but that the individual membership is generally more active. There are grounds for believing that this is an important factor in selection, pointing to not only the particular influence of individual trade unions, but also to the *general* influence of trade unions in the selection of candidates.[101]

It has, incidentally, become the practice in a number of constituencies for there to be a restriction on the number of delegates which any affiliated organization may send to the G.M.C.[102] The usual basis of affiliation is one delegate per fifty (or sometimes a hundred) members or part thereof, but over and above a certain number of delegates there is a restrictive maximum to prevent the domination of the G.M.C. by any one organization.

Table 5(4): The number of delegates to a G.M.C.

Constituency	Date	Delegates	Constituency	Date	Delegates
Islington North	1958	48	Rotherham	1963	320
St Helens	1958	175	Ilkeston	1963	199
North-East Derbys.	1958	220	Bromley	1964	52
Ebbw Vale	1960	200	Neath	1964	251
Paisley	1961	135	Kettering	1964	106
Chesterfield	1961	239	Shoreditch and		
Orpington	1961	32	Finsbury	1964	106
Hendon North	1962	41	Stepney	1964	66

The figures shown in Table 5(4) give some idea of the size of the G.M.C. of a C.L.P. The three Conservative-held seats included in the list, Orpington, Hendon North and Bromley, show lower totals than the Labour-held seats. Furthermore, most of the remaining seats lie in regions with high or relatively high trade union affiliations, whereas the three London seats, Islington North, Shoreditch and Finsbury, and Stepney, all have G.M.C.s numbering less than a hundred, and are in an area with lower trade union affiliations. This suggests that the larger the G.M.C. the larger the proportion of trade union delegates will be,

101. See Chapter Six below.
102. *Labour Organizer*, October 1958, p. 183. Since 1965, when the Model Rules were amended, all delegates to G.M.C.s, Ward Committees, L.L.P.s, etc., must be *individual* members of the Labour party. (Conference proceedings, APCR 1965, p. 174.)

although such a conclusion can only be tentative. What is clear is that, relative to the total membership, whether affiliated or individual or both, the number of delegates on the G.M.C. consists of only a small proportion of that membership.

Although the G.M.C. is the authoritative centre of any C.L.P., a smaller body, the executive committee (E.C.), elected by and from the members of the G.M.C., is generally responsible for the day-to-day running of the party. The size of the E.C. varies considerably, seldom falling below fifteen but often as high as forty. All officers of the C.L.P.[103] are members of the E.C. and the remaining members are divided proportionately between the party and affiliated organizations. As with the G.M.C. there is often a limit to the total number of members any one organization may have on the E.C.

It is these two bodies, the G.M.C. and the E.C. which are responsible for the selection of candidates. Once permission has been given by the N.E.C. for selection to proceed, the E.C. seeks authority[104] from the G.M.C. to secure nominations, and this having been given, the initiative reverts to the E.C. for the time being. The detailed procedure to be followed is laid down in Clause XII(3) of the C.L.P. Constitution.

The E.C. and the N.E.C. or its representative must now agree upon a timetable for the selection procedure. This is 'to ensure that every organization and delegate is given adequate time to take whatever steps are necessary at each stage of selection'.[105] For instance, it is normal for a period of at least twenty-eight days to be left between the invitation and closing date for nominations. Nominations are invited by means of a prescribed circular[106] sent to all affiliated and party organizations, and all nominations must be made on a prescribed form.[107]

The question of nominations often presents difficulties, if only because many of the affiliated and party organizations have no idea whom they wish to nominate, and little idea of how to find a suitable nominee. Generally speaking, List 'A' is left to the branches of the respective trade unions found on the list, whilst List 'B' is the principal source of nominations for ward committees, Young Socialists, women's

103. C.L.P. Constitution, Clause IX(2): president, two vice-presidents, treasurer, financial secretary, and secretary. There is also a chairman, of whom, curiously, no mention is made in either constitution.

104. *Labour Organizer*, January 1956, p. 13.

105. ibid.

106. Appendix I to the C.L.P. Constitution.

107. Appendix II to the C.L.P. Constitution. In the case of divided boroughs, any organization affiliated to the *central* party may nominate for a C.L.P. vacancy. (Model Rules (Set D), Clause XII (3).)

sections and so on. The information given on the lists is often felt to be totally inadequate and usually consists of brief biographical details:

FOLEY, M. A.   Company Director. Born 1925. Member of the Party
(address and   15 years. Member of T.G.W.U. and Fabian Society.
tel no.)   Held various Party and trade union offices. Urban
                   District Councillor. Contested Bedford 1959 General
                   Election. Special interests: European Affairs, Pan-
                   Africanism, Local Government and Industrial
                   Relations.[108]

There have, therefore, been attempts to meet this problem, principally by introducing the technique of interviewing *before* nomination. This is by no means an innovation: Hugh Dalton describes a similar technique prior to his selection at Bishop Auckland in 1928,[109] whilst there was a demand for a general introduction of pre-selection interviewing in 1948, and it was reported that some parties were following this suggestion.[110] In 1953 North Buckinghamshire C.L.P. made extensive use of preliminary interviews, though little encouragement was received from Transport House.[111] Further demands in 1955 fell upon deaf ears,[112] but by 1960 they began to receive attention: 'There is no reason why likely nominees should not be *introduced to the constituency and their abilities tested at public meetings, day schools, etc., before selection* is even started.'[113] This advice was echoed in the N.E.C.'s Report in 1960, when C.L.P.s were urged 'to invite likely nominees to address local meetings'.[114] This system is now fairly widespread, particularly in the Southern Region of the Labour party.

There have been other attempts to widen the field of possible nominations by advertising vacancies in party journals and national newspapers, but this has not been adopted.[115]

108. List B, April 1960, p. 8.
109. Hugh Dalton (Lord Dalton), *Call Back Yesterday*, London, 1953, pp. 201–2.
110. *Labour Organizer*, December 1948, pp. 4–5.
111. *Labour Organizer*, January 1953, pp. 14–15.
112. *Labour Organizer*, September 1955, pp. 171–2.
113. *Labour Organizer*, January 1960, p. 4. (Author's italics.)
114. N.E.C. Report, APCR 1960, p. 24. Ranney, in op. cit., p. 170, footnote 8, quotes the case of a safe Conservative seat in West Sussex, in which the local E.C. wrote to twenty-three persons on List B, none of whom wished to be considered. Eighteen more were approached, three consented and were nominated, but two dropped out. Similarly, 'for a safe Conservative seat in North-West London the executive wrote to 68 persons on List B, six responded favourably, four were nominated and all were put on the short-list,' (ibid.). See also Chapter 9, 'A Controversial Selection'.
115. *Labour Organizer*, January 1953. North Buckingham C.L.P. sought to advertise the vacancy in the *Daily Herald* and *Reynolds News* but neither newspaper co-operated. The author, R. Bellchambers, also suggested that the *Labour Organizer* could be used as an advertising medium, a suggestion which was repeated by C. Ford in another article in the issue of November 1955, p. 198.

The number of nominations a C.L.P. is likely to receive is often quite unpredictable. One agent confidently predicted receiving at least forty nominations, but in fact received only eighteen.

Table 5(5) shows that the number of nominations is not usually very high and a total of over twenty is uncommon in Labour-held seats. There is, of course, nothing to prevent interested persons from *approaching* affiliated organizations in the constituency and seeking their nomination. For example, Ranney quotes two cases in which such approaches were made: one concerned a safe Labour seat in Derbyshire in which some fifty individuals sought nomination through local groups, a process which culminated in fourteen official nominations; similarly, local organizations in Lincoln C.L.P. were approached by approximately thirty-five persons, resulting in eleven nominations.[116]

Table 5(5): *Average number of nominations in selected constituencies*

	Average number of nominations	
Number of constituencies	*Labour-held seats*	*Conservative-held seats*
10	17*	–
4	–	12†
9	13‡	–
3	–	5§

* Including Kettering, with 51 nominations.
† Including Central Norfolk, with 32 nominations.
‡ Excluding Kettering.
§ Excluding Central Norfolk.

Of course, the total number of nominations in Conservative-held seats is often much lower, and in these cases a total of more than a dozen is uncommon. It should be pointed out, however, that the relatively small number of nominations in Labour selections is due in part to the nomination procedure, in so far as each affiliated and party organization may only nominate one candidate, although most C.L.P.s in Labour constituencies will have at least fifty affiliated and party organizations, whilst some, such as Rotherham, have over a hundred. The principal limiting factor is the absence of any automatic forwarding of possible nominations from national level and local parties are left very much to their own devices in seeking nominees: 'the National Agent is willing to suggest names of those whom he thinks are worthy

116. Ranney, op. cit., p. 170, footnote 8.

of consideration. For obvious reasons he is not prepared to do this unless invited to do so.'[117] Possible nominees are therefore generally limited to sponsored candidates suggested by unions or the Co-operative party, to those on List 'B' and to any worthy local aspirants. To select a candidate from List 'B' may require a great deal of work on the part of the local members concerned: the list must be studied carefully, any likely persons must be approached, their consent secured, a choice made, perhaps by means of interviewing, and so on. All too often ward committees and other party organizations do not regard it as a worth-while effort, even in a Labour seat.

The E.C. has the right to nominate one candidate,[118] but this must be submitted in the same way as any other nomination. The G.M.C., being the eventual selecting body, may not nominate a candidate.[119]

When all nominations have been validated by the N.E.C. the E.C. proceeds to draw up a short-list, although it may, if it so wishes, recommend that all nominees should appear before the selection conference.[120] Most short-lists in Labour-held seats comprise five or six candidates, although occasionally the number may rise to ten[121] or fall to four.[122] Short-lists in Conservative-held seats average between three and four candidates. Occasionally, the E.C. in a non-Labour seat will invite a particular individual to accept candidature, subject to the approval of the G.M.C.[123]

The G.M.C. has a constitutional right to approve the short-list and a special meeting is called for this purpose before the actual selection conference. Normally the G.M.C. accepts the recommendations of the E.C., but it 'has the power *to accept, amend or reject* the short-list . . . [and] also has the power to decide that the nominees are unsuitable or inadequate . . . It can discuss at length the qualities of the nominees before deciding on the short-list.'[124] Although the G.M.C. invariably accepts the recommendations of the E.C. it is not uncommon for there to be changes or attempted changes in the composition of the short-list. At Ebbw Vale, for example, in September 1960, the G.M.C. added the names of Michael Foot and Alderman Frank Whatley to the short-list.[125] Similarly, at Paisley, in March 1961, the name of John Robert-

117. *Labour Organizer*, January 1953, p. 15.
118. *Labour Organizer*, January 1956, p. 13.   119. ibid.
120. e.g. Bromley, 1964.   121. e.g. Faversham, 1961.
122. e.g. Greenock, 1955, Wigan, 1958 and Wolverhampton, 1963.
123. e.g. High Peak, 1961, North Dorset, 1962. In the case of High Peak, the candidate had fought the constituency for Labour in the General Elections of 1950 and 1951.
124. *Labour Organizer*, January 1956, p. 14. (Original italics.)
125. *The Times*, 19 September 1960.

son was added after pressure from his union, the A.E.U.[126] Such attempts are not, however, always successful, and this was the case at Kettering where an unsuccessful attempt was made to substitute one nominee for another on the short-list.[127]

Apart from the formal adoption of the selected candidate shortly before the actual election, the final stage of selection, as far as the C.L.P. is concerned, is the selection conference. Under Clause XII(3)(f) of the C.L.P. Constitution, this is a special meeting of the G.M.C. 'convened by circular[128] in the terms prescribed by the National Executive Committee'.[129] The circular informs each delegate of the date and time of the meeting, lists the valid and, if any, invalid nominations, and stipulates that the basis of voting at the meeting shall be one delegate one vote. It is signed by the secretary of the C.L.P. and countersigned on behalf of the N.E.C. by the national agent.

Only accredited delegates to the G.M.C. may attend the selection conference: 'It is a special meeting of the General Committee and the delegates entitled to attend are the delegates who are appointed by organizations entitled to representatives on the General Committee, and who are appointed to attend the Annual Meeting and the General Committee meetings for the ensuing year.'[130] The question of the substitution of delegates has often been raised, especially by trade unions whose members are often engaged in shift work and are therefore unable to attend the conference. For instance, the former Area general secretary of the Derbyshire Miners' Association estimated that not more than 85 per cent of the N.U.M. delegation can be expected to attend any selection conference in his area. It is mainly in strong union areas that substitution is found, although Transport House does not encourage the practice: 'We strongly advise against substitution. ... However, when substitution is permitted, conditions of appointment must be clearly laid down. Written notification should be required prior to the meeting, signed by the secretary of the organization appointing a substitute, indicating the name of the delegate substituted.'[131]

It is also the normal practice for C.L.P.s to 'freeze' the affiliations of local organizations as soon as the timetable of selection has been fixed.

126. *The Times*, 6 March 1961.
127. *Daily Telegraph*, 31 August 1964.
128. Appendix III to the C.L.P. Constitution.
129. C.L.P. Constitution, Clause XII(3)(f).
130. *Labour Organizer*, January 1956, p. 14.
131. *Labour Organizer*, January 1954, p. 4.

This is to prevent any organization or group of organizations from increasing their number of affiliations and thus increase their number of delegates to the G.M.C. prior to the selection conference. This is in addition to any limitation there may be regarding the total number of delegates to which any one organization may be entitled.

A further problem which sometimes creates difficulty is whether delegates may be *mandated* at the selection conference. Transport House's view of this is that 'a member of a General Committee is in fact a *representative rather than a delegate*. As such he will take notice of the decisions made by the organization he represents, and generally will express its views. ... *He is not, however, bound by any mandate* from that body ...'[132] during the normal process of selection. This is a very difficult problem largely because of the federative nature of the Labour party and the very conditions under which selection takes place. It is almost impossible in practice to distinguish between a formal mandate and genuine group loyalty on the part of the delegate and the body he represents. That mandating occurs is known, but its extent is subject to a great deal of speculation, and the real problem is far more likely to be that of group loyalty which may override all other considerations in the selection: this is especially true of trade union delegates.[133]

Either before or at the selection conference, each delegate is given brief biographical details of the nominees on the short-list. The information contained in these biographies varies considerably, from the brief recital of the nominee's name, age, address, occupation, and trade union, to his response to a lengthy questionnaire previously sent to him by the secretary of the C.L.P. Most C.L.P.s, however, content themselves with a brief biography similar to that found in List 'B'. Unless the delegates are personally acquainted with any of the nominees or one or more of the latter is a well-known national figure in the party, the initial basis on which a choice must be made is small. This is in accordance with the theory of the selection conference: 'the delegates should vote on *the performance of* the nominees themselves ...'.[134] Moreover, just as the representative of the N.E.C. is not allowed to speak on the merits or demerits of any nominee, nor is any delegate and no discussion is allowed: 'a Chairman who permits any contribution to be made after the nominees have spoken is failing in his duties ...'.[135]

132. ibid., pp. 6–7. (Author's italics.)
133. See Chapter Six below.
134. *Labour Organizer*, January 1956, p. 14. (Author's italics.)
135. *Labour Organizer*, May 1952, p. 89.

Theoretically, therefore, the choice of candidate depends on their performance at the selection conference during the course of a speech and questions from the floor. Normally, each nominee speaks for between ten and twenty minutes and this is followed by a similar period for questions. The nominees must be seen according to a strict timetable, and prior to the meeting, lots are drawn to decide their order of appearance before the delegates. As soon as the last nominee has had his allotted time the meeting proceeds to a vote. Voting continues until one nominee has an absolute majority, the nominee at the bottom of the poll dropping out at each successive ballot. The chairman will usually announce the voting figures after each ballot, although a number of C.L.P.s avoid this practice and take a secret ballot. The practice of announcing the voting figures helps to maintain an atmosphere of democracy: delegates can see that as far as the voting figures are concerned democracy is being done. But it has the disadvantage of making inter-ballot manoeuvring easier: delegates can calculate the most effective way of switching votes in the following ballot and this facilitates the hurried canvassing which often occurs between ballots.

Should the balloting end in a tie the chairman does not have a casting vote: 'on the rare occasions when a tie occurs, the wise procedure to follow is for *a further selection conference to be convened*, when the same nominees would attend'.[136] Ties are, in the nature of things, infrequent, but when a tie occurred at a selection meeting attended by the author, a second conference was not held and the issue was decided by a further ballot.

As soon as one nominee emerges with an absolute majority, a resolution is proposed assuring him of the unnaimous support of the C.L.P. and recommending that his selection be endorsed by the N.E.C. It is most unusual for there to be any dissentients to this motion. Finally, the meeting must agree to a resolution accepting responsibility for the election expenses of the candidate in accordance with Clause IX(4) of the Party Constitution and a copy of this resolution must be attached to the application for endorsement.

This completes the process of selection as far as the C.L.P. is concerned, and only the endorsement of the N.E.C. is necessary to entitle the selected nominee to call himself a prospective Labour candidate.[137]

It occasionally happens, however, that a C.L.P. decides that it has chosen the wrong candidate or some disagreement has arisen between

---

136. *Labour Organizer*, January 1956, p. 14. (Author's italics.)
137. An adoption meeting is held shortly before the actual election campaign.

the candidate and the local party. In such circumstances the candidate may decide to resign, but if necessary the C.L.P. may demand his resignation, usually by securing a mandate from affiliated and party organizations and passing a vote of no confidence in the candidate. Such actions are rare, however, and no special provision is made to deal with this situation. This is not the case with M.P.s who find themselves in conflict with their local party: if the C.L.P. is represented in Parliament by a member of the Labour party, selection procedure as described above is not set in motion unless

(a) Such representative intimates his or her intention to retire, or
(b) The General Committee on securing a mandate from its affiliated and Party organizations intimates by resolution its desire that he or she must retire.[138]

The position under sub-section (a) merely allows for the normal selection of a candidate when the M.P. wishes to resign or retire, but sub-section (b) enables the C.L.P. to effect the removal of the M.P. should it be in conflict with him. It may simply be a matter that the M.P. in question is advanced in years and the C.L.P. wishes to secure a more effective representative,[139] but it is far more likely to be a disagreement over policy or over the political actions of the Member. It is not unusual for a C.L.P. to demand an explanation from its Member as to why he voted against the party in the Commons, or abstained or has been speaking against party policy in public, or has allowed his name to be associated with certain political régimes, and so on. Thus Woodrow Wyatt was asked to consult his local party before making any further suggestions about a pact between the Liberal and Labour parties. Maurice Edelman was asked to explain his attitude towards the Labour government's aircraft policies. Occasionally, such explanations prove unsatisfactory to the C.L.P. or further differences emerge until some members of the local party feel that the M.P. should be replaced and a candidate more amenable to their views selected.

According to one former Labour M.P., 'the signal for retirement begins around sixty-seven, and M.P.s who sit for safe constituencies are painfully aware that the drive to oust them begins long before they reach seventy years and that a long queue awaits the seat; and by

138. C.L.P. Constitution, Clause XII(7)(a) and (b).
139. e.g. N. Maclean (Glasgow – Govan), 1949 (cited by Ranney, op. cit., p. 185); J. Kinley (Bootle), 1955 (cited by D. E. Butler, *The British General Election of 1955*, London, 1955, p. 46). There are occasionally disputes in which the personal actions of the Member are subject to criticism, e.g. J. D. Mack (Newcastle-under-Lyme), 1950-1, and J. E. Glanville (Consett), 1953-5 (both cited by Ranney op. cit., pp. 186-8).

innuendo, hints and resolutions, his departure would be welcomed'.[140] It is not difficult for the M.P. to turn a deaf ear to such demands, although an open challenge under sub-section (b) is more difficult to resist, particularly when this challenge is based not on considerations of age but reflects a clear disagreement between the M.P. and his local party. For instance, 'some members of the Parliamentary Labour Party received threatening letters about their fate at the next selection conference if they didn't conform'[141] to the Scarborough Conference decision of 1960 on unilateral nuclear disarmament.

A number of C.L.P.s have attempted to remove their M.P.s by refusing them re-nomination for the next election. The most celebrated case is that of Mrs Bessie Braddock, whose local party, the Liverpool (Exchange) C.L.P., secured a mandate under sub-section (b) after she had refused to comply with a resolution of the G.M.C. demanding that she support Aneurin Bevan in his disagreement with party policy.[142] This was in June 1954. Mrs Braddock resisted this attempt to remove her with the help of the north-west regional organizer of the Labour party, but the G.M.C. persisted and passed a vote of no confidence in Mrs Braddock. The N.E.C. decided to set up an inquiry into the affair and eventually ordered a re-selection. At this second meeting Mrs Braddock's candidature was rejected by forty votes to thirty-nine, but it was subsequently discovered that seven of the delegates who had been present lived outside the constituency and were not entitled to vote. Mrs Braddock formally complained to the N.E.C., which, after a further investigation, ordered her re-adoption, and eventually caused the disbandment and re-forming of the G.M.C. of the Exchange party.[143]

Mrs Braddock's disagreement with her local party was not an isolated case, and a number of Labour M.P.s found themselves in conflict with their C.L.P.s at this time, especially over German re-armament. For instance, Arthur Skeffington had some difficulty in securing re-nomination by Hayes and Harlington C.L.P. in 1955, and was successful only with the assistance of Transport House.[144]

It is not only M.P.s whose deviation is to the right of their local parties who are likely to be subject to such challenges. In January 1963 William Baxter, M.P. for West Stirlingshire, from whom the whip

140. Jean Mann, op. cit., p. 157.
141. ibid., p. 208.
142. Jack and Bessie Braddock, *The Braddocks*, London, 1963, p. 90.
143. ibid., pp. 90–2.
144. Richards, op. cit., p. 21.

had been withheld since March 1961, found his position challenged by a resolution of the local branch of the Post Office Workers, demanding that he should give the necessary assurances to accept the Standing Orders of the P.L.P. and apply for the restoration of the whip. Should he fail to do so, the resolution demanded that the E.C. of the C.L.P. 'should take the necessary procedure to appoint a new candidate...'.[145] In May 1963 Baxter gave the necessary assurances to the P.L.P. and the whip was restored.

Another Labour M.P., John Baird, M.P. for Wolverhampton North-East, was less fortunate: in February 1963 the G.M.C. of the local party secured, by thirty-eight votes to twenty-one, a mandate under sub-section (b), informing Baird that he must retire at the next general election.[146] The reason for the GM.C.'s decision is a matter of dispute: the G.M.C. claimed that Baird had been neglecting his duties as an M.P., but Baird himself asserted that it was the result of his views on racial discrimination, which he strongly opposed.[147] Baird appealed to the N.E.C. against the decision, but the N.E.C. decided that 'the Wolverhampton party had acted within its rights as laid down in constituency party rules'.[148] Baird was refused re-nomination and was not short-listed for the ensuing selection conference.[149]

The position of the N.E.C. in such circumstances is often difficult: it may wish to help some M.P.s, who are threatened in this way, but unless the local party acts unconstitutionally it may be impossible for the N.E.C. to prevent his removal. There is some evidence that the N.E.C. is more disposed to help right-wing rather than left-wing M.P.s: in the cases of Mrs Braddock and Arthur Skeffington, the N.E.C. successfully intervened, but in the case of William Baxter it made no attempt to interfere, whilst in that of John Baird, whose position was certainly more left than right, it refused to uphold his appeal against the local party's decision. This evidence does correlate with that discussed on the expulsion of M.P.s from the Labour party.[150]

The principal initiative in selection lies with the C.L.P., both in the routine selection of a candidate and in the removal of a sitting M.P. Generally, such influence that the N.E.C. can bring to bear on selection is negative in character and consists largely of a watching brief over procedure, backed by the ultimate power of denying recognition to any candidate the C.L.P. might choose. This can, of course, prevent the

145. Quoted in *Daily Telegraph*, 14 January 1963.
146. *Daily Telegraph*, 9 February 1963.
147. *Daily Telegraph*, 28 February 1963.   148. ibid.
149. *Daily Telegraph*, 13 July 1963.   150. See pages 138–9 above.

C.L.P. from having the candidate of its choice, but it does not enable the N.E.C. to secure the selection of particular individuals. Furthermore, although the N.E.C. has greater powers over the selection of a candidate at a by-election, these powers are carefully used and often circumscribed in practice, if not in theory. Cases such as Leyton and Nuneaton are the exceptions which prove the rule, since they are usually made on an appeal to party unity and national interest.[151]

Within the C.L.P. selection is the prerogative of a relatively small group of the total party membership: even the G.M.C. is likely to consist of 200 or 300 members at the most, representing some 1,000 or so individual members and several thousand affiliated members, whilst the E.C. can hope to be representative only of the larger groupings within the C.L.P. Moreover, *no general meeting of the C.L.P. endorses the choice of the G.M.C.* until the formal adoption of the candidate immediately before an election. To reject a candidate at this stage is normally unthinkable and control over selection is retained by leading members of the C.L.P., whose decision, always provided that it has been effected constitutionally, is irrefutable. The factors which influence their decisions will be dealt with in the following chapters.

151. Especially true when the Labour party is in power.

CHAPTER SIX

The Trade Unions and the Selection of Candidates

One of the many features which distinguishes the Labour party from its opponents in the selection of parliamentary candidates is the practice of sponsorship by affiliated organizations, a practice which is frowned upon by the Conservatives and unknown among the Liberals. Any organization affiliated to the Labour party may sponsor a candidate, but the majority of such candidates are financially supported by the trade unions. Furthermore, these trade union candidates comprise an important minority of Labour candidates in general, and Labour M.P.s in particular: at every general election since 1950 approximately one Labour candidate in five, and at least one Labour M.P. in three, has been sponsored by a trade union.

Table 6(1) provides an overall picture of trade union sponsorship between 1950 and 1966, but it can be misleading to refer to the trade unions as though they are a united body. It is true that they do have

Table 6(1): Proportions of Labour candidates and M.P.s
sponsored by trade unions, 1950–66

	Number of candidates %	Elected %	Defeated %
1950	22·5(139)	34·9(110)	9·6(29)
1951	22·5(139)	35·9(106)	10·2(33)
1955	20·9(129)	34·7 (96)	9·7(33)
1959	20·9(129)	36·0 (93)	9·9(36)
1964	22·0(138)	37·8(120)	5·8(18)
1966	22·4(138)	36·3(132)	3·1 (6)

much in common in structure and organization, that they share a common interest in industrial and, to an important extent, political affairs, that many are members of the Trades Union Congress and in all these senses can be regarded as one of the three sections which form the Labour movement. Furthermore, the majority of trade unionists are, through their unions, linked politically to the Labour party, and as such form a vital part of that party's federative structure. In the selection of candidates, however, the unions are, as indeed in many other spheres, both partners and rivals. Candidates are sponsored not by the T.U.C., nor by those unions affiliated to the Labour party acting in concert but by *individual* unions who must compete for constituency nominations with those on the 'B' List, with the Co-operative party, and *with each other*. It is important to appreciate, moreover, the extent to which sponsorship is, in practice, confined to roughly a third of the unions affiliated to the Labour party, as shown in Table 6(2).

Table 6(2): Number of trade unions affiliated to the Labour party and sponsoring candidates, 1950–66

Election	Affiliated to the Labour party	Number of unions sponsoring candidates	Sponsoring M.P.s
1950	83	25	20
1951	82	24	20
1955	87	25	18
1959	87	23	19
1964	81	27	25
1966	79	28	25

Not only is trade union sponsorship dominated by a minority of the unions affiliated to the Labour party, but also, to a large extent, by the 'Big Six' unions (T.G.W.U., A.E.U., N.U.G.M.W., N.U.M., U.S.D.A.W., and N.U.R.). The extent of this domination is illustrated in Table 6(3).

In the six general elections between 1950 and 1966, the 'Big Six' unions were responsible for more than two thirds of the total number of seats sponsored by trade unions and three quarters of the seats sponsored successfully. Apart from the ability of individual union members to secure nomination, sponsorship depends on two factors: the willingness of each union to sponsor one or more candidates and its financial capacity to do so. Many of the smaller unions, with

Table 6(3): *The domination of trade union sponsorship by the 'Big Six', 1950–66*

	All candidatures %	Successful %	Unsuccessful %
'Big Six'	69·5(564)	75·8(498)	42·6 (66)
T.S.S.A.	6·4 (52)	5·5 (36)	10·3 (16)
	75·9(616)	81·3(534)	52·9 (82)
Other unions	24·1(196)	18·7(123)	47·1 (73)
Total	100·0(812)	100·0(657)	100·0(155)

memberships of less than 150,000, are unable to finance more than one or two candidates at any general election, and only the large unions, with their substantial political funds, are able to think in terms of a dozen or more candidates.

Much also depends, however, on the extent to which a union is committed to a policy of sponsorship, both in the sense of a general allegiance to the Labour party, of which sponsorship is a clear manifestation, and in the particular sense that unions feel the need for direct parliamentary representation. The value of the latter to individual unions is a matter of dispute: a case can be made out for those unions involved in the nationalized industries or public corporations, although the nature of parliamentary control of these undertakings is a limiting factor, since Ministers are not responsible for their day-to-day running; or again, union M.P.s may be regarded as *additional* channels of communication with the government of the day, supplementing the official and quasi-official contacts that unions have with Whitehall; or the unions may see their representatives principally as a form of political influence on the parliamentary Labour party in general and the leadership in particular; finally, a number of unions subscribe to the view that sponsored M.P.s fulfil the function of industrial or occupational representation – that mining areas should be represented by miners, rural areas by agricultural workers, the cotton towns by textile workers, and so forth.

Both these factors are important in accounting for a number of the characteristics of trade union sponsorship, in particular the distribution of candidatures among the various unions and the location of trade union sponsored constituencies. One of the major causes of the domination of union sponsorship by the 'Big Six' is simply financial – these unions can afford the necessary outlay, not only at election times, but throughout the inter-election periods in the form of constituency grants, whilst their smaller rivals must consider whether their political funds can adequately support even a single candidature. Thus it is that some small unions, like the Tobacco Workers' Union or the National Union of Furniture Trade Operatives, supported only one candidate each between 1950 and 1966; or others, such as the United Patternmakers Association or the National Union of Tailors and Garment Workers, were each represented by a single M.P. during part of this period. Conversely, finance accounts to a considerable extent for the ability of the N.U.M. to support nearly 200, the T.G.W.U. over a hundred, and the A.E.U. over eighty candidatures between 1950 and 1966.

Commitment to sponsorship is also extremely important: it accounts on the one hand for the active role played by the Transport Salaried Staffs' Association, which, though its membership is only 80,000 to 90,000, regularly sponsors about six candidates, averaging some 6 per cent of the total between 1950 and 1966; and, on the other, for the almost dominating role of the N.U.M., which was responsible for approximately a quarter of the candidates sponsored over the same period. In the case of the T.S.S.A. this is attributable to the union's representation of workers in a nationalized industry and to its firm belief in the value of direct parliamentary representation.[1] In the case of the N.U.M., not only is state control of the industry important, but there exists a strong tradition of political activity, pre-dating the formation of the Labour Representation Committee, which found its expression as early as 1874, with the election to Parliament of Alexander Macdonald and Thomas Burt, both of whom were miners. Moreover, the idea that mining areas should be represented by miners is strong, and the concentration of the N.U.M.'s membership has enabled the union to dominate many constituencies in the past. Despite the relative decline of mining as an industry, the political commitment remains and the N.U.M. continued to sponsor more candidates than any other union until 1966, when the T.G.W.U., for the first time, equalled the miners' total of twenty-seven.

The N.U.M. is, of course, the most obvious example of the close

1. See T.S.S.A. Pamphlet (11/60) illustrating 'help which has been rendered by the Labour party and by the *Association's M.P.s* through action in Parliament'.

relationship which may exist between a union and the constituencies it sponsors. It was not, in fact, until the General Election of 1964, when it supported the candidature of Eric Ogden in the West Derby division of Liverpool, that the N.U.M. sponsored a candidate in a non-mining constituency. There are, however, other unions in which sponsorship is related to the location of a particular industry: for example, the National Union of Agricultural Workers generally sponsors in agricultural areas, the National Union of Boot and Shoe Operatives in or nearby areas concerning that industry, the British Iron, Steel and Kindred Trades Association in centres of the steel industry, the United Textile Factory Workers' Association in the cotton towns, and so on. The concentration of the memberships of these unions accounts for the N.U.A.W.'s sponsorship of North Norfolk, the long-standing relationship between N.U.B.S.O. and the old Frome constituency, B.I.S.A.K.T.A.'s present connection with Neath, and the financial support given to Farnworth by U.T.F.W.A.

It is possible, however, to establish a general relationship between trade union membership and the distribution of union-sponsored constituencies. Trade union membership is not evenly distributed throughout the country, and this is reflected in the location of sponsored seats: nearly half (47 per cent) of the Labour-held constituencies and over a third (34·9 per cent) of the non-Labour constituencies which selected union-sponsored candidates between 1950 and 1966 were in the north of England.[2] An examination of the trade union affiliations to the regional councils of the Labour party shows that a correlation exists between the distribution of the affiliated membership and the constituencies in which union-sponsored candidates were selected between 1950 and 1966 (Table 6(4)).

With the notable exception of Wales, the rank order of affiliated union membership and of the proportions of sponsored candidates selected in each region is the same. The proportions for the three northern regions are particularly close, and each of the remaining regions is within a 3 per cent margin, except for Wales, where the difference is 6 per cent, and the South-West, where it is 4 per cent. The Welsh figure is a reflection of the relatively low turnover among Labour-held seats in the region, especially those held by the N.U.M. If the proportion of seats *held* by the unions in Wales, as opposed to the proportion in which they won selections, is taken into account, nearly 11 per cent of the seats sponsored by the unions are in Wales.

2. See Appendix A.

Table 6(4): Rank order correlation between trade union affiliation to the regional councils of the Labour party and the distribution of constituencies selecting union-sponsored candidates, 1950–66

Regional council	T.U. affiliated membership*	Union-sponsored constituencies
	per cent	per cent
Northern	9·1 ⎫	10·0 ⎫
Lancs. and Cheshire	18·4 ⎬ 37·8	18·6 ⎬ 39·4
Yorks. (East and West)	10·3 ⎭	10·8 ⎭
East Midlands	8·1 ⎫ 16·2	14·0
West Midlands	8·1 ⎭	
Scotland	10·4	12·7
Southern	9·3	11·7
Wales	9·2	3·2
South-Western	6·0	10·0
Eastern	5·6	5·4
London	5·5	3·6
Total:	100·0	100·0

* Based on the average affiliated membership to each council between 1950 and 1966.

NOTE: Rank order correlation coefficient = 0·8572 where the Northern, Lancashire and Cheshire, and Yorkshire Regional Councils are combined, and 0·8637 where they are treated separately.

The figure for the South-West region is the result partly of a number of non-Labour constituencies, such as Exeter and Bridgwater, which selected more than one sponsored candidate between 1950 and 1966, and partly of the extensive union interest in the Bristol constituencies: of the five Bristol seats which are or have been Labour-held over this period, four have now, or have previously had, union-sponsored candidates.

The distribution of trade union membership accounts, in part at least, for the location of union-sponsored seats, but there is another factor which plays a very considerable part in the selection of candidates as far as the trade unions are concerned. This is the question of the *electoral status* of union-sponsored constituencies.

The figures in Tables 6(1) and 6(3) suggest that the trade unions are reluctant to sponsor non-Labour constituencies: whereas at least one Labour M.P. in three was union-sponsored between 1950 and 1966, only one defeated candidate in ten, at its very highest in 1951, and only one in thirty in 1966, was financially supported by a trade union. Moreover, Table 6(3) shows that the smaller unions were responsible for a greater proportion (47·1 per cent) of these defeated candidates than the 'Big Six' (42·6 per cent). This would support the view that the unions are principally interested in sponsoring M.P.s rather than candidates.

The figures in Table 6(5) not only support this view, but further suggest that the unions tend to concentrate their efforts in Labour-held safe and impregnable seats. Although the C.L.P.s *select* candidates, the individual unions have the *right of nomination* through their branches, and are therefore able to decide in which constituencies they will seek to place candidates. The electoral pattern of union sponsorship shown in Table 6(5) is therefore a direct reflection of union policies. The contrast is considerable: of the Labour-held seats financed by the C.L.P.s, a third were marginal or semi-marginal (compared with just over a quarter of the union seats), and rather more than two fifths were safe or impregnable (compared with nearly three fifths of the union seats). The contrast is even greater among the non-Labour constituencies: here, less than a quarter of the C.L.P. seats were marginal or semi-marginal (compared with two thirds of the union seats), and three fifths (compared with less than one fifth) were safe or impregnable.

Table 6(5) is, in some respects, misleading, however, since it does not distinguish between individual unions or groups of unions. It suggests, in fact, that all unions pursue similar sponsorship policies. In the sense that the principal aim of almost every union is to secure the election of its sponsored candidates to Parliament, this is true, but the

Table 6(5): Comparison of the electoral status of constituencies in which candidates sponsored by the trade unions and C.L.P.s were selected, 1950–66

| Electoral status | Incumbent | | Non-Incumbent | |
	Trade unions	C.L.P.s	Trade unions	C.L.P.s
Marginal	12·0(10)	14·8(13)	33·3 (46)	10·1 (153)
Semi-marginal	15·7(13)	19·3(17)	31·9 (44)	13·8 (210)
Comfortable	14·5(12)	21·6(19)	17·4 (24)	16·2 (245)
Safe	25·3(21)	25·0(22)	11·6 (16)	36·4 (552)
Impregnable	32·5(27)	19·3(17)	5·8 (8)	23·5 (357)
Total:	100·0(83)	100·0(88)	100·0(138)	100·0(1,517)

price that individual unions are willing or possibly have to pay in order to fulfil that aim, varies. It varies in particular for the N.U.M. on the one hand and most other unions on the other.

The National Union of Mineworkers

The N.U.M. may be distinguished from its rivals in at least three important respects. Firstly, in the simple numerical weight of its contribution to union sponsorship: nearly a quarter of all union candidates and nearly a third of the trade union M.P.s selected between 1950 and 1966 were sponsored by the N.U.M. In further contrast to its rivals, the N.U.M. stands alone among the 'Big Six' in having sponsored only five seats unsuccessfully, less than 3 per cent of its total effort. Secondly, with the exception of Liverpool (West Derby), the N.U.M. confines itself to sponsoring seats in mining areas, whereas the majority of other unions place no comparable limits upon themselves. This is a fundamental difference since the vital link in sponsorship by the N.U.M. is the *constituency*, whereas the vital link for the majority of unions is the *candidate*. It is not simply that this limitation provides an explanation of the location of N.U.M.-sponsored seats: *location is the basis of sponsorship* (Liverpool (West Derby) is, of course, the exception that proves the rule). This self-imposed limit is also important, however, because mining constituencies are normally safe Labour seats.

This is the third feature which distinguishes the N.U.M. from its rivals: the concentration of its electoral effort in safe and impregnable seats. At every general election since the war, over 90 per cent of the constituencies sponsored by the N.U.M. have been safe or impregnable Labour seats. Moreover, of the twenty-one Labour-held seats which selected N.U.M. nominees, four were safe and seventeen impregnable.

The impact of the N.U.M. on the selection of candidates is therefore considerable, and the union makes, in many respects, a unique contribution to trade union sponsorship.

It is generally the practice to speak of the N.U.M. as a whole rather than its constituent organizations: in fact, the union comprises fourteen area bodies, together with six industrial associations. Only the area bodies are actively involved in the sponsorship of candidates, and of these, four only marginally. In practice, it is these area bodies[3] which are

3. Particularly the Derbyshire Miners' Association, the Durham Miners' Association, the Lancashire and Cheshire Miners' Federation, the Nottinghamshire and District Miners' Federated Union, the National Union of Scottish Mineworkers, the South Wales Miners' Federation, and the Yorkshire Mine Workers' Association.

responsible for selecting nominees, securing their selection and financing their candidatures, although the National Executive of the N.U.M. occasionally submits a nomination to the area[4] and has the right of veto over area nominees.[5] Apart from this, candidates must normally have worked in the area, in the mines or as an official, for a minimum of five years.[6] Each area is allowed one candidate for every 10,000 members:[7] in fact, only one area has reached its full entitlement since the war, and then for only one election.[8]

Although the miners are slowly but steadily losing ground, they are still a powerful force in the selection of candidates. But their power, once based on numerical superiority or equality, now often depends on being the largest organized minority. This has often been sufficient to retain seats when a new candidate is selected, but seldom to gain seats and often to lose them. The label 'miners' seat' often arouses the resentment and opposition of other unions.

Table 6(6): Number of Labour-held constituencies retained, gained, and lost by the N.U.M. at selection conferences between 1945 and 1966

Area	Retentions	Gains	Losses
Derbyshire	1	1	–
Durham	5	1	3
Lancs. and Cheshire	3	1	–
Northumberland	–	–	2
Nottinghamshire	1	–	–
Scotland	2	2	4
South Wales	4	1	7
Yorkshire	10	1	1
Total:	26	7	17

Table 6(6) shows how these retentions, gains, and losses were distributed among the areas of the N.U.M. Yorkshire is probably the strongest bastion of mining M.P.s, followed by Durham, but South Wales and Scotland show a steady decline, particularly the former,

4. e.g. R. W. Williams was nominated for Wigan in 1948.
5. Rules of the National Union of Mineworkers, No. 48(5).
6. ibid., No. 48(3).
7. ibid., No. 48(4).
8. In 1950 the South Wales area was entitled to eleven sponsored candidates and supported eleven M.P.s.

where the N.U.M. has found itself in fierce competition with the expanding steel industry. A few areas are seeking fresh seats outside the traditional mining areas. For instance, the Lancashire and Cheshire Miners' Federation successfully sponsored a candidate in 1964 in the West Derby division of Liverpool, whilst other areas are making determined efforts to recapture former miners' seats and any Labour-held seats which become vacant in the union area. The Derbyshire Miners' Association (D.M.A.) provides an interesting case-study of the retaining, the gaining, and the attempted capture of seats within its area.

Some months before the General Election of 1959, Henry White, M.P. for North-East Derbyshire since 1942 and an official D.M.A. candidate, announced his impending retirement. The constituency was a miners' stronghold, with some 8,000 members of the N.U.M. affiliated to the C.L.P. and a hundred delegates in the 220-strong G.M.C.[9] Some six nominations were received for the vacancy, among them Stanley Mellors, the D.M.A.'s candidate, Morgan Phillips, general secretary of the Labour party, and Arthur Else, the agent of the local Labour party.[10] The D.M.A. made it abundantly clear that they strongly resented Phillips's nomination, and he eventually withdrew. At the selection conference which followed, Mellors was chosen with the support of ninety-eight delegates out of 176 present.[11] In view of the traditional solidarity of the N.U.M. delegates' votes, there can be little doubt that a substantial proportion of Mellors's votes came from his mining colleagues.

In August, however, Mellors was forced to withdraw through ill-health,[12] and the process of selection had to begin again. Once again the D.M.A. nominated a candidate and once again Morgan Phillips sought selection, but this time he did not withdraw, and both he and the miners' nominee, Tom Swain, were placed on a short-list of four. On this occasion there were 184 delegates present, and in the final ballot Swain defeated Phillips by 103 votes to eighty-one. Once again, the closeness of the D.M.A. candidate's vote to the absolute total the miners could muster is evident.

If the dual selection in North-East Derbyshire was a triumph for the D.M.A., the capture of Chesterfield in 1961 was a greater one. Chesterfield had been held for Labour since 1935 by Sir George Benson, who had first won it in 1929 and then lost it in 1931. The

9. *The Times*, 19 September 1959. 10. *The Times*, 18 March 1959.
11. *The Times*, 6 April 1959. 12. *The Times*, 17 August 1959.

constituency had last been held by a D.M.A. candidate shortly after the First World War, when Barnet Kenyon had held the seat as a Liberal Coalitionist. During the 1920s and early 1930s, relations between the D.M.A. and the Chesterfield D.L.P. were strained, and the announcement of Benson's retirement in 1961 presented the D.M.A. with its first real chance of securing the seat since 1920.[13]

The general secretary of the D.M.A., H. W. Wynn, was determined to secure the selection of the miner's nominee, Eric Varley. Wynn therefore made a careful calculation of the number of delegates to which the miners were entitled on the G.M.C. of Chesterfield C.L.P. Unfortunately this fell short of an absolute majority when allowance was made for a 75–85 per cent attendance by miners' delegates. Wynn's solution to this problem was to approach the next largest union delegation, that of the A.E.U., and seek its support: this he did. In the meantime, all the D.M.A. branches in the constituency were fully briefed to ensure the maximum attendance and support for Varley, whilst members of the association who were individual members of the C.L.P. were encouraged to canvass discreetly on his behalf. There could be no guarantee that this plan would work: the A.E.U. delegation had agreed to support Varley, but a switch of votes at the conference could not be ruled out, whilst much depended on the turnout of the miners. In the event, Varley was successful by a margin of twenty-seven votes.

It was a different story at Ilkeston in 1963, however, though success seemed more likely there: at Chesterfield the D.M.A. had nearly 5,000 members affiliated to the C.L.P., but at Ilkeston the association had nearly 8,000 affiliated members. Wynn followed the same technique he had used at Chesterfield, but he was unable to secure the support of another union delegation. This was partly because the third largest union, the T.G.W.U., which had formerly held the seat, had itself nominated a candidate, Raymond Fletcher. The T.G.W.U.[14] had, moreover, sponsored Ilkeston since 1922, and consequently felt that it had a strong claim to the seat. The selection became a struggle between the D.M.A. and the T.G.W.U., neither of which could command a majority in its own right. Nevertheless, the D.M.A. had eighty-four delegates at the selection conference to the T.G.W.U.'s twenty-three, and, on the first ballot, Peter Heathfield, the D.M.A.'s nominee, had a lead of eleven votes and needed only a further sixteen

13. J. E. Williams, *The Derbyshire Miners*, London, 1962, pp. 807–30.
14. Then the Workers' Union.

votes for victory. But these votes were not forthcoming and victory went to Fletcher on the second ballot. It is not difficult to see why Heathfield failed to secure the nomination: the D.M.A. could be certain of the solid support of its members, but it had no allies, and, whether it was due to resentment of the D.M.A. or to a personal failure on the part of its candidate, the latter was unable to secure sufficient support from delegates outside the D.M.A. Fletcher, assuming that he had the full support of the T.G.W.U. delegates, had, on the other hand, secured no less than fifty votes from non-T.G.W.U. delegates in the first ballot, whereas his rival, assuming that he had the solid support of the D.M.A. delegates, had none.

The D.M.A. is typical of those areas of the N.U.M. which are active in sponsorship, although much depends, of course, on the area general secretary, as the examples given above indicate. In a few cases the miners can still ensure the selection of their candidate against all comers, but assaults on the miners' strongholds have become increasingly successful since the war. This is not entirely due to the decline of the coal industry (though a decline in affiliations to the Labour party of 100,000 between 1950 and 1962 cannot be ignored), for the N.U.M. has been slow to adapt its policy to changing conditions. The rule that candidates must normally work in the area in which they are seeking parliamentary nomination inevitably restricts the miners' choice. None of the areas of the N.U.M. train their candidates in any way, apart from encouraging them to attend W.E.A. or similar adult education courses, and only once since the war has the N.U.M. sponsored a candidate who was not a working miner or a full-time union official.[15] Although trade union candidates tend to be older than other candidates, those of the N.U.M. are often somewhat older than those from other unions and this is invariably reflected in educational background, a far higher proportion of N.U.M. candidates having had only an elementary education than is the case with other union candidates. All these factors tend to isolate the miners' candidate, whose claims are often limited to being the N.U.M. nominee and having strong local connections. In such circumstances the C.L.P. may, if faced with a choice between several sponsored candidates or sometimes where an outstanding non-sponsored candidate has been nominated, reject the miners' nominee. To this problem the N.U.M. has not found an acceptable answer: many of its rivals have.

15. R. W. Williams (Wigan), 1948, solicitor to the N.U.M., nominated by the National Executive of the N.U.M. Williams was the son of a miner.

The N.U.M.'s Rivals

Unlike the N.U.M., the majority of other trade unions very seldom find themselves as the largest organized minority in a C.L.P., least of all the dominant organization. Furthermore, the majority of unions do not restrict sponsorship to particular areas or constituencies and will normally seek candidatures in any area where the prospects of success appear reasonable. The principal consideration is, of course, the electoral status of the constituency, but this does not mean that the unions are interested only in safe and impregnable Labour seats, as Table 6(7) shows.

Table 6(7): Comparison of the electoral status of constituencies in which candidates sponsored by trade unions other than the N.U.M. and by C.L.P.s were selected, 1950–66

| | Incumbent | | Non-incumbent | |
| | Trade unions excluding | | Trade unions excluding | |
Electoral status	N.U.M.	C.L.P.s	N.U.M.	C.L.P.s
Marginal	16·1(10)	14·8(13)	33·8 (45)	10·1 (153)
Semi-marginal	21·0(13)	19·3(17)	30·8 (41)	13·8 (210)
Comfortable	19·4(12)	21·6(19)	18·1 (24)	16·2 (245)
Safe	27·4(17)	25·0(22)	11·3 (15)	36·4 (552)
Impregnable	16·1(10)	19·3(17)	6·0 (8)	23·5 (357)
Total:	100·0(62)	100·0(88)	100·0(133)	100·0(1,517)

It is quite clear from Table 6(7) that the unions other than the N.U.M. are by no means overwhelmingly committed to sponsoring only safe and impregnable Labour seats. In fact, nearly two fifths of the seats sponsored by these unions were marginal or semi-marginal, against just over a third of those financed by the C.L.P.s. Moreover, as far as safe and impregnable constituencies are concerned, the balance is even. The significant contrast is seen if the selections by non-incumbent C.L.P.s are examined: here it is quite clear that whilst the unions are prepared to sponsor non-Labour seats, they have a very strong preference for marginal and semi-marginal constituencies. Nearly two thirds of the non-Labour seats sponsored by unions other than the N.U.M. between 1950 and 1966 were marginal or semi-marginal, compared with less than a fifth which were safe or impregnable. For the C.L.P.s, however, the position is almost reversed: the overwhelming majority of hopeless seats are left to the C.L.P.s.

There are, of course, a number of unions who are prepared to sponsor candidates in constituencies where the likelihood of success is remote, partly to assist the Labour party's electoral effort and partly to give members of their parliamentary panels electoral experience. Both the T.G.W.U. and the A.E.U. have, for example, regularly sponsored candidates in strongly-held Conservative seats like Maidstone, Arundel and Shoreham, Esher, and Cirencester and Tewkesbury, whilst many smaller unions, such as the E.T.U. and D.A.T.A., have sponsored more unsuccessful than successful candidatures. The fact remains, however, that for most unions the *criterion* of sponsorship is not whether a constituency is safe or impregnable, but whether, to use the word used by the unions themselves, a seat is '*winnable*': the majority of trade unions are *primarily* interested in *winning seats not losing them*.

In practice this means that a union is willing to sponsor a marginal or semi-marginal Conservative seat in the hope that a favourable electoral swing will make it a Labour *gain*. Thus, in a period of electoral misfortune for the Labour party, the unions share in that misfortune by unsuccessfully sponsoring as many as thirty Conservative constituencies.[16] This was the pattern between 1950 and 1959, but with the reversal of electoral fortunes which occurred in 1964 and 1966, the unions reaped the benefit of their earlier efforts. Of the *thirty-one* Conservative-held constituencies sponsored by the unions in 1964, *fifteen* were Labour gains. Similarly, in 1966, the unions sponsored *twelve* Conservative constituencies, of which *six* were Labour gains. Moreover, the number of Labour gains in constituencies sponsored by the unions between 1951 and 1966 was disproportionate compared with the number financed by the C.L.P.s: 18·1 per cent of the seats sponsored by the unions were Labour gains, compared with 6·5 per cent of those financed by the C.L.P.s.

The principal object of trade union sponsorship is to secure parliamentary representation, and the unions fashion their policies accordingly; that sponsorship aids Labour's electoral effort is incidental, a secondary consideration which enhances the value of sponsorship over and above its primary purpose. In this context the value to the unions of direct parliamentary representation is of less importance than the

16. There is, of course, also a loss of union seats through the defeat of sitting Members, e.g. nine in 1950, three in 1951, five in 1955, and four in 1959.

fact that they *believe* it to be in their interests and therefore act on that belief. Perhaps the most important result of trade union sponsorship is that it provides the parliamentary Labour party with the overwhelming majority of its working class members: over 80 per cent of the union candidates selected for Labour-held seats between 1951 and 1966 came from an essentially working class background, compared with less than 6 per cent of the candidates financed by the C.L.P.s. This, at least, is the *apparent* result of sponsorship, but whether this may be due to the *financial* aspects of sponsorship, or to the fact that the majority of these candidates are representatives of the trade union movement in the sense that they reflect the characteristics of their constituents to a far greater extent than the majority of their colleagues at Westminster, remains to be seen.[17]

Trade Union Candidates

The way in which trade union candidates are selected by their respective unions varies considerably: some unions simply sponsor any member who secures the nomination in a Labour-held or 'winnable' Conservative seat; others have established formal parliamentary panels, to which members may be elected by the union membership, whilst others resort to examinations and interviews to select suitable individuals. This question is more fully discussed in Appendix C, however (pp. 291–4). What is of more immediate interest is the sort of candidate that unions seek to place in the House of Commons.

Because unions use different methods to select their candidates, differences among unions are bound to arise. Even if unions are grouped into categories like 'industrial' and 'white collar', certain differences in the type of candidate chosen emerge, whilst a comparison of N.U.M. candidates with those of other unions shows important divergences. For example, white collar union candidates are normally younger, but likely to have had previous electoral experience; N.U.M. and industrial union candidates have a similar age structure, but N.U.M. candidates seldom have electoral experience. Despite these differences, which are undoubtedly important, the fundamental difference is not within the union group of candidates, but the contrast between them and the candidates financed by the C.L.P.s.

Perhaps the most interesting difference that emerges is the substantial rebuttal of the general hypothesis (as earlier applied to Conservative candidates) that candidates selected by incumbent C.L.P.s and those

17. See Chapter Eight.

selected by non-incumbent C.L.P.s differ markedly. This hypothesis holds true for the C.L.P. but not for the union candidates.

In respect of previous electoral experience, occupational breakdown, and local government experience, the union-sponsored candidates selected by incumbent and non-incumbent C.L.P.s have identical characteristics, whilst in respect of age, education, and local connections in general, they are markedly similar.

In general, the trade union candidate differs from his C.L.P. colleague in that he is normally older, less well-educated in the sense that he is not a university graduate, is most likely to be a worker by occupation, have had local government experience, and to have been a member of the Labour party for more than twenty years. Local connections are especially important to N.U.M. candidates, of whom over 70 per cent had direct local associations with their constituencies; but for candidates of other unions there is no substantial difference in the demand for local connections compared with C.L.P. candidates. The principal differences between union and C.L.P. candidates are shown in Table 6(8).

It is clear from the figures in Table 6(8) that there is for many union candidates a clear route to Parliament: long service in the union coupled with faithful service to the party, part of which is local government service. The trade unions have, however, found it increasingly difficult to withstand the challenge of non-union candidates in the post-war period, and a number of unions have re-examined their sponsorship policies, with important and far-reaching results.

Prominent in this field is the A.E.U., which, since 1945, has become increasingly active, and successful, in the field of sponsorship. This is the result of a vigorous policy of expansion coupled with an extensive programme of training for members of the parliamentary panel. After they have been selected for the panel, all members undergo a week's training in public speaking: this course is run on behalf of the union by a qualified teacher of elocution. In addition to this, all members of the panel, except sitting M.P.s, must attend an annual educational course lasting five days.[18] The course involves a series of lectures on current political and party policy given by leading members of the parliamentary Labour party and members of the staff of Transport House, and candidates are required to submit daily essays on topics due to be discussed. In the summer of 1965 the A.E.U. enlisted the help of public

18. *Labour Organizer*, August 1963, p. 154. See also the *A.E.U. Journal*, March 1967, pp. 128–9.

Table 6(8): Comparison of the characteristics of trade union and C.L.P. candidates, 1950–66

| | Incumbent | | Non-incumbent | |
| | Trade unions per cent | C.L.P.s per cent | Trade unions per cent | C.L.P.s per cent |
Characteristics				
Previous electoral experience	52·9(69·4)*	67·0	51·4	42·6
Age				
Under 40	19·3	30·7	26·8	54·0
40–49	45·8	46·6	36·3	27·0
50 or over	34·9	22·7	36·9	18·2†
Education				
Elementary	28·6	5·7	39·4	8·5
Graduates	13·2	68·2	8·0	51·9
Public school education	3·6	37·5	2·9	23·0
Occupation				
Workers	82·0	5·7	84·9	16·4
Professional	6·0	46·6	4·3	41·5
Business	1·2	9·1	3·6	14·5
Miscellaneous	10·8	38·6	7·2	27·6
Local connections				
Direct	37·4(25·8)*	25·0	33·4	38·1
None known	22·9(30·6)*	29·6	17·4	13·8
Local government				
experience	67·5	39·8	69·5	46·7
Trade union membership	100·0	55·7	100·0	56·3
Party membership				
Over 20 years	66·3	45·5	50·0	24·9

* Excluding the N.U.M.   † Plus 0·8 per cent not known.

schoolboys in providing hostile audiences for the candidates.[19] This policy has paid dividends and the A.E.U. has more than doubled its number of M.P.s since 1950, when it secured the return of eight Members, compared with 1964, when this number had risen to nineteen.

The training of candidates was the A.E.U.'s solution to a problem which has been facing the trade unions in general, and industrial unions in particular, for a number of years. Before the Second World War, the

19. *Sunday Times*, 31 January 1965.

trade unions were the major source of financial support for M.P.s, especially after the disaffiliation of the I.L.P., but during the post-war period C.L.P.s became more independent both financially and in the selection of candidates. Although the question of finance often looms large in selection, the question of the quality of candidates has been playing an increasingly important part. The competition for seats became fiercer and unions could no longer rely on their 'pocket boroughs', in which, when they became vacant, the union would be 'invited ... to nominate a successor'.[20] Furthermore, the number of unions seeking candidatures has tended to increase: this is especially true of the 'white collar' trade unions, and the situation has, from the point of view of the unions, only been aggravated by the activities of the Co-operative party. It has become an increasingly frequent experience for nominees from industrial unions to find themselves defeated by better-qualified, more articulate Co-operative and non-sponsored nominees. The A.E.U.'s solution has been conspicuously successful, but it has only been possible because the union has been prepared and able to spend money training its candidates. A number of unions have followed the lead given by the A.E.U., notably the E.T.U., N.U.G.M.W., U.P.W., and A.S.W., but others have sought an easier and less expensive solution. Indeed, the N.U.G.M.W. has adopted both methods.

The two general unions, the N.U.G.M.W. and the T.G.W.U., have made increasing use of union members whose industrial connections with the union are often non-existent.[21] These are usually members of the Labour party who seek to fulfil the demand of the Party Constitution that they should, if eligible, belong to a trade union recognized by the T.U.C.[22] Neither union, especially the T.G.W.U., has been slow, moreover, to 'adopt' promising members as sponsored M.P.s or candidates. For instance, the T.G.W.U. has placed Dr Jeremy Bray, M.P. for Middlesbrough West, and Peter Shore, formerly head of the Labour party's Research Department and now M.P. for Stepney, on its panel. This policy has also paid dividends, and six out of seven such T.G.W.U. candidates were elected in 1964. But it is a policy which has met with protests and it is by no means an unusual occurrence at a selection conference for a solicitor or a teacher or a local government officer to be asked by an *industrial* trade unionist why he is a member of the

20. N.E.C. Report, APCR 1931, pp. 17, 18, and 21: Shipley (N.U.D.A.W.), Whitechapel (T.G.W.U.), Pontypool (M.F.G.B.), and Ogmore (M.F.G.B.).
21. This policy has also been adopted by other unions, e.g. the N.U.P.E. and C.A.W.U.
22. Party Constitution, Clause III(3)(b).

T.G.W.U. or the N.U.G.M.W.; whilst the rising proportion of 'white collar' workers on the T.G.W.U.'s parliamentary panel has been the subject of criticism among some sections of the union membership.[23]

Industrial unions have also been losing ground to 'white collar' unions: in 1945, only four 'white collar' unions sponsored candidates, but by 1964, this number had risen to seven. These unions have also helped some of their candidates by allowing them to stand in Conservative-held seats, thereby gaining electoral and political experience. It is perhaps significant that both the A.E.U. and the T.G.W.U. have followed this practice, especially the former, though it should be remembered that to sponsor an unsuccessful candidature is a luxury which smaller unions are often unwilling to indulge in or unable to afford.

Most unions still seek nominations in Labour-held seats for the most part, but they are coming to realize that, where they could formerly choose, they now have to compete with other, Co-operative or non-sponsored, candidates. The ultimate effect of this often unpalatable fact is that unions are being forced to look at the quality of their candidates, at the efficiency of their methods of selection, even at the very concept of sponsorship. How they have endeavoured to meet the Co-operative challenge is the subject of the next chapter, but in response to the general problem some will contract out, others will try to adapt themselves to the more demanding conditions; none will succeed, however, if they attempt to meet those conditions with the standards which were sufficient for the Labour party of the 1920s and 1930s.

23. *Daily Telegraph*, 26 February 1964.

CHAPTER SEVEN

The Co-operative Party[1]

The Co-operative party is the political wing of the Co-operative Movement and is technically a constituent part of and responsible to the Co-operative Congress.[2] It is organized on a basis similar to that of the Labour party, consisting of individual and affiliated members, the latter being members of Co-operative societies affiliated to the Co-operative at national level. Although there are over eleven million affiliated members, the total individual membership is only 18,000.

At local level there are both *society* and *constituency* parties,[3] and it is the *constituency* Co-operative parties which are affiliated to the C.L.P.s. There are various estimates of the amount of money spent on politics by the Co-operative Movement: Harrison suggests that it is 'at least £130,000, and possibly as much as £175,000';[4] others put it as high as £200,000 or more.[5] As Harrison points out, however, 'only about £30,000 reaches the Labour party',[6] and the Co-operative party's

1. Including the Royal Arsenal Co-operative Society. The R.A.C.S. is the only co-operative society affiliated to the Labour party at national level. To that extent it has a special role in Labour–Co-operative politics and normally has a representative on the N.E.C. of the Labour party. Since the last war the R.A.C.S. has financed its own candidates in constituencies within its trading area. Between 1945 and 1959, it sponsored J. Reeves, M.P. for Greenwich, and, since then, has sponsored his successor, R. W. Marsh (although Marsh has now become a sponsored member of the N.U.P.E.), and both he and Reeves were invited to attend meetings of the Co-operative Parliamentary Group in the House of Commons as observers. The society also sponsored two candidates in 1950, both unsuccessfully, at Lewisham West and Woolwich West, and has made grants to several Labour M.P.s and candidates in Greater London. Since the number of candidates it sponsors is very small and nominees are now taken from the Co-operative party panel, the R.A.C.S. has been included as part of the Co-operative party, to which, of course, it is also affiliated.

2. Constitution of the Co-operative Party (approved by the Co-operative Congress, 1951), p. 3.

3. Co-operative societies often cover several parliamentary constituencies.

4. Harrison, op. cit., p. 97.

5. *The Times*, 5 March 1963; *Daily Telegraph*, 11 April 1963; see also Proceedings of the Co-operative Party Conference, 1963, p. 18.

6. Harrison, op. cit., p. 97.

relationship with the Labour party has had a chequered career.[7] Whilst the vast majority of Co-operative societies are affiliated to the Co-operative party, their relationship to and role in the Labour party is somewhat tenuous.

The Co-operative party is not, however, affiliated nationally to the Labour party, despite considerable and long-standing pressure to do so. This has been a major source of grievance on the part of the Labour party:

> From the very beginning the Labour party made provision for the national affiliation of Co-operative organizations, but the Co-operative movement held aloof. Because it is not affiliated to the Labour party nationally [the Co-operative party] makes no contribution to the Labour party's national funds.[8]

The Co-operative party has always resisted the demand that it should affiliate on the grounds that it is responsible to the Co-operative Congress[9] and could not, therefore, accept the decisions of the Annual Conference of the Labour party should these conflict with the decisions of the congress:

> If we affiliate nationally, we should require to affiliate in such a way that we could be assured that we have, if not a dominating influence within the Labour party, a fairly decisive influence (at present affiliation would give the Co-operative party 800,000[10] votes at the Labour Party Conference, or one vote in seven) and you would be committed to the decisions of the Labour party without having an effective vote in its affairs.[11]

Apart from any scruples about its responsibility to the Co-operative Congress, however, the Co-operative party's financial position is such that it could not at any time during its history have afforded to affiliate its total membership to the Labour party on a national basis. Indeed, had it been able to do so, the Co-operative party would have been in a more powerful position than the whole trade union movement as far

7. See G. W. Rhodes, *Co-operative Labour Relations, 1900–62*, Co-operative College Papers, No. 8, Loughborough, 1962; and Barbara Smith and G. N. Ostergaard, *Constitutional Relations between the Labour and Co-operative Parties: An Historical Review*, Hansard Society, London 1961.

8. *Labour Organizer*, March 1957, pp. 46–8.

9. See *Monthly Letter of the Co-operative Party*, January 1950, pp. 9–10, and January, 1963, pp. 11–12.

10. Based on the then affiliation fee of 6d. per affiliated member, realizing a total of £20,000.

11. J. Bailey, then secretary of the Co-operative party, replying to a motion proposed by the R.A.C.S. urging national affiliation to the Labour party – Annual Conference of the Co-operative Party, 1949, pp. 76–82. (To be referred to as Party Conference.)

as the Annual Conference of the Labour party was concerned. In 1962 the unions paid the Labour party £207,426 in national affiliation fees based on 5,502,773 members:[12] if the Co-operative party affiliated on a similar basis, it would, in 1962, have cost the organization £420,220 for 11,392,546 members.[13] Yet, as early as 1948, local Co-operative parties were finding financial relations with C.L.P.s problematic: 'We as a [Co-operative] constituency party are not able to pay the sums asked, nominally 6d. per member for affiliation to the Labour party (at local level).'[14] For its part, the Labour party has not only sought the national affiliation of the Co-operative party, but also the extension of local affiliation through Co-operative societies. In 1955 the Wilson Committee recommended that Co-operative societies should be urged to follow the example of the R.A.C.S. and affiliate to C.L.P.s.[15] The financial advantage to the Labour party would be considerable and any large-scale affiliation of this sort would, of course, have an important impact on the selection of candidates. If only for financial reasons, however, the Co-operative Union and Co-operative party resisted this demand, since affiliations to C.L.P.s through constituency Co-operative parties were small and relatively inexpensive, whereas affiliations through societies would be much larger and more expensive. In fact, had the Labour party succeeded in persuading Co-operative societies to affiliate directly to C.L.P.s, the amount of money which the Co-operative Movement contributes to Labour's political effort would be increased considerably without the Labour party conceding any substantive control over its policy to the Co-operative Movement.

Table 7(1): Number of Labour–Co-operative candidates, 1950–66

| | Number of candidates | | |
Year	Successful	Unsuccessful	Total
1950	19	17	36
1951	17	22	39
1955	20	19	39
1959	17	14	31
1964	19	8	27
1966	18	6	24

12. N.E.C. Report, APCR 1964, pp. 49 and 55.
13. Based on figures given in the Report of the Co-operative Congress, 1963, p. 232.
14. Party Conference Proceedings, 1948, p. 17.
15. Report of the Sub-Committee on Party Organization (the Wilson Report), APCR 1955, pp. 85–6.

Numerically, the Co-operative candidates are relatively unimportant, as the figures in Table 7(1) demonstrate, but the relationship which has allowed between twenty-four and forty candidates at every general election since 1945 to call themselves 'Labour and Co-operative' has been stormy to a degree quite out of proportion to the numbers involved. Although the source of controversy between the Co-operative and Labour parties has been concerned with both policy and finance, it has manifested itself to a considerable extent in the question of the sponsorship of candidates by the Co-operative party.

The first national agreement between the two parties[16] was in 1927. The Cheltenham Agreement, as it was known, provided that 'local Co-operative parties and councils should be eligible for affiliation to Divisional Labour parties, that representation and voting powers of Co-operative parties should be in proportion to affiliation fees payable'.[17] The object of this agreement, however, was to establish a formal link at national rather than local level, in the form of a joint national committee drawn from the two parties. The provisions for local links merely recognized a state of affairs which existed since the inception of the Co-operative party in 1917 and sought only to encourage and extend the practice of local agreements. Despite difficulties over the position of Co-operative M.P.s under the Standing Orders of the P.L.P., the Hastings Agreement and the employment of constituency agents, the 1927 agreement remained in force until 1946, although negotiations on the settlement of outstanding differences had been continuing at irregular intervals for several years before the outbreak of war.

The Agreement of 1946 placed Labour Co-operative relations on a much firmer basis. As far as parliamentary candidates were concerned, Clause 19 of the agreement stipulated that Co-operative candidates were to be nominated and selected by the C.L.P. in accordance with the rules laid down by the Labour party,[18] and, furthermore, such candidates should sign the following declaration:

I accept nomination as a Parliamentary Candidate of the Co-operative Party running in association with the Labour Party. If elected to Parliament, I undertake to join the Parliamentary Labour Party and to accept and to act

16. Strictly speaking, these agreements are between the Labour party and the Co-operative Union.
17. Rhodes, op. cit., p. 30.
18. Agreement between the Labour Party and the Co-operative Union, APCR 1946, Appendix V, Clause 19.

in harmony with the Standing Orders of the Parliamentary Labour Party for the time being in force.[19]

The selection of Co-operative candidates was, of course, subject to the endorsement of the N.E.C. of the Labour party and it was agreed that they should be designated 'Co-operative and Labour Candidates'.[20] The agreement was approved by the Co-operative Congress in 1946.

For some years the relationship between the two parties was satisfactory, and the National Committee of the Co-operative party reported in 1951:

Cordial relations continue to exist between the Labour Party and ourselves. The majority of local Co-operative Parties have now affiliated to their respective Constituency Labour Parties. This has resulted in *a marked increase in the number of Parliamentary Selection Conferences before which a Co-operative nominee has appeared.*[21]

And:

By the end of the year we had secured, in addition to the 18 sitting M.P.s, the adoption of Co-operative nominees in 22 constituencies. This brings the total number of constituencies for which we have joint responsibility with the Labour Party to 40,[22] *a record.*[23]

The Co-operative party was, of course, very satisfied with this state of affairs, and again in 1952 the National Committee was able to report that 'continuous, close and cordial relations with the Labour party have continued throughout the year'.[24] There were expressions of regret that the Co-operative party had failed to secure the nomination in constituencies such as Droylsden, where there had been a long-standing association between the C.L.P. and the local Co-operative party,[25] but it was generally felt that such losses could be recuperated elsewhere. The party had long held the view that 'no nominating organization at a conference selecting a Parliamentary Candidate has any better right to the seat than other nominating bodies',[26] and, in 1950, the Party

19. ibid., Clause 20.
20. ibid., Clause 21. This was a curious condition, as it has been the practice for joint candidates to be known as 'Labour–Co-operative' and *not* 'Co-operative–Labour' since 1945; and until 1957 the Co-operative Movement habitually referred in its publications to a future 'Co-operative Labour Government'.
21. Report of the National Committee of the Co-operative Party, 1951, p. 21. (Author's italics.)
22. Before the General Election of 1951. This figure does not include J. Reeves, the R.A.C.S. M.P. for Greenwich.
23. National Committee Report, 1951, p. 22. (Author's italics.)
24. ibid., 1952, p. 11.
25. ibid., p. 30.
26. *Monthly Letter*, January 1945, p. 4.

Conference rejected a motion demanding the future allocation of seats currently held by Co-operative M.P.s to Co-operative candidates.[27] Ironically, it was this rejection of a controlled market in seats and the acceptance of a free market which led to the breakdown of relations between the Co-operative and Labour parties.

Between 1951 and 1957 not only did the Co-operative party demonstrate its ability to secure the selection of candidates in seats it already held, where the M.P. had died or intended to retire,[28] and to retain all its seats affected by the redistribution of 1954,[29] but also its capacity to win fresh seats, including a number formerly held by trade unions. In September 1952, A. M. F. Palmer was selected for Cleveland, a constituency previously held by the N.U.G.M.W.; in March 1953, Mrs Harriet Slater was selected for Stoke-on-Trent North, a constituency previously held by the T.S.S.A.; and in September 1954, W. J. Owen was selected for Morpeth, long a bastion of the Northumberland miners. This last capture resulted in strong protests from the N.U.M.; not only had the Co-operative party dared to challenge the supremacy of the miners (other unions had gone this far), but had, with Machiavellian cunning, chosen as their nominee an ex-miner and current employee of the National Coal Board. Coming so soon after the rejection of the N.U.M. nominee at Aberdare, where a non-sponsored candidate was selected, it is hardly surprising that the Co-operative party should be singled out as the object of the miners' wrath, especially as no *organization* could be regarded as responsible for their defeat at Aberdare. The fact that the traditional solidarity of the miners had broken down at Morpeth[30] was irrelevant.

Over the same period a Co-operative nominee also won the radically altered constituency of Romford, which had been unsuccessfully sponsored by the T.G.W.U. and was now a potential Labour seat, and another nominee with Co-operative connections, A. M. Skeffington,[31] was selected for Hayes and Harlington, a seat formerly held by the A.E.U. The seat at Greenock was also won against strong union opposition in November 1955.[32]

Trade union resentment reached a climax in January 1957, when

27. Party Conference Proceedings, 1950, pp. 76–8.
28. e.g. Birmingham (Small Heath), Wood Green, Bilston, and East Ham South.
29. Barons Court, Dartford, Erith and Crayford, and Glasgow (Govan).
30. See Harrison, op. cit., p. 301, footnote.
31. Labour Member for Lewisham West, 1945–50, sponsored by the R.A.C.S. in 1950. Skeffington was not, however, a sponsored candidate at Hayes and Harlington, although he was invited to attend meetings of the Co-operative Parliamentary Group.
32. *The Times*, 7 November 1955.

Wednesbury C.L.P. selected a Co-operative nominee in preference to a trade union member of the N.E.C., who was also an ex-M.P. It may not be without significance that the Wednesbury selection was endorsed by the N.E.C. at its *January* meeting and that on 1 *February* 1957 the Co-operative Union received 'an intimation by the Labour Party ... that the agreement ... dated September 24th, 1946, be terminated'.[33]

It should not be thought that the question of parliamentary candidates was the only matter over which the Co-operative *Movement* and the Labour party differed, for it was not simply a disagreement between the two parties. During the last three years of the 1945–51 Labour government there were policy differences over Labour party nationalization proposals, especially insurance. Nor did Labour's assumption of the role of Opposition lessen these differences, though they took on a less urgent aspect. In fact, fresh disagreements arose over Labour's policy statement, *Challenge to Britain*, in 1953, followed by others over agricultural and marketing policies.[34] None the less, it was the disagreement over candidates which brought matters to a head, and it was largely the inability of the two sides to agree on this issue which prevented a new agreement being reached until September 1958.

In the meantime, the Co-operative party continued to seek further nominations, securing the selection of a Co-operative nominee at Willesden West against competition from four trade unions in February 1958.[35] On the other hand, a year earlier the nomination at East Ham North, which had been a Co-operative seat since 1945, was lost to the T.G.W.U., who had nominated one of its ablest candidates for the seat. It was not without feeling that the *Monthly Letter* could report: 'The local Co-operative Party did not sulk ... or complain about Co-operative seats being taken by other organizations.'[36]

The unions complained that Co-operative nominees had been winning seats at the expense of union nominees, but the figures shown in Table 7(2) do not support these complaints, although no account is taken of seats which were not previously union-sponsored. It is clear that the unions lost several seats over a short period, and it is probably

33. Report of the National Policy Committee, Co-operative Congress Report, pp. 62–84.
34. Rhodes, op. cit., Chapter 5, pp. 85–94, and Chapter 6, pp. 95–102.
35. The A.S.W., which had held the seat since 1923, appealed in vain for trade union solidarity to ensure the selection of its nominee (see Harrison, op. cit., p. 303), whilst the T.G.W.U. was certain it had ensured the selection of its nominee (private communication).
36. *Monthly Letter*, July 1957, p. 15.

Table 7(2): Interchange of Labour-held constituencies between the Co-operative party and the trade unions, 1950–66

Inter-election period	Won from T.U.s	Lost to T.U.s
1950–1	–	1
1951–5	3	–
1955–9	1	1
1959–64	1	2
1964–6	–	–
Total:	5	4

significant that only one seat has been won from a trade union by a Co-operative nominee since any restriction was placed on the total number of Co-operative candidates.

After eighteen months of negotiation, during which the Labour party proposed that Co-operative representation in the House of Commons should be reduced to '*six* seats . . . allocated to Co-operative business leaders',[37] a new agreement was formally signed in January 1959.[38] The new agreement was a compromise and as such left unsolved the long-term problem of Labour–Co-operative candidates. Under Clause 9 of the 1958 Agreement, it was agreed that all the Co-operative M.P.s and candidates then endorsed would be sponsored at the next general election; and in the event of any withdrawals of candidature, it was agreed that joint consultations would take place. This meant that there would be thirty Co-operative party candidates at the next election. Clause 10 stipulated that the number of Labour–Co-operative candidates at ensuing elections would be the subject of further consultation. In future, joint candidates would be designated 'Labour–Co-operative', confirming the practice since 1945. Apart from the vague overall restriction on candidates, the most important section of the agreement from the point of view of selection was Clause 5(b), which said:

Where a Constituency Co-operative Party affiliates to a Central or Constituency Labour Party it shall be regarded as *the representative of the*

37. *Monthly Letter*, November 1957, p. 7. (Author's italics.)
38. Agreement between the Labour Party and the Co-operative Union, 1959. For full details, see Report of the National Policy Committee to the Co-operative Congress, 1959, pp. 61–4. This agreement is normally referred to as the '1958 Agreement', since negotiations were brought to a successful conclusion in September 1958.

wider Co-operative Movement, shall affiliate as a single unit and shall receive representation as such.[39]

The Co-operative party has never been in a position to dominate a selection conference in any constituency: this clause made sure not only that it could never do so, but that in relation to other affiliated organizations Co-operative representation was reduced to a minimum. Under normal C.L.P. rules, any trade union *branch* may affiliate to the C.L.P. and, whilst there may be a limitation on the total number of delegates any one branch may send to the G.M.C., there is no limitation on the number of *branches* which might affiliate. The Co-operative party, however, could affiliate only *en bloc* thereby incurring a possible limitation on its total number of delegates, since *branches* of the party were ineligible for affiliation. This could work only to the advantage of the unions and has been a source of bitter Co-operative complaint. Since this ruling, a former general secretary of the Co-operative party has estimated that no G.M.C. can boast more than a dozen Co-operative delegates, and most only half this number.[40]

The 1958 Agreement was accepted by the Co-operative Movement with reluctance: '. . . it must be appreciated that the new agreement has not been entered into with any degree of enthusiasm by the Central Executive [of the Co-operative Union]. It is believed, however, that the agreement represents the utmost which the Labour party was prepared to concede. . . .'[41] For the time being, however, electoral unity prevailed, but hard on the heels of the Labour party's defeat in 1959 came further criticism from the Co-operative party,[42] with the result that a supplementary agreement[43] was signed in June 1960, following a series of proposals by the Labour party in May of that year.

Under the supplementary agreement, it was agreed that there should be a limit of thirty on the number of Co-operative party candidates at the next election. In the meantime, the Labour party would raise no objection to the nomination of the four former Co-operative M.P.s, who were defeated in 1959, in the same constituencies, nor to the nomination of the ten unsuccessful Co-operative candidates, also in the same constituencies; but in all other constituencies *a Co-operative*

39. 1958 Agreement, Clause 5(b). (Author's italics.)
40. Private communication.
41. 1958 Agreement, Co-operative Congress Report, p. 61.
42. See proceedings of the Co-operative Party Conference, 1960, pp. 15–16 and 24–5.
43. See Co-operative Party Report to the Co-operative Congress, 1961, p. 191: Supplementary Agreement between the Labour Party and the Co-operative Union.

nomination would require the permission of the N.E.C. The permission of the N.E.C. would also be required for a nomination for *any by-election.* This, of course, referred to nomination for *selection* not simply as Labour candidates. To these restrictions was added the demand that the Co-operative party should 'take its share of the difficult constituencies'.[44] The Labour party also expressed dissatisfaction with the concentration of Co-operative candidates in the Southern Section of the Co-operative Union.[45]

At the Co-operative Party Conference the following Easter, a motion highly critical of the Labour party's attitude and treatment of the Co-operative party was passed against the advice of the National Committee,[46] but in urging the rejection of the motion, the secretary of the party introduced an air of unreality to the whole dispute: 'In practical terms our *present finances . . . would not enable us to run more than* 30 candidates.'[47] In fact, the National Committee was powerless in the face of Labour party pressure; whilst the Co-operative party needed the Labour party in order to maintain its parliamentary representation, the Labour party had no need of the Co-operative party. The admission that there was a practical ceiling on the number of Co-operative candidates equal to the limit imposed by the Labour party reduced the area of disagreement to one of the location of constituencies sponsored by the Co-operative party. To some extent, the differences between the two parties had narrowed, but the dispute was no less bitter.

The Co-operative party sought a modification of the 1960 Agreement which would facilitate the redistribution of Co-operative candidates throughout sections of the Co-operative Union. It was proposed that there should be a balance between favourable and unfavourable seats, and that the Labour party should withdraw the 1960 provision that the permission of the N.E.C. was necessary before a Co-operative nomination could be made in constituencies other than those sponsored in 1959 and where the same candidate was nominated. The Labour party rejected these proposals and offered no alternative solution.[48]

In the meantime the Labour party enforced the provisions of the 1958 and 1960 Agreements with considerable severity. In 1961 the Co-operative party was given the choice of *nominating a candidate for*

44. Supplementary Agreement, Clause (e).
45. See below, pages 198–200.
46. Party Conference Proceedings, 1961, pp. 114–18.
47. ibid. (Author's italics.)
48. Co-operative Party Report to the Co-operative Congress, 1962, pp. 220–1.

selection at *either* Warrington *or* Paisley. The party chose the former in the hope of increasing Co-operative representation in the north-west.[49] Between 1961 and 1962, the Co-operative party sought permission to submit nominations at Glasgow (Bridgeton), Middlesbrough East, Stockton-on-Tees, Hull West, Tottenham, Bristol Central, Poplar, and Swansea East, all of which were Labour-held seats, and at Liverpool (Kirkdale) and Darlington, both Conservative-held. In each case the N.E.C. refused the Co-operative party permission to nominate a sponsored candidate.[50] It was perhaps significant that *all* but two of the Labour-held seats, and one of the two Conservative-held seats, subsequently chose a candidate sponsored by a trade union.[51]

Eventually, in February 1962, a further supplementary agreement was negotiated by which the Co-operative party agreed that, of the ten candidates to which it was entitled, five should be in difficult and five in favourable constituencies. The timing of the nominations was to be such that a balance would be maintained between difficult and favourable constituencies, but the permission of the N.E.C. would no longer be required in any of the ten seats unless the seat was held by Labour.[52] Following this agreement, relations between the two parties became more amicable and the N.E.C.'s attitude towards Co-operative nominations was more in the spirit and less in the letter of the series of agreements.[53]

This was clear from the electoral agreements which followed the General Elections of 1964 and 1966.[54] Both agreements retained the overall limitation of thirty candidatures, including the sitting M.P.s, and restrictions continued to be placed on the remaining candidatures, eleven in the 1965 Agreement and twelve in the 1967 Agreement. In each case three of the candidatures could be in Conservative marginal or semi-marginal seats, the remainder being in Conservative seats with majorities of more than 5,000. There were, however, two relaxations

49. Party Conference Proceedings, 1961, pp. 114–18.
50. Report of the National Committee of the Co-operative Party, 1962, p. 9; Rhodes, op. cit., pp. 115–16; and Party Conference proceedings, 1962, p. 18.
51. It is ironical, however, that the union-sponsored candidate for Bristol Central later withdrew and the C.L.P. selected A. M. F. Palmer, nominated and sponsored by the Co-operative party.
52. Co-operative Party Report to the Co-operative Congress, 1963, pp. 234–6.
53. See Rhodes, op. cit., p. 117. Even as late as 1964, however, Co-operative party members were continuing to express doubts and dissatisfaction with Co-operative–Labour relations. See Party Conference Report, 1964, pp. 10–12.
54. For details of the agreements, see Report of the National Committee of the Co-operative Party, 1966, pp. 11–12, and *Platform* (successor to the *Monthly Letter*), No. 17, March 1967.

of the earlier restrictions: first, the specific permission of the N.E.C. to nominate a candidate was no longer required, merely that the Co-operative party should advise the Labour party of its intention to do so; and second, the 1967 Agreement allowed the Co-operative party to nominate a candidate for a Labour-held constituency. This last concession was to enable the Co-operative party to raise its number of M.P.s to the 1964–6 level, since it had been reduced by the retirement of Mrs Harriet Slater (Stoke-on-Trent North) in March 1966. But it also shows the willingness of the Labour party to allow the Co-operative party to maintain as many as eighteen Members, and is therefore a significant retreat from the proposal of 1957 that Co-operative representation should be reduced to six.

The question which always rankles in the mind of the Co-operative party is that, whatever its financial relationship with the Labour party, whatever financial limitation there may be on the number of candidates it can sponsor, there should be any limitation imposed from other than within its own ranks. The absence of any limitation on the number of candidates which may be sponsored by the unions is especially resented. The Labour party may be fully justified in imposing such limitations in the light of the *overall* relationship between the two parties, based as it is on conditions which do not pertain to the relationship between the trade unions and the Labour party. Nevertheless, by placing a limitation on the number of Co-operative candidates and their location, the N.E.C. of the Labour party has partially restricted the choice of C.L.P.s. Under certain circumstances a C.L.P. may not have the opportunity to select a *sponsored* candidate of the Co-operative party. It is true that under Clause 13 of the 1958 Agreement the right of locally affiliated Co-operative parties to nominate *non-sponsored* candidates is in no way curtailed, but so long as financial considerations are a factor in the selection of candidates in the Labour party, and so long as there is a restriction on the number of Co-operative delegates to a G.M.C., Clause 13 will remain an inadequate substitute for the real restriction of sponsorship; and the present selection procedure does not 'ensure equality of opportunity of nomination, and a representative method of selection'.[55]

The Pattern of Co-operative Sponsorship

The figures shown in Table 7(3) show that the electoral pattern of Co-operative sponsorship is similar to trade union sponsorship. As far

55. *Labour Organizer*, January 1956, p. 15.

as Labour-held seats are concerned, the Co-operative party is some-what more inclined to favour the safer constituencies, but compares favourably with the unions if account is taken of N.U.M. sponsorship. Nearly a third of the Co-operative-sponsored seats were marginal or semi-marginal, and rather less than three fifths were safe or impregnable. Taking all trade unions together, there is little difference, but if the N.U.M. is excluded, then the unions could argue that they are more willing to sponsor marginal Labour constituencies.

Table 7(3): The electoral status of constituencies in which Co-operative party candidates were selected compared with those in which trade union and C.L.P. candidates were selected, 1950–66

	Co-op party per cent	T.U.s (excl. N.U.M.) per cent	C.L.P.s per cent
A. *Incumbent C.L.P.s*			
Marginal	6·2 (1)	16·1(10)	14·8(13)
Semi-marginal	25·0 (4)	21·0(13)	19·3(17)
Comfortable	12·5 (2)	19·4(12)	21·6(19)
Safe	31·3 (5)	27·4(17)	25·0(22)
Impregnable	25·0 (4)	16·1(10)	19·3(17)
Total:	100·0(16)	100·0(62)	100·0(88)
B. *Non-incumbent C.L.P.s*			
Marginal	22·0(15)	33·8(45)	10·1 (153)
Semi-marginal	32·4(22)	30·8(41)	13·8 (210)
Comfortable	22·0(15)	18·1(24)	16·2 (245)
Safe	17·7(12)	11·3(15)	36·4 (552)
Impregnable	5·9 (4)	6·0 (8)	23·5 (357)
Total	100·0(68)	100·0(133)	100·0(1,517)

Turning to sponsored candidates in non-Labour constituencies, the balance is, if anything, slightly in the Co-operative party's favour. Proportionately, the latter sponsors slightly more safe and impregnable marginal seats. Nevertheless, the basic pattern found among the unions remains: both unions and the Co-operative party are primarily interested in securing parliamentary representation and therefore seek candidatures principally in either Labour-held seats, or marginally held

Conservative seats. Once again, this can be shown by the proportion of Conservative-held constituencies sponsored by the Co-operative party which were Labour gains in 1964 and 1966. The restrictions placed upon the Co-operative party after the 1959 General Election meant that it was difficult for the party to benefit substantially from a swing to Labour. However, of the eleven Conservative seats which the Co-operative party sponsored in 1964, three were Labour gains, and a fourth gain was made in 1966. This was some compensation for the losses the Co-operative party had suffered in the 1950s: in the General Election of 1950 four Co-operative M.P.s were defeated, two sponsored by the Co-operative party and two by the R.A.C.S.; the General Elections of 1951 and 1955 saw the defeat of a further three Co-operative M.P.s; whilst another four lost their seats in 1959, bringing the party's total loss to eleven over four elections.

The effect of the breakdown of electoral relations between the two parties had an important effect on the selection of Co-operative candidates between 1955 and 1959 and has done since 1959. Between 1951 and 1954 the selection of Co-operative candidates in Conservative-held seats continued steadily throughout the whole period, and the first Co-operative candidate was selected in March 1952 and the last in February 1955. Similarly, following the General Election of 1955, eight Co-operative candidates were selected for non-Labour seats between February and November 1956. A ninth candidate was selected in the New Year and endorsed by the N.E.C. in February 1957, but, with the exception of L. A. Pavitt's selection for the Labour seat of Willesden West in February 1958, *no Co-operative candidate was selected* between the termination of the 1946 Agreement in February 1957 and the selection of G. W. Rhodes at Battersea South, shortly before the General Election of 1959, following the sudden withdrawal of the previous candidate. Moreover, under the terms of the 1958 Agreement, the nomination of a Co-operative candidate at Battersea South required the N.E.C.'s permission.[56]

It is hardly surprising that the unions and the Labour party should feel that the Co-operative party was unwilling to sponsor sufficient of the 'difficult' seats, for, of the nine non-Labour constituencies which selected Co-operative nominees after the 1955 election and before the termination of the 1946 Agreement, two were marginal in 1955, five semi-marginal, one comfortable, and one safe. Neither the unions nor the Labour party were prepared to regard one comfortable and one

56. Co-operative Party Report to the Co-operative Congress, 1960.

safe constituency as a reasonable price for seven potential Labour seats, given a favourable swing at the next election.

Following the General Election of 1959, no Co-operative candidates were selected prior to the Supplementary Agreement of 1960. This was due, however, to the action of the N.E.C. in slowing the tempo of selection, rather than the N.E.C.'s refusal to approve the submission of Co-operative nominees to C.L.P.s. The 1960 Agreement was designed to clarify the general provisions of the 1958 Agreement, but in doing so it severely restricted the activities of the Co-operative party. Although the Labour party had agreed to raise no objection to the re-nomination of the Co-operative M.P.s defeated in 1959 in their former constituencies,[57] this did not result in the selection of any Co-operative candidates, since one of the former M.P.s retired and the other three decided to seek candidatures elsewhere. The other provision by which the Labour party would allow Co-operative nominations in the ten constituencies fought unsuccessfully in 1959, provided the same candidate was re-nominated,[58] resulted in the re-selection of three Co-operative candidates, one in a marginal, one in a semi-marginal, and one in a safe seat.[59] Only one candidate was selected under Clause (c) of the agreement, which provided that the permission of the N.E.C. was necessary in all other cases.[60]

The dissatisfaction of the Co-operative party led to the signing of the second supplementary agreement in February 1962, a month after the endorsement of the last of the re-selections. The 1962 Agreement laid down more detailed provisions for the nomination of Co-operative candidates, although no longer was the permission of the N.E.C. necessary for a Co-operative nomination in a non-Labour seat.[61] On the other hand, the Co-operative party was committed to sponsoring five of its ten remaining candidatures in 'difficult' constituencies[62] and to effecting a more even distribution of candidates throughout the sections of the Co-operative Union.[63] In fact, only seven of the ten candidatures were filled, and of these, one was marginal, two comfortable, one safe, and three impregnable. The balance of these was very much in the favour of difficult rather than favourable constituencies. As far as the distribution of candidatures was concerned, these selections

57. Supplementary Agreement, 1960, Clause (n).   58. ibid.
59. Manchester (Wythenshawe), Billericay, and Henley.
60. Birmingham (Yardley).
61. Co-operative Party Report to the Co-operative Congress, 1963, pp. 234-6: Supplementary Agreement between the Labour Party and the Co-operative Union, 1962, Clause (iv).
62. ibid., Clause (i).   63. ibid., Clause (vi).

did little to alter the overall pattern: with the exception of the Southern Section, which had two candidatures, and the Western and North-Western, which had none, the candidatures were shared out equally among the remainder.

The concentration of Co-operative candidatures in the Southern Section of the Co-operative Union had been causing the leaders of the Co-operative party concern for some time, and in 1960 an approach was made to the Labour party with a view to effecting a redistribution of seats within the Co-operative Union. The Labour party did little to meet this request, although the 1962 Agreement did allow the Co-operative party 'to indicate the number of candidatures it wishes to have in each of the divisions of the Co-operative Party'.[64] The concern of the Co-operative party over this question is understandable in so far as there was and is a heavy concentration of candidates in the Southern Section, but the overall distribution of Co-operative candidates does little more than reflect the overall distribution of Co-operative party membership (Table 7(4)).

Table 7(4): *Rank order correlation of Co-operative party membership and candidatures in the sections of the Co-operative Union, 1950–66*

Section – rank order membership*	Rank order candidatures†
Southern	1
Midland	2
North-Western	3
Scotland	3
North-Eastern	5
Northern	7
Western	8
South-Western	6

* Co-operative Congress Reports, 1950–60.
† Rank order correlation coefficient = 0·9226.

It is true, of course, that the concentration in the Southern Section is considerably heavier than can be accounted for simply in terms of membership, since approximately 30 per cent of the Co-operative party membership is found in the Southern Section against approximately 50 per cent of the candidatures, but this probably reflects the organization of the Co-operative party in that section as much as anything. For instance, the North-Western Section, which, though

64. ibid.

third in both candidatures and membership, is in fact under-repre-
sented. Generally speaking, the Co-operative societies in the North-
Western Section are relatively small, whereas the Southern Section
contains not only the largest Co-operative Society in Britain, but two
other large societies, the R.A.C.S. and the South Suburban. The
London Co-operative Society, with 1,283,000 affiliated members in
1959,[65] is extremely active politically, and, of the thirty-three
selection conferences won in the Southern Section between 1950 and
1959, no less than twenty-four were in the L.C.S. trading area.[66] The
secretary of the Political Committee of the L.C.S. keeps a tight rein
on sponsored candidatures in the area, and nomination is effectually
kept in the hands of the Political Committee and not left to the local
Co-operative party. The action of the N.E.C. of the Labour party in
withholding permission for the nomination of Co-operative candidates
in certain constituencies has resulted in a reduction in the number and
proportion of such candidates in the Southern Section. Since the
General Election of 1959, only twelve candidates have been selected in
the section, roughly two fifths of the total number of Co-operative
candidates. Inevitably, however, this is a slow process, and already the
Midland Section is slightly over-represented.

The pattern of Co-operative sponsorship bears some resemblance to
the pattern of trade union sponsorship: both the Co-operative party
and the unions are more interested in securing parliamentary seats than
fighting unsuccessful contests; where unsuccessful contests must be
fought both prefer relatively favourable seats; and the distribution of
Co-operative and trade union candidatures can be related to the
distribution of their respective memberships. To this extent there is a
general pattern of sponsorships which is as complex as the process of
selection itself and which is one of the most important factors in the
selection of parliamentary candidates in the Labour party.

The Co-operative Party Parliamentary Panel[67]

The Co-operative Party Panel is normally reconstituted after each
general election,[68] although nominations may be submitted to the
National Committee of the party at any time. Any society or Co-

65. *Monthly Letter*, January 1960, p. 15.
66. This extends from Uxbridge to Southend and from Rickmansworth to Crawley.
There are seventy-nine Co-operative party branches affiliated to the L.C.S. Political
Committee.
67. The R.A.C.S. now draws its nominees from the Co-operative party panel.
68. Co-operative Party Report to the Co-operative Congress, 1956, p. 187. After the
General Election of 1966 it was decided, as the election had followed so swiftly on that of
1964, not to reconstitute the panel.

operative organization[69] which is affiliated to the Co-operative party at national level may nominate individuals for the consideration of the National Committee. In 1963 there were seventy names on the panel, including sitting M.P.s.

As a result of an understanding with the trade unions, no nominee may be a member of another organization's panel.[70] All nominees are expected to have a detailed knowledge of the Co-operative Movement, to be conversant with trading methods and figures, and to have sufficient command of these facts to enable them to state the Co-operative case clearly and concisely: 'Persons nominated should have an intimate knowledge of the Co-operative Movement and be chosen because they are considered more suitable for the Co-operative Panel than any other. General political experience is not enough, nor even good service to the local society.'[71] In fact, political ability normally takes second place to Co-operative experience.[72] There is no lower age limit, but no nominee may be over sixty at the time of his first nomination to the panel.[73]

Although the panel is normally reconstituted after each general election, actual selection is made at irregular intervals, depending on the number of nominations received. The Executive Committee of the party examines their qualifications and decides whether any of the nominees should be interviewed. By no means all nominees are interviewed: for instance, the general secretary may already be acquainted with a nominee and may recommend that he is unsuitable and should not therefore be interviewed. Either the executive committee or the chairman of the party may reject this advice, however. There have been protests at the refusal of the executive to interview some nominees, but these have always been rejected.[74]

Each interview lasts about a quarter of an hour and is devoted principally to testing the nominee's Co-operative knowledge. The executive makes its decision immediately after the last of the interviews, although it may occasionally defer a decision by requesting a nominee to re-apply in six or twelve months' time.

69. Constituency parties must nominate through their society parties – Co-operative Party Report to the Co-operative Congress, 1951, p. 195.
70. Co-operative Party Report to the Co-operative Congress, 1956, p. 187.
71. The Organization of the Co-operative party, Manchester 1953.
72. Generally speaking, however, full-time national officials are ineligible for nomination.
73. See Report of the National Committee of the Co-operative Party 1966, p. 12. There is at present no basic qualification regarding minimum membership of the Co-operative party or trading membership of a society, although a resolution demanding this was passed at the Party Conference in 1959.
74. e.g. Party Conference proceedings, 1955, p. 19.

The whole panel is available to any constituency Co-operative party wishing to nominate a candidate to a C.L.P., subject to the approval of the National Committee[75] and to the agreement with the Labour party. Within these limits the local party has complete freedom of choice, although the general secretary will suggest names of suitable members of the panel if requested. Normally the local party will interview a small group drawn from the panel. The London Co-operative Society, however, adopts a slightly different procedure. The Political Committee of the L.C.S. reserves to itself the right of nomination in the case of *sponsored* candidates, though the local party is always consulted. Apart from this the same procedure is followed: the Political Committee interviews a number of members of the panel and recommends one candidate to the local party, which must, of course, be responsible for the actual nomination to the C.L.P. The local Co-operative party may reject the Political Committee's recommendation, but no alternative candidate may be sponsored. It is possible that the fairly strict surveillance which the L.C.S. maintains over the nomination of candidates in its trading area is responsible for its success in securing nominations.

What sort of candidates does this selection procedure produce? Generally speaking, Co-operative candidates occupy a position between the other two groups of candidates, having more in common in some respects with C.L.P. candidates and in others with trade union candidates.

The general similarity which was found among trade union candidates selected by incumbent and non-incumbent C.L.P.s is repeated. The Co-operative candidates, regardless of whether they were selected by incumbent or non-incumbent C.L.P.s, had an identical breakdown of characteristics in respect of education and occupation, and similar characteristics in respect of previous electoral experience. The obvious reason for this similarity in both groups of sponsored candidates is that they are subject to *pre-selection* by their sponsoring bodies. The screening process used by the N.E.C. is unlikely to produce any great uniformity of candidates, since the criteria used to decide applications are not especially severe and are essentially negative in character.

Although Co-operative candidates have specific characteristics in common with union candidates, such as local government experience (over two thirds of the trade union and three fifths of the Co-operative candidates) and length of party membership (half the union and a third

75. Co-operative Party Constitution, Clause 14.

of the Co-operative candidates had been party members for twenty or more years), in most respects they have more in common with C.L.P. candidates. For instance, three quarters of the Co-operative and C.L.P. candidates selected by incumbent C.L.P.s were aged under fifty, compared with two thirds of the union candidates. Similarly, among the candidates selected by non-incumbent C.L.P.s, over half the C.L.P. and over two fifths of the Co-operative candidates were under forty years of age, and in terms of education the latter had more in common with their C.L.P. than with their union colleagues: approximately three fifths of the C.L.P., one third of the Co-operative, and only a tenth of the union candidates were graduates. Finally, the occupational breakdown of the Co-operative candidates was considerably more diverse than that of the union candidates. Not only were the vast majority of union candidates workers by occupation, but the majority also had an occupational connection with their sponsoring organization, whereas less than a sixth of the Co-operative candidates were workers and the majority had no occupational connection with the Co-operative Movement. Half, in fact, came from miscellaneous occupations, whilst another third came from the professions, which, though different again from the occupational breakdown of the C.L.P. candidates, possesses in common with the latter the property of diversity not found among union candidates.

This analysis of candidates demonstrates the general tendency of the Co-operative candidates to have more in common with the C.L.P. than with the trade union candidates. The problem of assessing the quality of candidates is extremely difficult, but if age and, more particularly, education are used as a crude means of evaluation, it is not unreasonable to suggest that the Co-operative party candidates are generally superior in quality to trade union candidates. The Co-operative party itself is convinced that it is largely the quality of its candidates which is responsible for the party's post-war success in the field of selection. Geoffrey Rhodes, now a Co-operative M.P., writes:

Labour Constituency Selection Conferences are showing a marked tendency to select what they consider to be articulate, intellectually able, well-qualified (in the professional sense), parliamentary candidates. The Co-operative Movement *has planned for this* by deliberate recruiting from Co-operative families, younger Co-operators who, after service in the Co-operative Youth Organisations, and possibly study at the Co-operative College, or a university, are then placed on its parliamentary panel. An increasing number of Co-operative M.P.s and parliamentary candidates are university graduates.[76]

It is almost certainly significant that those trade unions which have sought to improve the quality of their parliamentary panels by drawing candidates from outside the industrial wing of the union and by extensive training of their candidates, are also the unions which can claim a measure of success in the selection of parliamentary candidates: so, too, can the Co-operative party.

76. Rhodes, op. cit., pp. 111–12. (Author's italics.)

CHAPTER EIGHT

The Factors which Influence Selection

The selection of parliamentary candidates is a much more complicated process in the Labour party than it is in the Conservative party. This is partly because of the machinery of selection which both reflects and emphasizes the federative nature of the Labour party, but more particularly it stems from the greater cross-pressures to which Labour selectors are subjected. In addition to the broad dichotomy between incumbent and non-incumbent C.L.P.s, other factors, such as age, education and social background, electoral experience, occupation, local connections, and local government service, all of which are important in influencing the selection of candidates in both parties, there exist in the Labour party cross-pressures notably or substantially absent from Conservative selections. The most important of these additional and often over-riding factors are political and financial in character.

The C.L.P. Candidates

The candidates financed by the C.L.P.s comprised 47 per cent of the candidates selected by incumbent and 88 per cent of those selected by non-incumbent Labour parties between 1950 and 1966. They therefore constituted in the first instance a substantial minority and in the second instance an overwhelming majority of the Labour candidates selected over the period. The extent to which these candidates differed from their sponsored colleagues has been noted in the earlier chapters on the trade unions and the Co-operative party. Furthermore, the dichotomy which existed between the candidates selected by incumbent and non-incumbent Conservative associations reasserts itself when applied to the non-sponsored candidates selected by C.L.P.s, as Table 8(1) shows:

Table 8(1) : *Comparison of the characteristics of the non-sponsored candidates selected by incumbent and non-incumbent C.L.P.s, 1950-66*

Characteristic	Incumbent C.L.P.s	Non-Incumbent C.L.Ps
	per cent	per cent
Previous electoral experience	67·0	42·6
Aged under 40	30·7	54·0
Public school education	37·5	23·0
Graduates	68·2	51·9
Local connections	77·1	86·2
Local government experience	39·8	46·7

What is of greater interest, however, is the relative resemblance between the C.L.P. candidates and *Conservative* candidates. Even where marked differences occur, the divergence is generally less sharp than that between sponsored and non-sponsored Labour candidates.

It is not suggested, of course, that the C.L.P. candidates are drawn from *precisely* the same background as Conservative candidates; it is suggested, however, that they are drawn from a broadly common source – the *middle class*. Just as the union-sponsored candidates provide the Labour party in general and the P.L.P. in particular with the majority of its working class members, so the C.L.P. candidates are the principal source of middle class recruits. It is, however, from the lower echelons of that class that the majority of these candidates come, as the *contrast* with the Conservative candidates shown in Table 8(2) demonstrates.

Table 8(2): *Comparison of the characteristics of non-sponsored Labour candidates and Conservative candidates, 1950–66*

Characteristics	Incumbents		Non-incumbents	
	C.L.P.s	Conservatives	C.L.P.s	Conservatives
	per cent	per cent	per cent	per cent
Previous electoral experience	67·0	64·2	42·6	41·3
Aged under 40	30·7	44·3	54·0	54·9
Public school education	37·5	78·0	23·0	53·9
Graduates	68·2	69·9	51·9	52·1
Local connections	77·1	62·8	86·2	79·4
Local government experience	39·8	34·1	46·7	37·3

Thus, whilst similar proportions of both the C.L.P. and the Conservative candidates have had a university education, the latter are drawn more substantially from a public school and Oxbridge background, whereas the former are more likely to be grammar school and Redbrick products.

This can be equally well illustrated by examining the occupational breakdown of the C.L.P. and Conservative candidates. There are important similarities between the two: for instance, both draw fairly heavily on professional groups and miscellaneous occupations, whilst there is a general diversity of occupations not found among the union-sponsored candidates. As would be expected, however, those with a business background are not very well represented among the C.L.P. candidates, whereas they form the largest single group among the Conservatives. Moreover, if the professional groups are broken down, further differences emerge: barristers are the most numerous professional group among the Conservatives, but teachers occupy that place among the C.L.P. candidates.

This basically middle class background of C.L.P. candidates is one of the most important factors in Labour selection. It is part of the fundamental class conflict which has beset the Labour party from its earliest days – the conflict between the working man and the intellectual. The fact that many of the middle class C.L.P. candidates have working class antecedents, that many would reject the label 'intellectual', is often irrelevant to the selectors: to the latter they appear to contradict the image of the Labour party as a political movement not only *for* the working class but *of the working class*. Taken to its extreme, this is a rejection of the Burkean concept of representation in so far as it can become a commitment to a view that a parliamentary candidate should be *representative of* those he purports to represent, and therefore of those who *select* him. It is, however, because this commitment is not total that the conflict exists: ability is not ignored but it is judged in the light of the views or prejudices of the selectors and it is these which differ markedly from those of Conservative selectors.

The Potential M.P.: Selection by Incumbent C.L.P.s

The analysis of the selection of candidates by incumbent Conservative associations revealed an important link between the type of constituency and the candidate selected for it. With incumbent C.L.P.s, however, the general uniformity of the types of candidate chosen compared with the types of constituency which selected them is, perhaps, surprising.[1] Differences did in fact exist when candidates were compared with the electoral status and regional breakdown of constituencies, but almost all of these differences appear to be related less to the relative safeness or marginality or the regional location of the seats concerned, and more to the *divisions within the Labour party* itself.

Some of these divisions have already been described in detail: the concentration of trade union candidates in the northern half of the country and the concentration of Co-operative candidates in the southern half. The division of the party into these physical groupings of trade unions, Co-operative parties, and C.L.P.s is of crucial importance in selection:

Recently we have selected a parliamentary candidate, and of the six people who came before the selection board by far the poorest of the candidates received the second highest number of votes, and received them because his trade union associates voted for him en bloc. Afterwards the same trade union members admitted that he was by far the poorest of the candidates; nevertheless they voted for him.[2]

There is a natural loyalty among trade unionists, among Co-operators, among the individual members of the party, but these loyalties are subject to cross-pressures: all are members, individual or affiliated, of the Labour party, all have political views which may or may not coincide with the views of their group, and some may belong to more than one group. It is the federative nature of the Labour party and its acknowledged political divisions which are vital in selection. Casting, as it were, a shadow over all these divisions, and introducing yet another cross-pressure, is the question of finance. Local parties need money and elections are often costly relative to their resources: sponsorship is often the solution.

It is against this federative background that the selection of Labour candidates must be seen, and it is within this context that Labour selectors judge the factors of political experience and party service, and the personal characteristics of nominees. A nominee's age, education, and occupation are in turn seen within the context of his political experience and party service. Of the three, age is the one criterion which is sometimes applied in relative isolation.

Generally speaking, the executive committee of a C.L.P. will not be

1. This does coincide, however, with the findings of Finer, Berrington, and Bartholomew, op. cit., p. 14.
2. Co-operative Congress Report, 1958, p. 285. See also pages 211–12 below

faced with as many names as its Conservative counterpart, and there is therefore less need to apply arbitrary criteria to the same extent as in Conservative selections. Inevitably age is one such criterion where such an exercise becomes necessary and the age structure of Labour candidates reflects this. The most important age group is forty to forty-nine, accounting for 46·5 per cent of the candidates selected by incumbent C.L.P.s between 1950 and 1966. Roughly equal proportions, 25·1 per cent and 28·4 per cent respectively, are drawn from those under forty and aged fifty or more. Age, however, cannot be divorced from a nominee's experience and party service: if a man is young the selectors will examine his claim to have proved himself in these two respects; if he is somewhat older they will expect him to have experience and party service commensurate with his age.

Similarly, a nominee's education and occupation cannot be separated from these basic criteria. They are, of course, an important means of judging a nominee's ability, especially during the early stages of selection, when the nominees are being considered on paper only, but any assessment of his ability will be measured against his political background.

Apart from known political views which may be attributed to the nominee,[3] his political background is judged in the light of the length of his party membership, whether he is a member of a trade union, and what electoral experience and local government experience he has had.

Individual party membership is, of course, a condition of selection, but the length of membership is often raised at selection conferences. A nominee in his forties will invariably be asked to explain his position if he has been a member of the party for less than ten years, certainly if it be less than five. The introduction of a minimum membership qualification of twelve months was sponsored by two local parties in 1948, and the Conference was asked to agree to a resolution which 'noted with regret the tendency to adopt as Parliamentary Labour Candidates persons of *quite recent conversion*'.[4] Thus well over four fifths of the candidates selected for Labour-held seats between 1950 and 1966 had been party members for eleven years or more, and half of these had been members for more than twenty years, so that cases like those of Dingle Foot, who joined the Labour party in July 1956 and was elected for Ipswich in October 1957, or Elystan Morgan, who

3. See pages 239–41 below.
4. Conference Proceedings, APCR 1948, p. 209. (Author's italics.) See the objection to the selection of I. R. Maxwell, pages 142–3 above – *The Times*, 6 February 1961.

became Labour Member for Cardigan within eighteen months of fighting Merioneth as a Welsh Nationalist, are exceptional.

Similarly, trade union membership is in one sense regarded as an indication of a nominee's commitment to the Labour Movement in general. Trade union candidates were all, by definition, union members though for some this was a relatively tenuous relationship strengthened by sponsorship. Taken as a whole, three quarters of the candidates selected by incumbent C.L.P.s were members of trade unions, including three fifths of the Co-operative candidates and well over half of the C.L.P. candidates. The latter were divided almost equally between 'white collar' and industrial unions, whilst of those for whom there was no record of union membership, over a third were members of the professions, mainly the legal profession, and many belonged to the Labour party's professional organizations, such as the Socialist Medical Association and the Society of Labour Lawyers. The division between 'white collar' and industrial unions was also significant: two thirds of the C.L.P. candidates belonged to a union which had *no connection with* their occupation, and the greater proportion of these belonged to *industrial* unions. Of course, this reflected to a large extent the desire of these candidates to belong to trade unions affiliated to the T.U.C., as urged under Clause III of the Party Constitution. But it also reflected the activities of some of the industrial unions in providing financial assistance to a number of candidates, though this assistance fell short of full sponsorship. At present the 'white collar' unions secure more representatives in Parliament through the non-sponsored candidates than through sponsorship: the extent to which this is a reflection of the relative quality of 'white collar' union candidates and *sponsored* industrial union candidates is difficult to gauge, but the fact that the majority of industrial union candidates are sponsored is not without significance. In this connection two factors suggest that the influence of trade unions at some selection conferences is important: first, marginal and semi-marginal seats showed a greater preference for 'white collar' candidates than did safe and impregnable seats, the reverse being true of industrial union candidates; second, more trade unionists among the C.L.P. candidates in general were chosen in the northern region. These facts suggest that where the trade unions in general are fairly strong they are likely to favour a unionist rather than a non-unionist, and that where the industrial unions are strong, in safe and impregnable seats, they are likely to favour a member of their own type of union, the 'genuine' trade unionist.

Previous electoral experience is no more a prerequisite of selection for Labour than it is for Conservative candidates: two fifths of the candidates selected by incumbent C.L.P.s had had no electoral experience, an equal proportion had fought one or more unsuccessful parliamentary contests, and the remaining fifth were former M.P.s. Once again, electoral experience is seen as part of a nominee's political background. For example, the author attended one selection conference where a nominee, who had fought one constituency in 1950 and a second in 1959, was asked what he had been doing in 1951 and 1955. As it happened, he had a satisfactory answer, but the selectors had taken note of the apparent gap in his political career.

It is possible, in fact, to posit two broad types of candidate, with the Co-operative candidates occupying an intermediate position. The trade union candidate is normally a fairly long-standing member of the party, a member who has demonstrated his loyalty and served his apprenticeship in party committees, and, possibly, in local government service; and who is likely, because of this apprenticeship, to be older than his C.L.P. rivals. Conversely, the C.L.P. candidate is usually able to establish himself in a secure occupation which he can use as a stepping-stone to a political career the initial stages of which can be embarked upon well before the age of thirty. *Active* service in the party is often regarded as an adequate substitute for long service, whilst to *contest* several local elections will often satisfy demands for local government experience. Probably the key difference between the union-sponsored and the C.L.P. candidate is that the latter usually has *political ambitions* at a relatively early age in his adult life, whereas the former may only conceive such ambitions after a period of party and, possibly, local government service, often at the direct or indirect suggestion of others.[5]

The dichotomy between the union and C.L.P. candidates does not appear to be explained by any factor other than the influence of the trade unions in selection. At a selection conference, the union delegate will, if there is a nominee from his union, normally support that nominee, but if there is not, he becomes subject to a number of cross-pressures: there may be a candidate from another union in his industry; there may be one or more 'intellectuals', whom he may resent; there may be a 'white collar' candidate and an industrial union candidate; there will be

5. Co-operative candidates are subject to similar pressures, at least in the sense that the Co-operative party demands that members of its panel have a knowledge and experience of Co-operative affairs.

candidates of varying abilities and varying political beliefs; and so on. Trade union loyalty is strong, not only as a member of a particular union, but as a trade unionist. If the union delegate's nominee is eliminated in an early ballot, for instance, he must decide to whom he wishes to transfer his vote, and he may decide that any unionist is better than no unionist. The feeling that there can be no better representative than one of their own is often strong enough to override questions of ability and quality.

The Standard-Bearer: Selection by the Non-Incumbent C.L.P.

The selection of candidates by non-incumbent parties is basically similar in the two major parties in so far as the three-fold object of nominating candidates at all in constituencies held by the opposing party is, first, to capture any seats which are electorally vulnerable; second, to engage as high a proportion as possible of the opposition's electoral forces in order to prevent them being thrown into marginal seats; and finally, to sustain the morale of party workers by raising the party's *national* vote to its maximum. In both parties the relationship between candidate and local party is potentially short-term in all but a few of the constituencies held by the opposition, and the principal consideration in the minds of the selectors in non-incumbent C.L.P.s is, therefore, the ability of each nominee to fulfil the demands of an election campaign. This means that one of the first considerations must be *when* to select.

The Timing of Selection

The principal difference between the two parties in the timing of selection is that the Labour party has suffered in the past, and still does compared with the Conservative party, from a greater incidence of withdrawals of candidature. In practice the Labour parties re-select their candidates more frequently, but because a substantial proportion of these candidates withdraw before the subsequent election the proportion of candidates who are re-selected and actually contest the same constituency more than once is similar in the two parties: approximately a fifth, but varying considerably from election to election. The general turnover of candidates is also similar at least to the extent that it is fairly high. The turnover of candidates in the Labour party has tended to increase between 1951 and 1966: in 1951 76·8 per cent of the candidates were fighting their first parliamentary contests or had had no electoral experience prior to the previous general election in 1950; but by 1966 this turnover had risen to 86·6 per cent and become similar to the Conservative figure of 83·4 per cent. In other words, the majority of candidates selected by non-incumbent C.L.P.s – and it was an increasing majority over the period – normally fight one or two elections unsuccessfully and then retire from what is the centre of the political arena at constituency level.

The timing of the actual selection depends, as with the Conservatives, on the circumstances of the previous election: when the gap between the parties is narrow, as it was after 1950, 1951, and 1964, then selection begins soon after the election.

It was fairly clear after the General Election of 1950 that another election would not be long delayed, and by November 1950, 226 candidates had been selected in Conservative and Liberal-held seats. A similar situation existed following the General Election of 1951, when the Labour party fully expected another election within two years. The result of this attitude was that by September 1952 over half the necessary candidates had been selected, by the end of that year over two thirds, and by April 1953, four fifths. After the General Election of 1955, however, the pace slowed: the Conservatives now had a comfortable majority and an early election did not seem likely. Nevertheless, the tendency was for selections to proceed at a fairly rapid pace as Table 8(3) shows.

Table 8(3): *The timing of the selection in non-Labour constituencies, 1951–66*
Proportion of candidates

Inter-election period	$\frac{1}{2}$	*selected* $\frac{2}{3}$	$\frac{4}{5}$	
1951–5	10	12	17	Months after each election
1955–9	19	22	24	
1959–64	44	48	50	
1964–6	9	11	12	

In 1957, the N.E.C. reported 'it is expected that by the *end of the year* nearly all C.L.P.s will have selected their candidates for the next General Election'.[6] The figures shown in Table 8(3) illustrate quite clearly the general relationship between the possibility of an early election and the timing of selection. Thus the period after the General

6. N.E.C. Report, APCR 1957, p. 13. (Author's italics.)

213

Election of 1959 saw an almost complete lull in the selection of candidates, although this was largely due to the refusal of the N.E.C. to grant permission for selection procedure to begin: 'the National Executive Committee decided that instead of hurrying selection, constituency parties should be encouraged first to build up their organization to full strength . . .'.[7] There were two reasons for this action by the N.E.C.: first, the problem of quality, and second, the problem of withdrawals of candidature. In replying to criticism of the N.E.CC. attitude, Harold Wilson said:

Obviously, we do not want to delay things too long; but it would be a great mistake immediately after the election to rush into the selection of candidates unless we can be certain that the right people are going to be selected.

In one constituency in the last Parliament I went to *three* adoption conferences of *different* candidates between the two elections.[8]

Wilson's remarks in 1960 on the inadvisability of early selection contrast sharply with the recommendation of the Sub-Committee on Party Organization in 1955, of which he was chairman: 'We do recommend, however, that every possible step be taken to ensure that *candidates are selected early*.'[9] In 1955 Wilson and his committee laid great stress on the importance of the quality of candidates and asserted not only that many constituencies had had the 'greatest difficulty in finding a suitable candidate',[10] but that many votes had been lost in the general election of that year as a result of the poor quality of candidates. They were therefore concerned with the problem of ensuring that not only were candidates of suitable quality, but that candidates were selected sufficiently early to enable them to make themselves well known in their constituencies. This led them to be particularly concerned with the turnover of candidates, and thus led the Wilson Committee to argue that the sooner selections began after an election, the more likely it was that candidates who had previously fought the seat would be re-selected, giving them the advantage of already being known in the constituency.

The figures shown in Table 8(4) show clearly the effect of the timing of selection on the re-selection of candidates. With just under 100 and

7. N.E.C. Report, APCR 1960, p. 24. To what extent this action delaying the selection of candidates was also politically motivated is a matter of conjecture, but the delay did coincide with the struggle in the party over Clause IV and defence.

8. Conference Proceedings, APCR 1960, p. 242.

9. Report of the Sub-Committee on Party Organization (the Wilson Report), APCR 1955, p. 74.

10. ibid.

Table 8(4): *The re-selection of candidates by non-incumbent C.L.P.s*
A. *The re-selection of candidates, 1945–66*

Inter-election period	Later withdrew	Fought both elections	Total
1945–50*	16	26	42
1950–51*	22	72	94
1951–55†	64	62	126
1955–59†	23	45	68
1959–64†	3	34	37
1964–66†	5	48	53

* Based on Labour Party Annual Conference Reports, 1946–51,
† Based on lists of endorsed candidates published in the *Labour Organizer*, 1951–66.
NOTE: the totals in column 2 of candidates who fought both elections are correct for all periods, but the figures for 1945–50 and 1950–1 in column 1 and, therefore, column 3 may be below the actual figures, since they are based on annual and not monthly returns.

B. *The re-selection of former M.P.s in the same constituencies, 1950–66*

Inter-election period	Number of former M.P.s selected for same constituency
1950–1	19, of whom 14 fought both elections and 5 withdrew
1951–5	17, of whom 13 fought both elections and 4* withdrew
1955–9	5† of whom 4 fought both elections and 1 withdrew
1959–64	1 who fought both elections
1964–6	None

* Including one seat redistributed, 1954.
† Plus two who fought their former constituencies in 1950 or 1951 and *not* in 1955.

over 100 re-selections following the 1950 and 1951 General Elections respectively, but only two thirds this figure after 1955, and little more than a third after 1959, the importance of timing is readily apparent. This is due in part to the re-selection of defeated M.P.s.

The number of defeated M.P.s re-selected for their former constituencies declined sharply after 1955, and after 1959 only one, Mrs Lena Jeger, was re-selected. None the less, whether the candidates concerned were defeated M.P.s or unsuccessful candidates in non-Labour constituencies, the fact remains that early selection and re-selection go hand in hand. Thus, by December 1952, of the 126 candidates re-selected between 1951 and 1955, 111 had already been selected, and, of the sixty-eight candidates re-selected between 1955 and 1959, fifty-four had been selected by the end of December 1957. The action of the N.E.C. in delaying the selection of candidates after the General Election of 1959, limited the number of re-selections to thirty-seven and, of these, thirty were selected by the end of 1962, some eighteen months after the N.E.C. allowed selection to start on a fairly large scale.

Generally speaking, it is the C.L.P.s in marginal constituencies that are most likely to re-select candidates who have fought the constituency before, especially when another general election is expected fairly soon. After the General Election of 1964, for example, half the re-selected candidates were in marginal constituencies.

The question of re-selection is also linked to the problem of withdrawals of candidature (Table 8(5)).

The problem of withdrawals of candidature reached a peak between

Table 8(5): *The number of withdrawals of candidature compared with the number of re-selected candidates, 1945–66*

	Number of withdrawals of candidature	
Inter-election period	Re-selected candidates	Total*
1945–50	16	47
1950–1	22	46
1951–5	64	154
1955–9	23	86
1959–64	3	47
1964–6	5	17

* Figures for 1945–50 and 1950–1 based on APCR 1946–51, and the remainder drawn from the *Labour Organizer*, 1951–66.

the elections of 1951 and 1955, and the extent to which this was due to the number of re-selections after 1951 can be seen in Table 8(5), when, of the total number of withdrawals, over two fifths were accounted for by the withdrawal of re-selected candidates. Clearly the speed with which selection proceeded was responsible for this, since nearly *half* the withdrawals between the two earlier elections of 1950 and 1951 were by re-selected candidates. The tendency for the local party to re-select the candidate who had just fought an election in the same constituency is understandable: the organizational advantages are considerable. Nor is it difficult to envisage the reaction of many candidates when offered the opportunity of re-selection: it must often appear to them as an endorsement of their recently fought campaign, a vote of confidence in their ability and a recognition of their suitability as parliamentary candidates. To refuse re-selection may appear churlish, to say nothing of a lost opportunity of fulfilling parliamentary ambitions, and under such circumstances refusal may be difficult. But when the early reactions of self-satisfaction and gratitude are replaced by the more sober thoughts of canvassing, meetings, the maintenance of public relations, the prospect of 'nursing' the seat for perhaps a year or possibly two or three, even four years, is much less attractive. Being a conscientious parliamentary candidate is a time-consuming process, bad enough when the prospect of becoming an M.P. is assured, but often disheartening for the candidate faced with a hostile majority of several thousands. It may not be a coincidence that during the spring and summer of 1953 the number of withdrawals in general rose sharply and that in May of that year Labour lost the by-election at Sunderland South, the first seat to change hands at a by-election since the war. All this applies, of course, to all candidates in non-Labour seats, but how much more apparent must it be to the re-selected candidate, with some experience of political fortunes, who has already sustained one defeat?

Between 1951 and 1955, *144* C.L.P.s had to select candidates *twice*, *nine* had to select *three* times, and *one*, Kingston-upon-Thames, had to select *four* times because of the withdrawal of candidates. The majority of the withdrawals of candidature occurred, as might be expected, in safe or impregnable seats: of the sixty-two C.L.P.s which suffered from more than one withdrawal of candidature between 1951 and 1966, twenty-nine were safe or impregnable and a further eighteen comfortable Conservative-held constituencies. The extreme case is the impregnable Conservative seat of East Surrey, which has had to select more than one candidate during every inter-election period between 1951 and 1966.

It does not seem unreasonable to connect not only re-selection with the timing of selection, but, to some extent, the problem of withdrawals of candidature. After the General Elections of 1955, when the tempo of selection was slower, and 1959, when the N.E.C. applied the brake on selections, the subsequent number of withdrawals was substantially lower. Of course, withdrawals still occurred: one candidate was selected for Warwick and Leamington on 17 March 1962 and withdrew on the 19th,[11] for example, but a certain number of withdrawals are inevitable, and the N.E.C.'s success in reducing their

11. *The Times*, 20 March 1962.

number is important. It marks a somewhat changed attitude on the part of the N.E.C. towards selection: in the past the N.E.C. had been only too happy to shelter behind the constitutional right of the C.L.P. to play the substantive role in selection. Now it realized that some control over the twin problems of quality and withdrawals could be exercised at national level. The first problem has been approached by a new attitude towards the two lists of candidates, whilst the second has been largely solved by a judicious exercise of the N.E.C.'s powers to refuse permission to proceed with selection.

It is impossible to be certain why candidates withdraw, although the reasons suggested may play a significant part. In all probability it is a combination of these reasons with the impact of the candidature on the individual's personal affairs. For instance, shortly before the Becken-ham by-election in 1957, the Labour candidate was forced to with-draw because he could 'not obtain leave from his work to fight a by-election campaign';[12] whilst, in January 1962, the candidate at West Derbyshire withdrew because of pressure of business commitments.[13] Many Labour candidates probably find that their normal occupation and being a parliamentary candidate are almost incompatible, and the strain which the latter imposes on the former may often be too great.

The question of timing is also important in one other respect: the type of constituency. Generally speaking, a certain amount of control over timing is exercised by the regional organizer of the area in which the constituency lies, since he cannot deal with too many selections at one time. Nevertheless, the normal sequence of selection is that marginal and semi-marginal seats select earlier than the comfortable, safe, and impregnable seats (Table 8(6)).

Twelve months after the election of 1955, over three fifths of the marginal non-Labour seats had selected their candidates, and after eighteen months, nine tenths. Similarly, over the same period of eigh-teen months, nearly three quarters of the semi-marginals had selected their candidates, but less than half of the comfortable seats, two fifths of the safe, and little more than a tenth of the impregnable seats had selected their candidates. Conversely, during the twelve months *before* the General Election of 1959, only two marginal seats and five semi-marginals (all in fact, second selections following the withdrawal of candidates) selected candidates, against seven comfortable, eight safe, and twenty impregnable constituencies. The number of impregnable seats constituted a fifth of the total number. Naturally, C.L.P.s in

12. *The Times*, 30 January 1957.   13. *The Times*, 16 January 1962.

Table 8(6): The timing of selection compared with the electoral status of constituencies, 1955–59

Period after election	Number of selections					Total
	M	S–M	C	S	I	
After 12 months	23	15	11	17	5	71
During following 6 months	10	21	15	26	5	77
After 18 months	33	36	26	43	10	148
During 12 months prior to 1959 General Election	2	5	7	8	20	42
Vacancies	36	48	55	108	89	336

marginal and semi-marginal seats, often formerly held by Labour, feel that *next* time they can win and the sooner they are in the field with their candidate the better. C.L.P.s in Conservative strongholds know that, even with a Labour victory of the scale of 1945, their chances of success are negligible in the eyes of the optimist, non-existent in the eyes of the pessimist.

The action of the N.E.C. in delaying selection after 1959 did not alter the *sequence* of selection among the various types of constituency, and marginals and semi-marginals again tended to select earlier than comfortable, safe, and impregnable seats. There is, in fact, some evidence that the N.E.C. not only controlled the timing of selection in general, but went as far as granting permission to select to marginal and semi-marginal *rather than* safe and impregnable seats once selection began again on a large scale late in 1961.

Twelve months after selection was permitted 47·2 per cent of the C.L.P.s in marginally held Conservative constituencies had selected candidates, compared with 1·1 per cent of the impregnable seats. Conversely, in the eighteen months before the 1964 election, *nine* of the C.L.P.s in marginal seats selected candidates, compared with 26·9 per cent of the impregnable seats. The sequence was no different after 1964: six months after selection was permitted 95·1 per cent of the marginals had selected candidates against 51·1 per cent of the impregnable constituencies.

The timing of selection is important because it may have a considerable effect on the quality of the candidates chosen. Hasty selection after an election may result in the more or less automatic re-selection of the previous candidate, or in a failure on the part of the C.L.P. to approach the matter rationally. Too little consideration may be given to the type of candidate required; too little time may be allowed for the consideration of possible candidates; too much attention may be given to the need to select a candidate; too much consideration may be paid to the party's financial position; too much weight may be given to a man's politics. These are some of the factors which affect selection in the Labour party: they cannot be ignored.

The Candidates

The contrast between the candidates selected by incumbent and non-incumbent C.L.P.s has already been pointed out in Table 8(1): candidates selected by non-incumbent C.L.P.s are normally drawn from a broader age group, fewer have been to university and they have less electoral experience, but they normally have more local government experience and are more likely to have local connections than the candidates selected by incumbent C.L.P.s. Although these characteristics are usually judged on the assumption that the candidate will be fighting an unsuccessful contest, selectors in marginal constituencies take into account the possibility that a favourable electoral swing could result in a Labour gain. The fact that less than *9 per cent* of the seats fought by non-incumbent C.L.P.s between 1950 and 1966 were gains is irrelevant in this context – if a constituency is marginal it is a potential gain.

Table 8(7) illustrates the general factors which influence the selection of candidates by non-incumbent C.L.P.s and, in particular, the extent to which a local party in a marginal seat will act as if it is choosing a *possible* M.P.: the more justification a C.L.P. has for believing that it may be selecting an M.P., the more likely it is that the selection will be controlled by factors which the selectors hope will influence the electorate.

Thus electoral experience is almost a condition of selection in so far as only a fifth of the candidates selected for marginal constituencies were fighting their *first election*, the reverse being the case in impregnable seats. Similarly, less than 5 per cent of the candidates chosen for marginal seats were under thirty, against nearly 20 per cent of those chosen for impregnable constituencies: youth is an asset only in relative terms and the younger a candidate the less likely he is to have had the

Table 8(7): *Comparison of the characteristics of candidates selected by non-incumbent C.L.P.s in marginal and impregnable Conservative constituencies, 1950–66*

Characteristic	Marginal constituencies	Impregnable constituencies
	per cent	per cent
Previous electoral experience	77·6	23·0
Aged under 30	4·7	17·6
Graduates	53·7	42·6
Public school education	24·3	17·9
Local connections	76·6	87·5
Direct connections	34·1	22·2

requisite experience. Marginal constituencies also select more graduates and this would suggest that the possibility of the candidate being elected is an important consideration in the minds of the selectors. In the same way *direct* local connections are more in evidence in marginal seats in response to the view that the local man starts with an initial advantage. This is further emphasized by the fact that local connections *in general* are more in evidence in impregnable seats.

Apart from the differences between marginal and impregnable constituencies, however, important changes have taken place in the characteristics of the candidates selected by non-incumbent C.L.P.s between 1950 and 1966. The candidates selected over this period have tended to be younger at each successive election: in 1951, 41·9 per cent of the candidates were under forty years of age and 28·2 per cent aged fifty or more; in 1966, 67·8 per cent were under forty and only 12·6 per cent aged fifty or more. Candidates have also become better educated: 15·8 per cent had had only an elementary education in 1951 and 42·9 per cent a university education; by 1966 those with only an elementary education had fallen to 5·6 per cent and the proportion of graduates had risen to 56·6 per cent. Finally, the occupational pattern of the candidates selected by non-incumbent C.L.P.s also changed: the proportion of workers has fallen from 22·5 per cent to 14·6 per cent between 1951 and 1966, and there has been a significant decline in the number of candidates with a business background. Conversely, there has been a dramatic increase among the representatives of the professions from 29·5 per cent in 1951 to 48·0 per cent in 1966, an increase which was reflected in the influx of members of the teaching profession in the General Elections of 1964 and 1966 in particular.

Women and Selection

Although there have only been three general elections since 1923 when more Conservative than Labour women M.P.s were returned,[14] the proportions of women selected in the two parties does not differ very much. Between 1950 and 1966, 3·9 per cent of the candidates selected by incumbent Conservative associations were women, compared with 3·2 per cent of the candidates selected by incumbent C.L.P.s. Similarly, 5·6 per cent of those chosen by non-incumbent Conservative associations were women, compared with 6·6 per cent of the Labour candidates. The majority of these candidates were supported by the C.L.P.s, although the Co-operative party sponsors a significant minority of women candidates. Two women Members, Mrs Harriet Slater (Stoke-on-Trent North), and Mrs Joyce Butler (Wood Green), were sponsored by the Co-operative party during this period, whilst a further seven women, none of whom were elected, were Co-operative candidates between 1951 and 1966.

Since 1950, however, the trade unions have sponsored only one candidate, Mrs Renée Short (Wolverhampton North-East), in a Labour-held seat, and two other candidatures, both involving the same candidate, Mrs Margaret McKay (now M.P. for the Clapham Division of Wandsworth).

The success of the Labour party in securing more women Members than their opponents owes much to the apparent willingness of C.L.P.s in marginal non-Labour constituencies to adopt women candidates. Only one of the eighty-eight women selected by non-incumbent Conservative associations between 1950 and 1966 succeeded in winning the seat from Labour, but ten of the Labour women candidates over the same period won the seats for Labour. The two General Elections of 1964 and 1966 saw no less than seven Labour gains involving women candidates, so that in 1966 of the twenty-six women Members, nineteen were Labour and only seven Conservative.

None the less, the proportion of women who stand for Parliament as Labour candidates is not very high, and as with the Conservatives the explanation appears to be twofold: a commitment, ill-defined but

14. In 1924, 1931, and 1935. As a result of by-election changes, however, there were thirteen Conservative compared with twelve Labour women M.P.s between 1961 and 1964, but in 1964 Labour resumed its lead with seven more women than the Conservatives and this was increased to twelve in 1966.

genuine, to the belief that being an M.P. is a man's job and the simple question of supply – there does not appear to be any more would-be women candidates than are in fact selected, if the Labour party's own list of available candidates is an accurate reflection of the situation. Of the 171 candidates on the 'B' List of April 1960, and its supplement of April 1961, only 5·3 per cent were women.

The Influence of Religion

The influence of religion is always difficult to establish. There is no evidence to suggest that there is any *general* prejudice in the Labour party for or against any particular religion. It is known, however, that *certain constituencies* are affected by religious factors. For instance, Martin Harrison reports a case in which religion played a part in a selection: 'The attempt to select a single [N.U.M.] candidate sometimes breaks down on religious differences – notably at Sedgefield, where bitter opposition between backers of a *Methodist and a Roman Catholic* N.U.M. candidate gave another union the nomination.'[15] The two religious groups, however, which are most likely to have any affect on selection are Jews and Catholics, although the influence of the former is not, of course, entirely a matter of religious faith.

It is extremely doubtful whether Jewish influence is at all important in selection in any positive sense. Poale Zion, the Jewish Socialist Labour party, is affiliated at national and local level to the Labour party. The distribution of the constituent societies of Poale Zion is fairly closely related to the general distribution of Orthodox Jews in Britain (Table 8(8).

In 1963 there were twenty Jewish M.P.s[16] in the parliamentary Labour party, and ten represented constituencies with significant Jewish populations: five in the London area, four in the North-West, and one in Glasgow. There was also a Jewish Labour candidate in one of the Leeds constituencies in 1950. The figures shown in Table 8(8) suggest that this might not be due entirely to coincidence. Nonetheless, the fact that there are less than half a million Jews in Great Britain and Northern Ireland, of whom over half are found in London, suggests that any question of Jewish pressure at a selection conference is extremely doubtful. The explanation probably lies in the distribution of branches of Poale Zion, which would have the right of nomination in any of the C.L.P.s to which they were affiliated. This may go some way in explaining the distribution of Jewish M.P.s in the Labour party.

15. Harrison, op. cit., p. 280, footnote.   16. *Jewish Year Book*, 1963, p. 217.

Table 8(8): *Distribution of the constituent societies of Poale Zion compared with the distribution of Orthodox Jews in Britain, 1963*

Branches of Poale Zion	Numbers of Orthodox Jews
London (several)	280,000
Manchester	28,000
Leeds	25,000
Glasgow	13,400
Liverpool	7,500
Birmingham	6,300
Southend	3,500
Southport	3,000
Cardiff	3,000
Luton	1,160

Source: *Jewish Year Book*, 1963.

The distribution of Catholic M.P.s in the Labour party also appears to bear some relation to the distribution of the Catholic population (Table 8(9)).

Table 8(9): *Distribution of Catholic M.P.s in the Labour party compared with distribution of Catholic population, 1963**

Region	Number of M.P.s	Catholic population†
North-West	3	1,180,000
Home Counties and South‡	3	1,126,000
Scotland	3	799,000
Midlands	2	407,500
North-East	1	365,000
Yorkshire (West Riding)	2	250,000
Western	—	139,000
Eastern	—	132,000
Wales	1	128,500

* Excluding Northern Ireland.
† *Catholic Directory*, 1963.
‡ Including London.
NOTE: Rank order correlation coefficient = 0·8709.

It is, of course, difficult to be certain whether the selection of Catholics in those areas with a relatively large Catholic population is due to Catholic influence at selection conferences, or to the greater likelihood of a Catholic *nomination*. The Scotland division of Liverpool is often mentioned as a constituency in which the selection of a Catholic candidate is inevitable, both in the Labour *and* the Conservative parties. Certainly, at the by-election in June 1964, *both* candidates were Catholics. It is likely, however, that such constituencies are exceptions and that in most cases the selection of a Catholic is either accidental, in that the question of the candidate's religion has no bearing on the selection at all, or the result of the increased probability of a Catholic nomination in areas with an above average Catholic population. The fact that in certain areas there may be one or more Catholic nominees does not ensure the selection of a Catholic candidate, but makes it possible or more likely. A case in point is the St Helens by-election in 1958.

Following a report in *The Times*[17] explaining his rejection by the St Helens C.L.P., Tom Driberg, then chairman of the N.E.C., wrote a letter to the editor in which he said that he regarded it as surprising that the political correspondent had failed to notice the presence of 'at least *four and probably five . . . Roman Catholics*' on the short-list, which 'can hardly be due to coincidence . . . [and] it would be interesting to know how many of those not short-listed are not Roman Catholics'.[18] On the eve of the selection the secretary and agent of the C.L.P., Alderman J. E. Hughes, resigned in protest against the short-list, on the grounds of alleged religious discrimination. He pointed out that of the six nominees on the short-list, four were Catholics and only one a member of the Church of England.[19] A few days later the Reverend V. L. Tucker-Harvey, Anglican vicar of the largest parish in St Helens, wrote to *The Times*:

it is widely accepted in this constituency that the selection of a short-list of candidates for nomination in the forthcoming by-election is the culmination of a '*Catholic action*' campaign and ungenerous criticism of our former member. The leading local newspaper contained these statements on Saturday, April 26th: 'For some time now it has been well-known that a small but highly organized clique, operating under the cloak of a *particular religious belief*, has been seeking to obtain control of the local Labour Party.'[20]

In the event a Catholic was not selected and the Anglican was successful. The extent to which this was the result of anti-Catholic feeling is

17. *The Times*, 28 April 1958.
18. Letter to *The Times*, 1 May 1958. (Author's italics.)
19. *The Times*, 1 May 1958.
20. Letter to *The Times*, 5 May 1958. (Author's italics.)

uncertain, since cross-pressures were considerable. Four of the six nominees on the short-list were trade union sponsored candidates, and one union, the N.U.M., made an especially strong bid for the candidature, claiming that St Helens was a miners' seat.[21] None the less, the selection demonstrates not only that religion may be a factor in selection, but that certain constituencies in strong Catholic areas, of which St Helens is part, may have several Catholic nominees, increasing the possibility of a Catholic candidate.

The reference, by the Reverend V. L. Tucker-Harvey in his letter to *The Times*, to the group known as 'Catholic Action', may be important. During the Parliament of 1959–64, a number of Catholic candidates were nominated for by-elections, and it has been alleged[22] that their selection was the result of a concerted effort by Catholic Action to increase the Catholic representation in the House of Commons. It may be significant that in four of the five instances these candidates were selected in areas with a somewhat lower Catholic population. Two were selected in Yorkshire, one in the Midlands, and one in Wales. There can be little doubt that, in at least two of the cases, religion played no *positive* part in their selection, but in all these cases it may have played a part in their nomination to the C.L.P. It may be that some attempt is being made to secure not only a larger Catholic representation, but a more widely spread distribution of that representation.

The Individuality of Selection

Because selection is the prerogative of the local party, and because a relatively small section of the local party is directly involved, the factors which influenced any particular selection are often obscure and subject to speculation. The nomination, for instance, of a member of the staff of Transport House almost always gives rise to rumours of pressure on the local party. There are eight departments at Transport House, or seven prior to 1958, which have since 1945 been headed by twenty-six persons, of whom five have become M.P.s and one has unsuccessfully sought nomination.[23] Three of the five were heads of the Research Department[24] and the other two heads of the International Department.[25] Only one of these candidates was selected for a by-

21. Harrison, op. cit., p. 304.
22. Private communication.
23. Morgan Phillips, then general secretary of the Labour party, at North-East Derbyshire, in 1959. See pages 147 and 174 above.
24. W. Fienburgh (Islington North), 1951; D. Ginsburg (Dewsbury), 1959; and P. Shore (Stepney), 1964.
25. D. Healey (Leeds South East), 1952 and D. Ennals (Dover), 1964.

election,[26] thus limiting the possibility of official pressure by the N.E.C. It would appear that two of the departments at Transport House are useful springboards for a parliamentary career: they are likely to attract the potential candidate and also provide him with extremely useful experience. However, since 1951, headquarters officials have not been allowed to fight parliamentary elections unless they have been members of the staff for at least five years. Thus Peter Shore, head of the Research Department from 1959 to 1964 and a member of Transport House Staff since 1951, was unable to fight an election between his unsuccessful contest at St Ives in 1950 and his attempt to wrest Halifax from Maurice Macmillan in 1959.

A similar case may be made out for the position of general secretary of the Fabian Society. The last three successive secretaries of the society have been elected to Parliament,[27] but this is probably nothing more than a reflection of the type of person who becomes general secretary of the Fabian Society. The position provides useful experience and is undoubtedly an indication of ability and loyalty to the Labour Movement. Again, it is doubtful if there is anything significant in the selection of Carol Johnson for South Lewisham in 1959, when he was secretary to the parliamentary Labour party: this would normally be regarded as a recommendation, though it might give rise to some suspicion.

There are, in fact, selections which do at least suggest that some particular factor has played a significant part. There is nothing quite comparable to the 'family seat' in the Labour party, but it is not unknown for the wife of a Labour M.P. to succeed her husband on his death or resignation. In 1930 Lady Noel-Buxton succeeded her husband as M.P. for North Norfolk, on his elevation to the peerage.[28] Following the death of Hector McNeil, M.P. for Greenock, in 1955, it was rumoured that his wife might seek nomination,[29] whilst Mrs Lena Jeger was selected for Holborn and St Pancras South following the death of her husband in 1953. Similarly, Frank Pakenham fought Oxford unsuccessfully in 1945 and his wife fought the same seat in 1950, also unsuccessfully. These cases are not difficult to explain, given that the wife of an M.P. or candidate becomes well known, and often

26. Healey, February 1952.
27. W. D. Chapman (Birmingham (Northfield)), 1951: general secretary 1949–53; W. T. Rodgers (Stockton-on-Tees), 1962: general secretary 1953–60; and Mrs Shirley Williams (Hitchin), 1964: general secretary 1960–4.
28. N.E.C. Report, APCR 1930, p. 17.
29. *The Times*, 26 October 1955.

well liked, in the C.L.P., and, should she possess the qualities and ambition to become an M.P., she often has a distinct advantage when she appears before the selection conference, as Mrs Jean Mann has pointed out:

When Dr Jeger died, quite a number of carpet-baggers were mentioned for the vacancy, and it was a matter for surprise when his widow, Mrs L. M. Jeger, was chosen to take his place. Those closest to the hard-working M.P. knew his wife and her worth. She had all the qualities for the job; had worked in the constituency, a member of the local authority; canvassed for him; dealt with his cases; well-educated and a good platform style. It would have been wrong to have passed her over.[30]

The nominee with strong local connections is often in a similar position: the desire for a local candidate may be considerable, and should one or more of the nominees be a member or former member of the local authority, official or former official of the C.L.P., *and* possess sufficient qualifications in the eyes of the local party to become a candidate or M.P., then his position is invariably strong. It is possibly because such cases are fairly infrequent that they may be the subject of speculation. As far as candidates in Labour-held seats are concerned, there have been only seven cases between 1950 and 1964 where the C.L.P. has selected a candidate with strong local connections. The selection of S. Mahon for Bootle in 1955 is probably typical. The previous member, J. Kinley, had been under pressure to retire on grounds of age, and it may well be that the C.L.P. was dissatisfied with his performance of his duties in the constituency. Furthermore, the constituency lies in a strongly Catholic area. The then chairman of the C.L.P., Simon Mahon, was a member of the Bootle Borough Council and a Catholic. His selection may not have been inevitable, but it was probably predictable.

Sponsorship and Finance

The question which is far more likely to play a positive part in selection is that of finance. This is a difficult question because it is bound up with the general problem of trade union and Co-operative candidates. It is often difficult to distinguish between the candidate who has been chosen for financial reasons, the candidate who has been chosen because he is a trade union or Co-operative nominee, and the candidate who is chosen for neither of these reasons.

30. Jean Mann, op. cit., p. 47.

Prior to the Hastings Agreement between the trade unions, the Co-operative Union, the National Union of Labour Organizers and Agents, and the Labour party, the amount of financial assistance which an *individual* or an *affiliated organization* could contribute to a C.L.P.'s funds and to the election expenses of the candidate was unlimited. Thus, in the first volume of his biography, Lord Dalton relates:

Mrs Webb puts up £250 towards my expenses from Sir Arthur Acland, who wishes his son, Sir Francis, had gone Labour and makes this gift for 'a young University man standing for Labour'. This makes it possible to say that I can guarantee expenses anywhere.[31]

Sponsorship was not therefore limited to affiliated organizations and self-sponsoring by candidates was fairly common before the Second World War. For instance, by 1923 it had become the established practice to declare the financial responsibility for by-elections in the reports submitted by the N.E.C. to the Annual Party Conference, and with the establishment of a By-Election Fund, it also became the practice to declare whether a grant had been made from this fund. Normally, if a seat was sponsored by an individual or an affiliated organization it was recorded that no appeal or grant had been made, although sponsorship did not rule out any financial assistance from the fund. If the seat was fought on the responsibility of the local party, it was recorded that a grant had been made. In either case, whether a grant had been made or not, this fact was normally declared, and where a grant had been made, the amount recorded in the accounts presented to the conference.

Between 1926 and 1931 there were five recorded instances where the *candidate* paid his or her own election expenses at a by-election,[32] and between 1926 and 1934 two cases where the N.E.C. Report states that no appeal was made under the By-Election Fund[33] and four cases where there is no record of any appeal.[34]

The Hastings Agreement sought to limit the contributions which either an individual or affiliated organization could make towards election expenses and constituency organization. In its original form, the agreement stipulated that the 'C.L.P. shall itself undertake to pay not less than 20 per cent of the election expenses of [the candidate]',[35] thus limiting any candidate or affiliated organization to 80 per cent of

31. Dalton, op. cit., p. 139.
32. See N.E.C. Report, APCR 1926, p. 25; 1929, p. 25; 1931, pp. 13 and 26.
33. N.E.C. Report, 1930, pp. 14 and 17.
34. N.E.C. Report, 1927, pp. 9 and 10; 1934, pp. 33 and 34.
35. Clause 1(a), The Hastings Agreement on Parliamentary Candidatures and Constituency Finance, N.E.C. Report, APCR 1933, p. 36.

the total. A further limitation was imposed in that no candidate or affiliated organization was allowed to contribute more than '80 per cent of 60 per cent of the maximum expenses allowed by law'.[36] As far as contributions towards the maintenance of the constituency organization were concerned, there was a limit of £150 per annum in borough constituencies, and £200 per annum in county constituencies.[37] These financial conditions have been altered three times since the original agreement. In 1944 the grants to boroughs and counties were raised to £200 and £250 respectively,[38] and then, in 1948, the figures were raised to £250 and £300, and affiliated organizations were to be allowed to pay up to 80 per cent of the legal maximum.[39] Finally, in 1957, the grants were again raised, this time to £350 for boroughs and £420 for counties.

Apart from placing a limit on the amount which an individual might contribute to his election expenses and to constituency funds, and generally regularizing the procedure, the Hastings Agreement did not preclude the practice of self-sponsorship. Martin Harrison cites several cases after the Second World War in which candidates supported themselves financially.[40] In 1955 Wilfred Fienburgh alleged, 'the Labour party is the only party in Britain in which you can buy a seat',[41] whilst a month earlier a former Labour candidate wrote: 'it is most difficult for a member of the Labour party to reach the benches of the House of Commons unless he is supported either by an organization *or from his own resources*'.[42] In January 1956, however, the assistant national agent reported: 'Most of these grants are modest and only a very small number of candidates contribute anything like the maximum permitted under the Hastings Agreement.'[43]

In 1955 the Wilson Committee on Party Organization expressed its concern at the number of candidates,

who, out of their own pockets, are required to make annual contributions towards Constituency Party finances. Quite apart from the undesirability of this practice, on general grounds, the dependence of Constituency Labour Party finances on such a source of income has a detrimental effect on organization. We recommend that early steps be taken to end this practice and that

36. ibid., Clause 1(b).   37. ibid., Clause 1(c).
38. Conference Proceedings, APCR 1944, p. 142.
39. N.E.C. Report and Conference Proceedings, APCR 1948, pp. 10 and 209.
40. Harrison, op. cit., p. 276.
41. W. Fienburgh, 'The Future of Labour Party Organization', *Fabian Journal*, November 1955.
42. C. Ford, in *Labour Organizer*, October 1955, p. 198. (Author's italics.)
43. *Labour Organizer*, January 1956, p. 15.

it shall be an instruction to N.E.C. representatives at Selection Conferences, that any attempt to influence a Selection Conference by personal promises of money, or any attempt to exact a financial pledge from a possible candidate shall invalidate the conference.[44]

The N.E.C. did not adopt these recommendations until 1957, when it proposed a number of amendments to the Hastings Agreement. As a result of two of these amendments, candidates were not allowed to contribute more than their personal expenses towards the election expenses and were limited to a maximum contribution of £50 towards constituency organization.[45] A third amendment stipulated, 'That a Constituency Labour Party selecting a Parliamentary candidate shall make *no enquiry or reference* to the financing of the candidature until *after selection* when the written agreement between the Constituency Labour Party and the selected Candidate is completed.'[46]

In explaining these amendments, Transport House pointed out:

Not all C.L.P.s who have M.P.s sponsored by trade unions, or the Co-operative Party, receive the *maximum* financial assistance permitted under the regulations, and some of the C.L.P.s who sponsor their own candidate *receive financial assistance from their M.P.s and a few up to the permitted maxima or near to it* . . . [the new regulations] would strengthen the existing safeguards against *rich men using their wealth to buy seats*.[47]

These comments confirm earlier evidence that self-sponsorship had continued since the war, but persisted in making what is in many respects a false distinction between self-sponsorship and sponsorship by an affiliated organization. This distinction was reflected in the objections of constituency delegates to the limitation on the financial contributions of candidates. One delegate 'felt there was a *discrimination* in limiting the amount which non-sponsored candidates could contribute to constituency funds'.[48] Another 'suggested that the proposed *maximum* contribution by candidates should be a *minimum* contribution'.[49] With the exception of the N.U.M. and a few smaller unions, the question of sponsorship is *related to the candidate and not the* constituency. When a sponsored nominee presents himself at a selection conference, the delegates are normally aware that, *if they select him,*

44. The Wilson Report, APCR 1955, p. 74.
45. Amended Clauses 2(a) and (b), Hastings Agreement, N.E.C. Report, APCR 1957, p. 14; adopted by Conference, p. 126.
46. ibid., new Clause 3.
47. *Labour Organizer*, September 1957, pp. 163–4. (Author's italics.)
48. Conference Proceedings (private session), APCR 1957, p. 125. (Author's italics.)
49. ibid. (Author's italics.)

his nominating organization will support him financially, but *only* if they select him. The difference between the self-sponsored and the organization-sponsored candidate is simply a matter of the *source* of financial support. Before this ruling, it was acknowledged that the 'rich man' might be able to 'buy a seat'; this privilege is now limited to the rich union and the rich Co-operative party.

Does the question of finance actually influence selection? The fact that the Wilson Committee felt obliged to recommend that any attempt on the part of a nominee or affiliated organization to influence a selection by promises of money, or attempts on the part of the C.L.P. to exact such promises, should invalidate the selection, suggests that it did, prior to the ruling of 1957. The N.E.C. did not, however, adopt the Wilson Committee's recommendation in its entirety: it proposed that any enquiry or reference to the financing of the candidature by the *C.L.P.* should be prohibited. No direct prohibition was imposed on references to the financing of the candidature by any of the *nominees*, and Harold Wilson, speaking in the debate on the proposals, made it clear that it was a 'rule forbidding *questions about finance at selection conferences*'.[50] Furthermore, as Transport House explained, 'the adoption of this proposal would regulate what, in the majority of cases, is already *established practice*'.[51]

The author has attended two selection conferences at which delegates asked direct questions about the financing of the candidature. Neither selection was declared invalid, although in one of the two cases the delegate concerned was declared out of order by the regional organizer. Against this, the author has attended eight selection conferences at seven of which one or more *nominees* made direct reference to the fact that they were sponsored. However much a selection conference may or may not be swayed by financial considerations, it seems clear that some nominees think and hope that it will be. It is, in fact, doubtful whether the delegates at any selection conference are primarily concerned with the problem of finance. A few, perhaps those conversant with the financial position of the C.L.P., may be, but the majority will be swayed by the performance of the nominees on the platform, by trade union and other loyalties, and by political considerations, though not necessarily in that order.

Although, as Harrison points out, 'in only a handful of constituencies – mostly safe Labour seats where individual membership is minute

50. ibid. (Author's italics.)
51. *Labour Organizer*, September 1957, p. 164. (Author's italics.)

– do union affiliations exceed members' subscriptions',[52] the tempta-tion for C.L.P.s with small individual memberships and, therefore, relatively small incomes to choose a sponsored candidate is not as strong as might be suspected. The figures in Table 8(10) show that the imbalance between C.L.P.s with below average individual membership

Table 8(10): *Average individual membership* of constituencies which selected sponsored candidates, 1950–5*

Sponsoring organization	Individual membership		
	Below average	*Average*	*Above average*
All sponsored seats	51·1(91)	5·1(9)	43·8(78)
Trade union seats	55·6(65)	3·4(4)	41·0(48)
Co-operative seats	42·6(26)	8·2(5)	49·2(30)

* Based on Annual Conference Reports, 1950–5.

and those with above average membership is not excessive. In fact, with Co-operative seats the balance is in favour of the above average constituencies. To stress the point further, of the eighty-nine con-stituencies with a Labour majority in 1955 of 10,000 or more, 61·8 per cent had below average individual memberships, 5·6 per cent average memberships, and 32·6 above average memberships. Rather more than half of the eighty-nine, 56·3 per cent, were sponsored and 68·9 per cent of these had below average memberships, but well over two thirds of these were sponsored by the N.U.M., constituencies whose average membership was only 942.[53] Constituencies sponsored by other unions in fact showed a balance in favour of above average membership. Such evidence as can be brought to bear suggests that the selection of a sponsored candidate in a constituency with a small individual member-ship is far more likely to be the result of the location of the constituency than of financial considerations at the selection conference. In other words, constituencies in strong union areas, or those with substantial Labour majorities or both, are likely to have a small individual member-ship. This may mean that their position is financially precarious, despite union affiliations, but any question of adopting a sponsored candidate is likely to be considered at an earlier stage than the selection conference.

Some indication of the extent to which a C.L.P. is likely to select

52. Harrison, op. cit., p. 79.   53. ibid., p. 84.

a sponsored candidate can be seen in the number of constituencies which have selected *consecutive* sponsored candidates. Between 1945 and 1966, seventy-nine C.L.P.s in Labour-held seats selected consecutive sponsored candidates. In forty-seven cases, the candidates came from the *same* sponsoring organization, and in the remaining thirty-two from a different sponsoring organization.

The prominence of the N.U.M. in securing the selection of consecutive candidates is shown clearly in Table 8(11) but it is also important to note the relative positions of the Co-operative party, which has

Table 8(11): *Number of incumbent C.L.P.s selecting consecutive sponsored candidates, 1945–66*

Sponsoring organization	Number of constituencies
A. *Sponsored by the same organization*	
N.U.M.	25
Co-operative party*	7
U.S.D.A.W.	3
T.G.W.U.	3
A.E.U.	2
N.U.G.M.W.	2
N.U.A.W.	1
R.A.C.S.	1
U.P.W.	1
N.U.R.	1
U.T.F.W.A.	1
Total	47
B. *Sponsored by different organization*	32
Total	79

* Excluding the R.A.C.S.

incurred the resentment of many unions; U.S.D.A.W., a semi-white collar union, and the T.G.W.U., A.E.U., and N.U.G.M.W., all of which have sought to meet the challenge of changing circumstances in selection. Apart from the obvious case of the N.U.M., which sponsors constituencies in which loyalty to the union is often strong, the fact that ten other sponsoring organizations succeeded in securing the selection of consecutive candidates is an indication of the part often played by loyalty in the selection of candidates. For instance, it is invariably the practice for the E.C. of the C.L.P. to place the nominee of the former sponsoring organization automatically on the short-list, if only to avoid bitter recriminations. Once on the short-list, his chances of selection will vary: too loud a proclamation that this is a 'miners' seat' or a 'T. and G. seat' may cause resentment; a strong challenge from a rival union may introduce an unknown factor; the last candidate from the organization may or may not have been satisfactory; and so on. None the less, tradition plays an important role: several unions make it a general rule not to nominate if the incumbent union is again seeking the selection of its nominee. Inter-union agreements are by no means unknown in the general nature of things, but where a union seat is involved, such agreements may play an important part. For instance, Carlisle was sponsored by T.S.S.A., one of the railway unions, from 1950 to 1955, when the then M.P., A. Hargreaves, was defeated. After his defeat, Hargreaves sought re-selection, and the N.U.R. did not nominate for the vacancy,[54] but following his second defeat in 1959 and his decision not to seek re-selection, T.S.S.A. stood down and the N.U.R. secured the selection of its candidate. The A.E.U., T.G.W.U., A.S.W., and several areas of the N.U.M. have made agreements with other unions to avoid clashes of interest, though such agreements normally apply only to particular selections.

Between 1950 and 1966, thirty-two Labour-held constituencies which had previously been sponsored selected non-sponsored candidates, and twenty-one which had not been previously sponsored selected sponsored candidates. Thus the turnover of sponsored candidates is related largely to particular constituencies: where a C.L.P. previously had a sponsored candidate it is quite likely to choose another. It is likely that this is the result of the distribution of the affiliated organizations rather than any deliberate choice of a candidate because he is sponsored.

The question of Conservative-held constituencies is somewhat more complicated, since the number of selections involved over the period is greater. The number of C.L.P.s which select sponsored candidates for two elections *running* is fairly high, and this accounts for the majority of the constituencies in Table 8(12), but the number of C.L.P.s selecting sponsored candidates for three or more elections is extremely small.

If finance were the *principal* consideration in the minds of delegates

54. See ibid., p. 303.

Table 8(12): *Number of non-incumbent C.L.P.s selecting more than one sponsored candidate, 1945–66*

	Number of elections					
	2	3	4	5	6	7
Number of constituencies	52	8	5	2	1	–

at selection conferences, it would seem reasonable to assume that more than fifty-two C.L.P.s would have selected a sponsored candidate for two out of seven elections, and more than eight C.L.P.s would have selected a sponsored candidate for three out of seven elections. There may be constituencies of the sort cited by R. T. McKenzie,[55] where

Table 8(13): *Number of non-incumbent C.L.P.s selecting consecutive sponsored candidates from the same organization, 1945–66*

Affiliated organization	Number of consecutive elections					
	2	3	4	5	6	7
Co-operative party	16	–	–	1	–	–
A.E.U.	6	–	–	–	–	–
T.S.S.A.	4*	1	–	–	–	–
T.G.W.U.	3	–	–	–	–	–
E.T.U.	2	–	–	–	–	–
N.U.A.W.	2	–	–	–	–	–
D.A.T.A.	1	–	–	–	–	–
A.S.L.E.F.	1†	–	–	–	–	–
U.P.W.	1	–	–	–	–	–
U.S.D.A.W.	1	–	–	–	–	–
N.U.M.	1	–	–	–	–	–
U.F.T.W.A.	–	1	–	–	–	–
N.U.R.	–	1	–	–	–	–
Total	38‡	3§	–	1**	–	—

* Including two defeated M.P.s re-selected.
† Defeated M.P. re-selected.
‡ Twenty-six cases involved the *same* candidate, twelve a *different* candidate.
§ Two cases involved the *same* candidate; the other, two candidates, one selected *twice*.
** This case involved three candidates over five elections, i.e. the re-selection of the *same* candidate occurred *twice*.

55. McKenzie, op. cit., p. 554.

finance appears to play at least a prominent role, but probably fewer than is often supposed.

It is important to note that the majority of the cases involved the re-selection of the *same* candidate. The incentive to re-select a candidate is strong provided he has proved satisfactory and it is likely that this, rather than financial considerations, is the principal factor in such cases. The most celebrated case of a constituency which appears to have a strong preference for a sponsored candidate is Billericay, which, ever since its creation in 1948, has had a sponsored candidate. The extent to which this can be explained in purely financial terms is questionable, however, since at five of the six elections the sponsoring organization was the same – the Co-operative party – and the C.L.P. has twice re-selected candidates. The Co-operative Movement in general is strong in the area, whilst the local Co-operative party is particularly active. Moreover, the provision of the Supplementary Agreement of 1960 by which the Co-operative party could re-nominate the *same* candidate in the constituency which he or she fought unsuccessfully in 1959, without seeking the permission of the N.E.C., was an incentive to the local Co-operative party to retain its hold on the seat, quite apart from the fact that the general incentive to re-select a candidate is often strong. The selection in 1965 of Eric Moonman, who is sponsored by the National Graphical Association and who won Billericay in 1966, is probably attributable as much to his local connections as to any financial benefit which his candidature involved. In addition to political and local government ties with East London, Moonman had fought the neighbouring constituency of Chigwell in 1964, having 'nursed' the seat from early in 1962.

This is not to say that the financing of the candidature is ignored, and the question of sponsorship may loom larger in the choice of non-incumbent, than in the choice of incumbent C.L.P.s. It seems certain that cross-pressures are greater in Labour-held seats: it matters far more who is selected since the candidature of the unsuccessful candidate lapses after his defeat; that of the M.P. continues until retirement, death, or defeat intervenes. It may be far more important in non-Labour seats that the election expenses are assured, than the fact that the candidate is a trade unionist or is on the left or right wing of the party. Furthermore, the delegates to the G.M.C. of the non-Labour constituency are far more likely to be aware of the C.L.P.'s financial position, since they represent to a much greater extent than G.M.C. delegates in Labour seats the hard core of local party workers, con-

THE SELECTION OF PARLIAMENTARY CANDIDATES

versant with the problems of running a political party in a relatively unsympathetic area, and probably less well-supported by local union affiliations.

In most Labour selections the question of finance will almost certainly be considered at an earlier stage, unofficially in the pre-nomination period, officially at the meetings of the executive council. In the course of a fairly recent selection at Abertillery, a prominent member of the C.L.P. said:

Money is the main consideration. The party draws a great deal of financial support from the unions, particularly the miners' union. Naturally, the unions would like to have a say in the choice of candidate and Mr Gordon Walker *is not union sponsored.*[56]

Speaking of a possible candidature at Dundee in 1945, Jean Mann commented:

Dundee was short of cash: indeed at that time in a perpetual state of debt. I was a penniless lass and there were others anxious for Dundee adoption, good men *with cash*. I was not so anxious to offer any. Indeed, I flatly refused ... in no circumstances would I buy a nomination.[57]

In 1964, a prominent member of the Co-operative party alleged that he had been asked by a local party *how much money he could offer*, as the C.L.P. needed money to pay for the new premises it had recently acquired.[58] Such cases may be rare, but they occur.

The influence of the E.C. is at its greatest in the drawing up of the short-list. Between 1953 and 1964 the average number of nominees on the short-lists of twenty-two Labour-held constituencies was *five* and the average number of sponsored candidates on each short-list was *three*. The corresponding figures for five Conservative-held constituencies between 1955 and 1964 were *four* and *one*. Some Labour-held seats, such as Islington North in 1958, had no *sponsored* nominees on the short-list; others, such as one C.L.P. in the period before the 1964 election, had no *non-sponsored* nominees on the short-list. The E.C. of any C.L.P. knows its financial position and knows which of the nominees are sponsored, and the temptation to place one or more of the sponsored nominees on the short-list may be considerable. It is difficult to dismiss as a coincidence that the second of the two C.L.P.s mentioned above sent a questionnaire to all nominees which included

56. *Sunday Times*, 7 February 1964. (Author's italics.)
57. Jean Mann, op. cit., p. 23. (Author's italics.)
58. Private communication.

the comment: 'This is not a 'rich' constituency . . .',[59] and that, of the two short-lists which were eventually compiled, one had *four* sponsored nominees out of a possible *six*, and the other *eight out of eight*.

Political Factors and Canvassing

To the major cross-pressures of the federative nature of the Labour party and sponsorship must be added the question of political considerations. That *politically aligned groups*, as distinct from particular affiliated organizations, seek the selection of their members is clear enough. The clash between C.D.S. and C.N.D. is evidence of this.[60] In the early 1960s one of the most frequent questions at selection conferences was, 'Are you a member of C.N.D.?' or, 'Do you support the party's nuclear policy?' One Labour candidate, selected for a by-election in 1962, said that at his selection the C.L.P. had the choice between two C.N.D. nominees and one of two outsiders.[61] Prior to the clash over nuclear defence, there was the dispute over Clause IV, and before that German rearmament, and so on. The post-1964 clashes have been over Vietnam and prices and incomes – *political* divisions between left and right are an acknowledged feature of Labour politics, but it is wrong to assume, as Harrison has pointed out,[62] that the federative and political divisions of the party coincide. There is no reason to believe that individual members favour left-wing candidates any more than there is reason to believe that the unions favour right-wing candidates. Seldom is selection so simple.

Michael Foot was selected for Ebbw Vale in 1960, a close friend (and later biographer) of his predecessor, Aneurin Bevan. Shortly before the selection, Ebbw Vale C.L.P. had passed a motion supporting unilateral nuclear disarmament:[63] Foot is a supporter of C.N.D. But the E.C. of Ebbw Vale C.L.P. omitted Foot from the short-list and one member of the E.C. remarked: 'Nye was a world figure and we did not mind if he hardly ever came to see us. We kept the party going for him ... But Michael Foot is not Nye. ...'[64] Pressure from various quarters of the G.M.C. ensured that Foot was placed on the short-list, and he was eventually selected after three ballots. The challenge from the miners and the steelworkers was strong, and, had they combined forces, might have been in a position to prevent Foot's selection, but the steelworkers were split. B.I.S.A.K.T.A.'s official nominee had not

59. Private communication.
60. See *Guardian*, 28 August 1964.
61. Private communication.
62. Harrison, op. cit., pp. 238–57.
63. *The Times*, 16 September 1960.
64. ibid.

been short-listed, but a second member of the union had. The executive of B.I.S.A.K.T.A. sent a letter of appeal to local branches urging support for this nominee. The situation was further complicated, however, by the fact that Foot had been nominated by a branch of B.I.S.A.K.T.A.,[65] whilst the steelworkers' adopted nominee was also the constituency agent.

It would be unrealistic to assume that Foot's known left-wing views did not play an important part in his selection, but it would be equally unrealistic to assume that his undoubted speaking ability, that local union rivalries, that clashes of personality were not also important. In fact, the political views of the nominees cannot be ignored: it was not a coincidence that the C.D.S. nominee at Birmingham (Small Heath) received fifty-six votes to the C.N.D. candidate's none;[66] nor was it a coincidence that Clive Jenkins, the left-wing general secretary of A.S.S.E.T. (now A.S.T.M.S.), was attacked in a circular by 'non-Communist and non-Trotskyist members of A.S.S.E.T.',[67] when he sought selection at Shoreditch and Finsbury in 1964. [68]

The various cross-pressures which affect selection are such that canvassing on behalf of particular nominees before the selection conference is almost inevitable. In fact this has always been so – describing a selection conference in 1924 Stella Davies notes: 'It was a good example of democracy in action, with just the amount of *wire-pulling* to make it credible as the action of men and not angels.'[69] Another writer, who has since become a Labour M.P., alleged, in 1955, that in safe seats 'the selection conference is usually only a ritual endorsement of what has already been achieved by *systematic canvassing*'.[70] At Ebbw Vale in 1960, one short-listed nominee requested a list of G.M.C. delegates from the Executive Council but this was refused and there were, at the time, general accusations of canvassing.[71] Similarly, it was reported from the Woodside division of Glasgow, in 1962, that

65. *The Times*, 30 August 1960.
66. See Chapter Five, page 140 above.
67. *Daily Telegraph*, 9 September 1964.
68. Richards, in op. cit., p. 23, also suggests that the rejection in 1955 of Sir Frank Soskice by Manchester (Gorton) C.L.P. in favour of Konni Zilliacus was a triumph for the left, and that the selection, also in 1955, of Frank Tomney for Hammersmith North in preference to W. T. Williams was a triumph for the right.
69. C. Stella Davies, *North Country Bred – A Working Class Family Chronicle*, London, 1963, p. 226. (Author's italics.)
70. R. Fletcher, M.P. for Ilkeston since October 1964, in the *Labour Organizer*, September 1955, p. 171. It is ironical that one of Fletcher's rivals for the candidature at Ilkeston should subsequently have accused him of '*lining up 68 votes before the selection conference*'. (Private communication.)
71. *The Times*, 23 September 1960.

'supporters of one of the nominees are planning to organize a shuttle service of cars to ensure maximum attendance of their group at the selection conference'.[72] The selection of a candidate at Shoreditch and Finsbury, in 1964, was marked by accusations and counter-accusations of canvassing on the part of supporters of rival candidates.

The Factors which Influence Labour Selection

The most serious problem which the Labour party faces in the selection of parliamentary candidates is not the efficacy of sponsorship as a means of financing candidatures, but the extent to which *sectional* considerations should determine selection. It is neither inconceivable nor indeed unknown for an able would-be candidate to be rejected in favour of a less able but stolid trade unionist. Occasionally the prospect of the financial support which the unionist or Co-operative nominee brings with him may play a significant part in his selection, but in the long term the question of the selection of an individual who may be more *representative of* his selectors than his rivals, but of lesser ability, strikes more deeply at the concept of representative democracy in the Burkean tradition than any question of financial influence. Should parliamentary candidates in general, and potential M.P.s in particular, be selected on the grounds that they are *representative of* their selectors? Or should they be selected in the light of their ability *to represent the views* of their selectors? The two are not easily distinguishable, whilst the question of a would-be candidate's ability to fulfil the role of an M.P. may not even be considered. It is not, of course, true to say that all union candidates or even a majority are less able than their non-sponsored colleagues: one need only point to members of the various Labour administrations to demonstrate this. None the less, the author has attended more than one selection conference at which a union candidate has been selected in preference to a more able non-union candidate. This is a reflection less of the system of sponsorship and more of the federative nature of the Labour party. In other words, the price that the Labour party has to pay for the continued representation within its ranks of one of the great sections of the Labour Movement is the possible exclusion of young and often more able candidates, who are discouraged by their rejection at the hands of local parties which prefer to be represented by one of their own kind.

There is no better way of illustrating this than by pointing out that many of the young and able Labour candidates who entered Parliament

72. *The Times*, 16 October 1962.

in 1964 and 1966 did so because they *won* seats from their Conservative and Liberal opponents. Over half these candidates were under forty, three fifths were graduates, and nearly half were members of the professions. In contrast, little more than a fifth of the candidates who were selected by *incumbent* C.L.P.s and entered Parliament at the same time were under forty, only a third were graduates, and little more than a quarter members of the professions. It should not be forgotten that many of these young and able candidates benefited from the favourable electoral atmosphere of 1964 and 1966 and that the majority remain Members for *marginal and semi-marginal* constituencies: what was the Labour party's gain in 1964 and 1966 may be its loss at the next two general elections.

The abolition of sponsorship is no solution, since this would only affect those selections in which finance is a factor. In the past sponsorship has undoubtedly enabled many extremely able men to enter Parliament, but whilst finance is no longer a real barrier, *sectionalism* is. Some C.L.P.s remain committed to the belief aptly expressed by a member of Abertillery C.L.P.: 'This ought to be a miner's seat. There are enough lawyers, school-teachers, economists and journalists in the Commons.'[73]

As long as this remains the case, the Labour party will continue to suffer from a basic conflict in selection, and this must leave open to serious doubt that, as a former national agent has asserted, 'Clause XII of the Model rules ... ensures the widest possible choice and an extremely democratic method of selection.'[74]

73. *Sunday Times*, 21 February 1965.
74. Sara Barker, in the *Labour Organizer*, January 1956, p. 13.

CHAPTER NINE

Three Case-Studies

A Controversial Selection

The constituency in this selection is in a mining area in the Midlands. The seat has been Labour-held since 1950, when there was a comfortable Labour majority, but the effects of the redistribution of 1955 and the anti-Labour swing of the 1950s reduced it to a marginal seat and left Labour with a relatively small majority to defend in 1964.

The greater part of the constituency is rural, and, apart from one town of under 30,000 inhabitants, has a widely dispersed population, scattered in a large number of small villages. Labour's strength in the constituency lay not in the one urban area, but was derived from the importance of the coal-mining industry.

Mining, of course, is a declining industry, but it is still this area's most important one: in 1961 five colleries in the constituency employed 8,224 men, which means that the miners are still the most important *single* group from which the Labour party draws its support.

The importance of the miners is reflected in the composition of the trade union section of the G.M.C. of the C.L.P. (Table 9(1)).

The miners constitute by far the largest group, with eighteen delegates from the N.U.M. and one from the Overmen, Deputies, and Shotfirers (N.A.C.O.D.S.). The A.E.U. has the next biggest delegation, with half the number of the N.U.M., followed by the T.G.W.U. with six, and the N.U.A.W. with three. There is no question, of course, of the miners being able to dominate even the union delegates, let alone the whole G.M.C., but their position is a strong one and any N.U.M. candidate is likely to be a strong challenger. In a questionnaire sent to the nominees for the candidature, the secretary of the C.L.P. pointed out that the constituency's most important industries were coal-mining, engineering and agriculture. This is borne out by the figures shown in Table 9(1) and is reflected in the distribution of trade union

Table 9(1): *Composition of the trade union section of the G.M.C.*

Trade union	Number of delegates
N.U.M.	18
A.E.U.	9
T.G.W.U.	6
N.U.A.W.	3
N.U.R.	2
D.A.T.A.	1
N.U.G.M.W.	1
C.O.H.S.E.*	1
A.S.L.E.F.	1
N.A.C.O.D.S.†	1
U.P.W.	1
U.S.D.A.W.	1
T.S.S.A.	1
Total	46

* Confederation of Health Service Employees.
† National Association of Colliery Overmen, Deputies, and Shotfirers.

delegates to the G.M.C. The latter does not, of course, provide a mirror-image of the industrial pattern of the constituency since only two industries are represented entirely, or almost entirely, by a single trade union: the miners by the N.U.M. and the N.A.C.O.D.S., and the agricultural workers by the N.U.A.W. The remainder of the industries support several unions: railwaymen may belong to one of three unions,[1] workers in engineering to at least three,[2] despite the importance of the A.E.U.; building trade workers appear to be unrepresented on the G.M.C., whilst there is probably competition for workers in distributive trades among several unions.[3]

Not only is no one union in a position to dominate the G.M.C., but the forty-six trade union delegates are outnumbered by those from party organizations. Approximately two fifths of the G.M.C. are union delegates, a factor which makes their position powerful but not all-powerful, influential but not dominant – always assuming, of course, that the union delegates act as a single group, which in most cases they do not. The initial stages of the selection were, in fact, marked by inter-union rivalry rather than union solidarity.

1. A.S.L.E.F., N.U.R., and T.S.S.A.
2. A.E.U., T.G.W.U., N.U.G.M.W., and, possibly, D.A.T.A.
3. U.S.D.A.W., T.G.W.U., and, possibly, C.A.W.U.

Table 9(2): Composition of the G.M.C.

Party or affiliated organization	Number of delegates
Local Labour parties (L.L.P.)	52
Women's sections	11
Young Socialists	2
Trade unions	46
Total	111

The retiring member was sponsored by the T.G.W.U. and remained so throughout his tenure of the seat. By the General Election of 1959 he was sixty-nine years of age, and by the next election he would clearly be well over seventy. Early in 1963, therefore, he announced his intention of retiring at the end of the current Parliament.

Although there were the usual rumours of an autumn election, no attempt was made to speed the selection, which took three months from the time of the Member's announcement to the selection conference, and four months by the time the selection had come before the N.E.C. for endorsement. Early in April the prescribed circular requesting nominations was sent to all party and affiliated organizations. Those Labour parties which asked for them were given copies of the 'B' List from which to select suitable nominees,[4] but no preliminary interviews were conducted by any party or affiliated organization prior to nomination. It is important to remember that, since this was a Labour-held constituency, the C.L.P. had had no experience of selecting a candidate since its selection of the retiring Member before 1950, and the same applied to the L.L.P.s, who were now asked to make nominations to the C.L.P. According to the secretary of one of the L.L.P.s, this was a most difficult task, a complaint which was echoed by several party organizations. In the first place, each L.L.P. was supplied with only one copy of the 'B' List which made effective comparison and selection of potential nominees by local executive committees difficult. Furthermore, the general feeling among the local committee was that the information supplied on the list was inadequate and that no guidance was given on how to select one or two candidates from a list of over

4. The 'A' List was left to the respective unions.

200 names. Several local committees were unsure of their rights in respect of nomination and naturally fell back on the advice of the agent, the one man in the C.L.P. who had had recent experience of selection.

The role of the agent was a curious one, for there is a strong suspicion that he sought to play a more positive role in the selection than that of a purely procedural guide. The agent's main preoccupation, it appeared, was to avoid what he called 'double nomination' – that is, the nomination of the same candidate by more than one party or affiliated organization. The avowed purpose of this was to secure as large a number of nominations as possible in order to widen the field of choice from which the candidate would be chosen.

In the meantime, only one L.L.P. had made any extensive use of the 'B' List. The local secretary had noted the names of fifteen possible nominees from the list and placed them before his executive committee. Eight of the twelve members of the committee attended and there followed a general discussion of the type of candidate they wanted. The advantages of a local candidate were discussed, but it was decided that this was not a vital qualification. The question of electoral and political experience was also discussed. These preliminary discussions were handicapped by the possession of only one 'B' List. Later, two further copies were secured from Transport House and the local executive committee eventually drew up a list of twelve names. There was a tendency for teachers to dominate the list, since a preference was expressed for a candidate with a good education but a working class origin, characteristics which tended to favour the teaching profession. Dissatisfied by the amount of information on the 'B' List, the local secretary wrote to each of the potential nominees requesting further information and asking whether they wished to be considered. Two or three were eliminated, either because they had already been adopted elsewhere or because they did not wish to be considered, and the remainder were placed before the committee when it came to draw up a short-list to present to its G.M.C., both meetings being scheduled for the same evening. Only seven members of the E.C. attended on this occasion[5] and the C.L.P. agent was also present. Eventually a short-list of four names was agreed, but the agent pointed out that two of these had already been nominated by other party organizations. This left the local G.M.C. with a choice of two. The G.M.C. meeting consisted of the seven members of the E.C. and one

5. The meetings coincided with a local council meeting and several members of the E.C. were also councillors; the weather was also bad.

delegate, making a total of eight. After a short discussion, one of the two candidates was chosen as the L.L.P.'s nominee to the C.L.P.

Other L.L.P.s had taken less trouble: some had found their own local nominees and a few made a random choice from a wider field; but several relied on the advice of the agent. As far as general qualifications were concerned, the latter stressed only age – saying that no one born before 1920 should be considered – and electoral experience, pointing out that the constituency had been removed from Transport House's list of marginal seats. When pressed for further advice, however, the agent suggested that the L.L.P. might consider Mr Long, whose name appeared on the 'B' List. This suggestion was made not to one L.L.P. but to several, in spite of the agent's earlier advice against 'double nomination'. Long, the agent urged, was an able man with considerable electoral experience, and, at thirty-nine, was the right age.

At the closing date for nominations a month later, eighteen nominations were received. Of these, seven were trade union nominated and sponsored, the remainder being nominated by party organizations. Only one candidate, however, was *nominated by more than one party or affiliated organization*: *Long*, who was nominated by three L.L.P.s.

The number of nominations was later reduced to sixteen, first by the withdrawal of one candidate, because his union had made an official nomination, and then by the action of the N.E.C. in declaring another nomination invalid because the candidate in question did not belong to her appropriate trade union. This also meant the elimination of the only woman candidate.

Table 9(3): Composition of the Executive Committee

Party or affiliated organization/position*	Number of representatives
Chairman	1
Vice-chairman	2
Treasurer	1
L.L.P.s	6
Women's sections	2
Young Socialists	–
Trade unions	6
Total	18

* The secretary/agent is also a member of the E.C., but without voting powers.

There is no rule restricting the number of members of the E.C. which may belong to any one affiliated organization, but this E.C. is not dominated by one union, although several members are miners. Any influence that an individual union may possess stems from the size of its local affiliation and from the advocacy of its representative on the E.C. This last asset is often important, especially at the drawing up of the short-list.

The remaining sixteen nominees were each asked to complete a questionnaire comprising eleven questions, in five groups as follows:

1. Two questions asking about the nominee's family and whether his wife would be able to help in the constituency.
2. One question asking whether the nominee belonged to any party groups, such as the Fabian Society, C.D.S., and so on.
3. Six questions on the relations between the nominee and the C.L.P. should he be selected. These related to the amount of time the nominee could be available; the extent to which the C.L.P. would be liable for his expenses; whether he would live in the constituency; whether he would be a full-time M.P.; and whether he had his own transport.
4. One question on the nominee's assessment of the electoral position in the constituency, his knowledge of local industries, and his views of the party's policies which affected these industries.
5. A final question asking for any further comments.

Each nominee was also asked to state his present address and age.

The questionnaire was largely a substitute for interviewing prior to short-listing and supplied members of the E.C. with a fair amount of detailed information about each nominee. This included a question about expenses: 'This is not a "rich" constituency. To what extent would the party be liable to meet the expenses of your visits?'

The fact that the enquiry was made suggests that financial considerations were not entirely absent from the minds of the C.L.P. during the selection. In fact, the agent admitted to the author that the *question of selecting a sponsored candidate was 'one of a number of important factors to be considered'*.

The E.C. reduced the sixteen nominees to a short-list of six, of whom four were sponsored candidates. It is difficult, of course, to be certain what factors determine the composition of a short-list, since so much depends on what sort of candidate the various members of the selecting body are looking for, on what cross-pressures they are subject to, and on their subjective evaluation of the nominees. Despite the information supplied through the questionnaire, one member of the E.C. remained unimpressed by the way in which the short-list was chosen. He pointed out that the sixteen nominees were considered in alphabetical order and that a preliminary decision was reached on each name before going on to the next. Five candidates were eliminated in this way and the process continued until six were left. The principle criticism was that no attempt was made to *compare* the nominees so that a number of able candidates were eliminated at an early stage. The six were:

Mr Baker, nominated and sponsored by D.A.T.A.
Mr Butcher, nominated by a Women's Section.
Mr Clark, nominated and sponsored by the N.U.M.
Mr Cooke, nominated and sponsored by the T.G.W.U.
Mr Cooper, nominated and sponsored by the U.P.W.
Mr Long, nominated by three L.L.P.s.

It was alleged that the first two candidates had benefited from being high on the alphabetical list; that Baker and Cooper had benefited from the forceful advocacy of their union representatives on the E.C.; that Clark had benefited from being a local man and the miner's nominee; that Cooke had been short-listed out of deference to the T.G.W.U., which had sponsored the seat since 1950; and that Long was most impressive on paper and had been nominated by three L.L.P.s, which made it difficult to exclude him.

None of the nominees was seen by the E.C. prior to short-listing, and only one, Clark, was known to all members of the E.C.: the whole process had been conducted thus far on paper.

This was the background to the selection conference. There were eighty-five delegates present out of the possible 111, and the chairman of the C.L.P. presided. The N.E.C. was represented by the regional organizer. The meeting opened with the chairman giving an outline of the procedure to be followed: each nominee would address the meeting for a maximum of fifteen minutes' questions. When all the nominees had appeared before the delegates, there would be an immediate ballot. Each delegate had been supplied with a copy of each nominee's biographical particulars and his answers to the questionnaire prior to the conference.

None of the nominees' biographical details occupied more than half a foolscap sheet of single-space typing, and only a superficial impression could be gained of each nominee from these particulars. Since the nominees were themselves responsible for these details, their content is of some interest. Naturally, each nominee sought to present himself in a favourable light: party experience was clearly regarded as important, as was local government experience, and, where applicable, considerable stress was laid on trade union experience. Four of the nominees could claim experience of parliamentary elections and each made this a central part of his biography. The other two nominees, however, were forced to rely more on long-standing party loyalty, union activity, and, in the case of Cooper, local government experience. Only Clark was able to point to a close connection with the local party and the constituency. Of the four sponsored nominees, only Clark and Baker mentioned membership of their respective union panels.

The remainder of the information provided to delegates before the conference comprised the nominees' answers to the questionnaire. These were fairly straightforward, with the exception of question ten, which asked for the nominee's assessment of the electoral situation in the constituency and for his experience of local industries. Every nominee answered this question at some length.

It is important to remember that all the information supplied to the delegates *originated from the nominees* and that the delegates did not, therefore, possess any *objective evaluation* of the latter.

Before the first of the nominees addressed the meeting,[6] a delegate asked whether either Butcher or Long were sponsored candidates, since both belonged to the N.U.G.M.W. and there was no reference to sponsorship in their biographies. Ignoring the ruling of 1957, the chairman did not rule the question out of order and replied that neither was sponsored: the regional organizer remained silent.

The topics of the speeches ranged fairly widely (Table 9(4)), but four of the six nominees chose to open with personal references, whilst the other two began by stressing their electoral experience. Only one candidate, Clark, mentioned specifically local problems, although two, Baker and Long, referred to the need for a national fuel policy, and one, Baker, mentioned agriculture. All the nominees spent most of their allotted time speaking about party policy, although two, Cooke and Long, devoted several minutes to attacking the Conservative government. Only one nominee, Cooper, did not speak for the full fifteen minutes, and this because he preferred to leave more time for questions.

In spite of the fact that he had left more time for questions, Cooper

6. They had previously drawn lots to decide the order of appearance.

Table 9(4): Details of speeches given by nominees

Cooke	Clark	Cooper	Butcher	Baker	Long
Personal	Personal	Personal	Personal	Electoral experience	Electoral experience
Party intellectuals	Local problems	Incomes	Socialism	Fuel policy	Attack opposition
Party unity	Education	Trade unions	Economy	Agriculture	Education
Attack opposition	Transport	Transport	Education	Economy	Economy
Industrial conditions	Housing		Party unity	Electoral experience	Transport
Social services	Defence			Personal	Fuel policy
Nationalization					

251

Table 9(5): *Questions asked by delegates per nominee*

Nominee	Number of questions	
Cooke	9	
Clark	6	
Cooper	8	Average
Butcher	9	7·8
Baker	7	
Long	8	

did not receive more than any other nominee. This was a reflection of his tendency to reply to questions at length. With the exception of Clark, each nominee received almost the same number of questions. In Clark's case, however, not only was there a gap in the questioning during which delegates appeared to have no further questions, but the questioning fell short of his allotted period.

Table 9(6): *Subjects of the questions asked by delegates*

Subject	Number of questions
Foreign affairs and defence	14
Home affairs	27
Local problems	–
Personal	4
Miscellaneous	2

Generally speaking, questions were related to the current political problems, some to specific issues, others to broader aspects of policy, but, in both cases, usually arising either from immediate or recent events or current party policy discussion. Table 9(6) shows that home affairs tended to predominate, with twice as many questions as foreign affairs and defence. There was, in fact, only one question on defence, and those on foreign affairs were divided equally between the Common Market and the United Nations, both relatively topical subjects at the time. Three of the four personal questions were to Butcher.[7] It is not uncommon for all or most of the nominees to be asked the same

7. See page 256 below.

question by the same delegate: for instance, five out of the six nominees were asked about the United Nations, and four out of the six about the Common Market. Nor was it surprising to find transport fairly high up on the list of subjects, since the Beeching Report had been published less than three months previously.

It is, however, difficult to assess the influence which a nominee's performance has on the selection conference: a nominee may make a popular speech but receive few votes; a nominee may enter the conference with a previous reputation, good or bad, which will lead delegates to expect a certain level of performance; and, in any case, delegates may already have made a decision about one or more of the nominees on the basis of previous knowledge. Any assessment of the nominee's performance can only be subjective; nevertheless, in the author's view, the order of nominees in terms of performance was as follows: Long, Butcher, Baker, Cooper, Cooke, Clark. The result of the five ballots was as follows:

Table 9(7): *Result of the balloting*

Nominee	1	2	3	4	5
Long	26	24	28	38	41
Butcher	18	22	23	28	43
Baker*	15	19	18	18	–
Clark*	12	12	15	–	–
Cooke*	10	7	–	–	–
Cooper*	3	–	–	–	–
Total	84	84	84	84	84

*Sponsored nominees.

Table 9(7) illustrates a number of interesting features of the selection, and provides some indication of the factors which appeared to influence the decision of the selection conference. Whatever significance the presence of four sponsored nominees on the short-list may have had, it appeared to have little influence on the voting of delegates, unless in a negative sense. What can be seen from Table 9(7) is that two factors appear to have been important: ability and sectional support. A third factor may be added, though this is not apparent in the table: this is the influence of political views.

Only one of the four sponsored nominees, Baker, managed to survive until the third ballot, when he too was eliminated. It may be that the delegates were impressed with Butcher's success in running a football pool for his local party, a fact which he placed some emphasis on during his speech; and they may also have been impressed by Long's declaration in his replies to the questionnaire that the C.L.P. would not be liable for his personal expenses. None the less, it is difficult to avoid the conclusion that the first three nominees in the first ballot owed their positions to ability and performance rather than to any financial considerations. It is far more likely that the latter were regarded as additional rather than sole assets.

On the other hand, the continued presence of Clark until the third ballot was not a reflection of his ability nor his performance. The N.U.M. was entitled to eighteen delegates: Clark received twelve votes in each of the first two ballots and fifteen in the third. It is unlikely that the full N.U.M. delegation was present, and it is possible that some of the miners voted against their nominee: one delegate was heard to remark that 'some of the miners are unhappy about their selection'. The fact remains, however, that Clark had a firm nucleus of support consistent with the number of N.U.M. delegates who could have been present. Similarly, Cooke's support was consistent with the support he would receive from the T.G.W.U. delegation, which could muster a maximum of six: in the second ballot Cooke received seven votes. The second largest delegation, the nine members of the A.E.U., probably divided their vote between Cooke and Baker, both of whom worked in the engineering industry. It would appear that Cooper lacked the necessary nucleus of support needed to carry him past the first and, in many respects, vital ballot. It is in this ballot that trade union delegations are most likely to vote *en bloc* for their nominee, and they will continue to do so, so long as their nominee remains in the running. Nominees such as Cooper, with the potential support of only one delegate, have to rely entirely on their ability to carry them through and for the average nominee this may be asking too much against the nominees of the larger unions.

The extent to which the political views of the nominees affected the result is difficult to judge with certainty. It is clear, however, that both Butcher and Baker were left of centre in their views: both had expressed themselves strongly on the independent deterrent and nationalization, were opposed to the Common Market, and had laid stress on the party's Socialist policies. On the other hand, Long was probably centre or even right of centre: he favoured membership of the Common Market on the right conditions; his views on education accorded with those of Anthony Crosland; and he tended to follow an orthodox line of supporting party policy. This may well be the explanation of Long's failure to secure the additional five votes he needed for victory after the fourth ballot, when he already had a ten-vote lead over Butcher.

After the fifth and final ballot, the chairman called for a motion expressing the party's unanimous support for Butcher, followed by a motion approving the necessary financial agreement.[8] Both were carried unanimously.

There seems little doubt that the delegates at the conference were subject to a variety of cross-pressures. It also seems fairly clear that these pressures were not of equal importance throughout the selection. For instance, the questions of ability and political views were probably less important in the first two, possibly three, ballots, when the sectional support that some of the candidates could bring to bear played a crucial role, if only in preventing the emergence of a successful nominee at an earlier stage. To this extent, sectional voting may not have been very important in so far as it did not ultimately decide the selection. Nevertheless, this was due to the inability of any one group to dominate the conference: had the trade union delegates so wished, they could have at least ensured the presence of one of the union nominees in the final ballot. It is not without significance for the process of selection in the Labour party that some delegates are prepared to place sectional interests before the criterion of ability: there can be no other explanation of the ability of the N.U.M. nominee to reach the third ballot. The question of ability had a fairly even application throughout the ballots in so far as the leading contenders were separated largely on this matter, but as the voting came nearer to a result, it seems clear that political considerations played a vital role. Butcher's recovery from a ten-vote deficit in the fourth ballot was remarkable: there was probably not a great deal to choose between him and Long in terms of ability and performance, but there were important political differences. The political views of Butcher and Baker coincided fairly closely, and this seems to have been borne out by the fact that Butcher succeeded in securing fifteen of Baker's votes to Long's three. That Butcher was helped by one of his supporters

8. In accordance with Clause IX(4) of the Party Constitution, and Clause XII(6) of the C.L.P. Constitution.

attempting to rally support for him between the fourth and fifth ballots is important, but it is doubtful whether this could account for his success in securing five sixths of Baker's votes. In fact, it is probably more significant that Butcher's supporter was a *left-wing member of the C.L.P.*

The rest of the selection procedure was now, it seemed, a mere formality – usually it is, but not in the case of Butcher. A complaint was made to the N.E.C. 'of undue pressure before . . . the selection'.[9] Despite attempts by left-wing members of the N.E.C. to have the matter referred to the organization sub-committee, the N.E.C. ordered a new selection. The grounds of the complaint were that Butcher had entered the constituency after he had been short-listed and that some members of the C.L.P. had been canvassing on his behalf prior to the selection conference. Normally, nominees, in order to avoid accusations of this sort, are not expected to enter a constituency for which they have been short-listed. In Butcher's case he was invited to a private meeting by one of the members of the E.C. of the C.L.P. *after* he had been placed on the short-list, but *before* he had been informed. The member of the E.C. and several of his colleagues had decided that Butcher seemed the most attractive of the nominees on the short-list and therefore sought a meeting with him to confirm their views. In fact, it would appear that both parties acted innocently: there was no intention on the part of Butcher to seek any advantage over his rivals, nor did the members of the C.L.P. who had invited him seem aware that they had offended normal procedure. The national agent of the Labour party was sent to investigate the complaints and the result of her enquiries was that several members of the C.L.P. were reprimanded and a new selection ordered.

The whole process of selection began again. This time only twelve nominations were received. The questionnaire used in the first selection was again sent to all the nominees. The E.C. eventually drew up a short-list of eight nominees:

Mr Baker nominated by D.A.T.A.
Mr Clark nominated by the N.U.M. and two L.L.P.s.[10]
Mr Miller nominated by the E.T.U.

9. It has never been revealed who complained to the N.E.C.: it could have been an aggrieved nominee; or possibly a union, resentful at the rejection of its candidate; or a member of the C.L.P., either a supporter of another nominee or someone in disagreement with the successful nominee's political views.
10. Both mining villages.

Mr North nominated by an L.L.P.
Mr Short nominated by the T.S.S.A.
Mr Cooke nominated by the T.G.W.U.
Mr Cooper nominated by the U.P.W.
Mr Taylor nominated by the A.E.U.

All eight nominees were trade union sponsored, and four had been on the earlier short-list.

At the second selection conference there were sixty-five of the 111 delegates present. As before, the chairman opened the meeting and outlined the procedure to be followed. Since there were eight nominees to be seen, speeches were to be ten and not fifteen minutes, and the same applied to questions: each nominee would therefore be seen for a total of twenty minutes instead of thirty. Delegates were supplied with biographical details and nominees' replies to the questionnaire on similar lines to the first conference.

Personal preferences were again the opening gambit of the majority of nominees, and only one, Cooper, chose to make no personal reference at all. Again topics varied widely, but probably the most interesting feature was the speeches of those nominees who had appeared at the first conference. Clark can, however, be discounted, for he devoted his speech to an attack on the N.E.C.'s handling of the earlier selection. Of the other three, Cooke's speech contained much of this earlier performance, Baker's perhaps a third to a half, and Cooper's none. As before, most nominees spent their time speaking on party policy, and only Cooper chose to forego part of his time in order to receive more questions (Table 9(8)).

The shorter period allowed for questions at the second conference accounts for the lower average of questions per nominee. Both Cooper and Taylor tended to give lengthy answers and therefore had below-average totals (Table 9(9)).

Questions were again related to current political problems, but interest in foreign affairs and defence appears to have waned. At the time nine months had elapsed since Britain's failure to enter the Common Market, fears that the United Nations was in danger of disintegration had lessened, the Nuclear Test-Ban Treaty had been signed in August, and the summer had been dominated by the 'Profumo Affair' and 'Rachmanism'. The high number of personal questions is accounted for by the action of a small group of dissidents among the G.M.C., who persisted in asking questions about sponsorship and the

Table 9(8): *Details of speeches given by the nominees*

Cooke	Clark	Cooper	Baker	Short	Taylor	Miller	North
Personal	Personal Sponsorship	Economy	Personal	Personal Sponsorship	Personal Socialism	Personal Socialism	Personal Socialism
Party intellectuals		Industrial conditions	Electoral experience	Electoral experience	Nationalization	Education	Attacking opposition
Unemployment	Personal	Socialism	Trade unions	Attacking opposition	Party unity	Unemployment	
Social services		Nationalization	Socialism	Housing			
Economy			Local problems			Economy	

Table 9(9): *Questions asked by delegates per nominee*

Nominee	Number of questions	
Cooke	7	
Clark	7	
Short	8	
Taylor	3	Average
Miller	6	6·0
Cooper	5	
North	5	
Baker	7	

ability of the nominees. The chairman, on the advice of the regional organizer, ruled direct questions on sponsorship out of order. The dissidents therefore asked seven of the eight candidates whether they regarded their ability as being responsible for their presence on the short-list. Only Baker was spared this question (Table 9(10)).

The chairman then called for a motion that the meeting move to the

Table 9(10): *Subjects of questions asked by delegates*

Subject	Number of questions
Foreign affairs and defence	2
Home affairs	27
Local problems	–
Personal	15
Miscellaneous	4

selection; this was proposed and seconded. Before the vote, however, one of the dissident members of the G.M.C. alleged that Baker had been given more than ten minutes for questions. The regional organizer denied this and said that he had timed each nominee strictly. The motion that the meeting proceed to the selection was then put: fifty-seven delegates voted for the motion and seven against.[11] At the request of several delegates, the nominees were again brought before the conference and identified. In the author's view the order of the nominees in terms of performance and ability was as follows: Baker and Short (equal first), Taylor, Cooper, Cooke, Miller, Clark, and North. The result of the voting is shown in Table 9(11).

11. The chairman did not vote.

Table 9(11): Result of balloting

Nominee	1	2	3	4	5	6	7
Baker	16	23	25	25	N/A	31	39
Clark	14	11	11	11	17	–	–
Taylor	9	10	11	11	33	11	–
Cooke	8	7	–	–	–	–	–
Short	7	9	13	13	N/A	18	21
Miller	3	–	–	–	–	–	–
Cooper	3	–	–	–	–	–	–
North	nil	–	–	–	–	–	–
Abstentions	5	5	5	5	15	5	5
Total	65	65	65	65	65	65	65

* After each ballot it is normal to eliminate either the bottom candidate, or, if applicable, the two or three candidates at the foot of the poll whose total vote is less than that of the candidate immediately above. This was not possible after the third ballot, since two candidates, Clark and Taylor, each had eleven votes, and the next highest candidate, Short, only thirteen. The position was explained to the conference without revealing the names of the candidates involved and a fourth ballot was held, with exactly the same result. It was therefore decided to hold a special ballot between Clark and Taylor, and this resulted in the elimination of Clark.

The characteristics which marked the balloting at the first conference were again apparent. Ability and sectional support tended to dominate the voting, with a hint of political views playing some part towards the end. In the early ballots sectional views predominated: Clark remained a leading challenger until the special ballot in which he was eliminated; Taylor maintained his challenge on a combination of ability and sectional support; but Cooke lasted only as long as his sectional support kept him from the foot of the poll. The three nominees eliminated at the first ballot all lacked a nucleus of sectional support: Cooper's union, the U.P.W., had one delegate present, but neither Miller nor North could claim any support from their own unions, and neither had the means to overcome this handicap. The votes of these three do not appear to have gone to any particular nominee in the second ballot, in which there was a considerable shifting of support. In the third ballot over half of Cooke's votes appeared to go to Short: this was probably a reflection of Short's ability as much as anything. Clark's votes were split evenly between Baker and Short in the sixth ballot, but in the final ballot Taylor's votes swayed the selection decisively in Baker's favour: one delegate suggested that this was the result of a common industry, engineering. This seems reasonable, but it is possible that Baker's known political views also played a part. It does not seem unreasonable to suggest that once sectional loyalties have been given their full rein and expression, the choice becomes one of ability and political views. On the whole, Short's political views appeared to be more moderate than those of Baker; furthermore, there was little to choose between them in ability, and Short may well have had a slight lead in this respect. The fact that this was the second occasion on which the delegates had had the chance to see Baker may also have told in his favour. On the other hand, it was noticeable that the dissidents refrained from attacking Baker as they had done every other nominee, and the dissidents were left-wing members of the C.L.P.

Short's position in the succeeding ballots illustrates plainly the handicap with which the nominee who cannot rely on a firm nucleus of support is faced. His union, T.S.S.A., had only one delegate, and, therefore, had he not succeeded in securing the support of six other delegates in the first ballot and eight in the second, Short could easily have been eliminated. Oddly enough, it was probably the length of the short-list which saved him, for it was the inability of three of the nominees to attract more than six votes between them which raised Short to fifth place in the first ballot. Had one or more of these three candidates been able to command a greater nucleus of *sectional* support, then Short's position would have been precarious. Indeed, he escaped elimination by a mere two votes in the second ballot, and yet became Baker's most serious challenger.

After the seventh and final ballot, the chairman moved a motion calling for an expression of unanimous support for Baker, three delegates voted against this motion and four abstained. The same occurred when the motion approving the necessary financial agreement was put to the meeting. It is, of course, most unusual for these formal motions to be opposed, and that they were, was a sign of the dissatisfaction, continually expressed during the meeting, that some members of the C.L.P. felt over the previous selection. Subsequently the secretary of one of the L.L.P.s resigned in protest against the selection.

The dual selection in this constituency was a complicated affair, if only because it was the subject of much dispute within the C.L.P. Apart from the rejection of Butcher after he had been selected by the G.M.C., the main complaint was that finance had influenced the selection. There is little evidence that the G.M.C. was unduly influenced by financial considerations, but *the same is not necessarily true of the*

Executive Committee. Before short-listing in the first selection, the agent made it clear that the question of finance could not be ignored. Four out of six nominees on the first short-list were sponsored, and all the nominees on the second. A short-list of eight is unusual; a short-list of eight sponsored nominees is probably unparalleled. This C.L.P. may have been exceptional in this respect, but it illustrates clearly the complicated nature of selection.

Selection in a 'Hopeless' Seat

The constituency in this second case-study lies in a strongly Conservative area in London's commuter belt. Not even the favourable opinion polls which were then current could give Labour any hope of doing more than reducing the massive Conservative majority – victory, even in the long term, was out of the question.

The C.L.P. had in fact selected a candidate over a year earlier, but found itself disagreeing more and more with his views, until he eventually resigned and the process of selection began again. Six nominations had been received by the closing date and shortly afterwards the local executive committee met to draw up a short-list.

The executive committee has nineteen members, of whom eight attended the meeting.[12] Two of the eight were late, however, so that the meeting was not quorate during the early discussion. The secretary read out the names and biographical details of the nominees. These details were the same as those given on the 'B' List. There was some brief discussion which was mainly concerned with whether all six should be invited to the selection conference, or whether the number should be reduced. It was eventually agreed that all six should be short-listed.

Discussion now turned to the arrangement for the conference. After various proposals had been made, it was decided that each nominee should address the conference for ten minutes, followed by fifteen minutes' questions.

The meeting of the G.M.C. to discuss and approve the decisions of the E.C. was held the same evening. Of the fifty-two members eligible to attend, ten were present, including the eight members of the E.C. The secretary reported the committee's decisions to the meeting and they were approved unanimously.

It seems quite clear that the committee took the line of least resistance in recommending that all the nominees should be seen by the

12. The weather was bad.

selection conference: there is every indication that the information on which they had to make their choice was quite inadequate for doing so. Moreover, the fact that each of the nominees had been seen by his nominating body tended to reinforce the committee's decision.

The regional organizer, who acted as the representative of the N.E.C., confined his role to that of procedural adviser. Only once, when a question was asked about sponsorship, did he make a categorical statement. The chairman and the secretary did no more than their offices demanded, and only one other member of the E.C. said anything: the rest seemed content to play a passive role.

The selection conference was held a week later: twenty-five of the fifty-two members of the G.M.C. were present. The delegates were supplied with brief biographical details of the nominees, giving their name and address, age, nominating body, occupation, length of Labour party and trade union membership, local government experience, and marital status. The details for all six nominees were contained on a single quarto sheet.

The speeches of the nominees did not differ markedly in content from those heard in the first case study (Table 9(12)).

There was rather less emphasis on personal qualifications and more on policy matters: each nominee appeared to deliver his speech as though he were preaching to the unconverted rather than to the converted.

Although each nominee had been allotted fifteen minutes for questions, the chairman asked delegates to minimize their questions to save time. Instead of receiving between seven and nine questions, therefore, the nominees had only four or five questions each. Again home affairs predominated, but nearly a third of the questions concerned defence. This was probably a result of the emphasis which the Conservative party was then placing on the independent nuclear deterrent. In home affairs nearly half the questions dealt with education, probably reflecting the recent publication of the Newsom and Robbins Reports. Trade unions also figured prominently, possibly a result of Conservative pressure for an enquiry into the unions (Table 9(13)).

There was, however, no great enthusiasm on the part of the delegates in response to the nominees' speeches, nor in asking questions. This was, it appeared, part of the necessary ritual of selection.

Only two ballots[13] were held: in the first, East, South, West, and Williams were eliminated, leaving Roberts and Jackson; in the second

13. The voting figures were not announced.

Table 9(12): Details of the speeches given by the nominees

Roberts	South	East	West	Jackson	Williams
Personal	Economy	Education	Personal	Attacking opposition	Personal
Electoral experience	Social services	Housing	Electoral experience	Defence	Defence
Socialism	Transport	Social services	Socialism	Housing	Housing
Defence	Education	Nationalization	Industrial conditions	Social services	Racial discrimination
Housing	Nationalization		Social services	Education	
	Incomes policy		Education	Economy	
	Industrial conditions		Housing	Defence	
	Local problems			Foreign affairs	

ballot, Jackson was selected. There could be little doubt that the conference had selected the ablest of the nominees and Roberts was deservedly runner-up. Clearly the delegates' main concern was to select the best 'standard-bearer', the nominee who was most likely to reduce the Conservative majority and further Labour's cause in the area. Although there was one candidate who had some financial backing from his union, this factor was ignored by all but one of the delegates.

Table 9(13): *Subjects of the questions asked by delegates*

Subject	Number of questions
Foreign affairs and defence	8
Home affairs	12
Local problems	—
Personal	3
Miscellaneous	2

This selection illustrates the position of all C.L.P.s in non-Labour seats: whatever chances there may be of winning the seat, the C.L.P. must go through the proper selection procedure, unless, with the agreement of the N.E.C., the seat is not fought at all. Obviously, a C.L.P. in a Labour-held seat always assumes, and the C.L.P. in a marginal Conservative seat always hopes, that it is selecting an M.P., and the selection is conducted in that belief. In the comfortable, safe, or impregnable non-Labour constituency, the C.L.P. knows that it can offer little more to a candidate than electoral experience and the chance to make some inroad into the anti-Labour majority. In this case, and in many constituencies like it, this means that the C.L.P. has had to select a fresh candidate after each election – sometimes more than one candidate, as in this instance. But there was no sign that the C.L.P. had had any great experience of selection and the local officials relied heavily on the regional organizer for advice, although there was, throughout the proceedings, an air of 'we have been through all this before'.

A Normal Selection

The final case-study concerns a constituency in the north-west of England. The constituency has returned a Labour Member since 1945, and Labour's hold on the seat was probably strengthened by the 1948 boundary redistribution. By 1955, however, the seat had become semi-marginal, and remained so in 1959, although the constituency was one of several in the north-west which showed a pro-Labour swing in 1959.

Much of the constituency's work force is concerned with shipping, and its associated industries, but the concentration of workers in these industries does not, however, enable one or two unions to dominate the trade union section of the G.M.C., partly because the C.L.P. has placed a constitutional limitation on the number of delegates any one affiliated organization may have,[14] and partly because no one union can claim the membership of all or most of the port workers. The latter are, in fact, split among several unions, the most important of which are the T.G.W.U., the Ship-Constructors and Shipwrights' Association, the A.E.U., and the E.T.U.

Table 9(14): *Composition of the trade union section of the G.M.C.*

Trade union	Number of delegates
T.G.W.U.	9
A.S.W.	4
U.S.D.A.W.	3
E.T.U.	2
A.E.U.	2
Plumbers' Trade Union	2
Shipwrights' Association	2
C.A.W.U.	1
U.P.W.	1
A.S.S.E.T.	1
T.S.S.A.	1
T.A.	1
Total	29

Several other unions are prominent on the G.M.C., however, as Table 9(14) shows, but none is in a position to dominate the committee, and this is also true of the trade union section in general (Table 9(15)).

Over three-quarters of the delegates represent party organizations compared with less than a quarter for trade unions, whilst the Co-operative party is limited to two delegates as a result of Clause 5(b)

14. A maximum of two delegates per trade union *branch*.

Table 9(15): *Composition of the G.M.C.*

Party or affiliated organization	Number of delegates
Ward parties ⎫ Women's sections ⎬ Young Socialists ⎭	98
Co-operative party	2
Trade unions	29
Total	129

of the 1958 Agreement[15] and the delegate limitation mentioned earlier.[16]

The retiring Member had represented the seat since 1945. He was a sponsored candidate, but his union ceased to finance its candidates beyond the Parliament in which they became sixty-five. Furthermore, the Member did not enjoy good health, and his parliamentary and constituency duties had become increasingly onerous. There was no formal move on the part of the C.L.P. to force him to retire, but the announcement of his impending retirement was privately welcomed in the party.

The prescribed circular requesting nominations was sent to party and affiliated organizations, and, by the closing date, sixteen nominations had been received. One of these, nominated by U.S.D.A.W., subsequently withdrew prior to short-listing. Of the remainder, nine were sponsored and one partially sponsored. None of the nominating bodies, apart from the Co-operative party, which held its own selection conference, interviewed possible nominees prior to nomination. According to the secretary of the C.L.P., the local party was unaware of the recommendation of Transport House that possible nominees should be invited to constituency and ward meetings.[17] One ward selected three persons from the 'B' List, sent them a questionnaire, and selected one on the basis of the replies. At the ward meeting following the selection conference, however, all the ward delegates reported that they had not been impressed with their nominee and had voted for someone else.

15. See Chapter Seven, pages 191–2 above.   16. See page 266 above, footnote 14.
17. *Labour Organizer*, January 1960, p. 4. See also Chapter Five, page 155 above.

The twenty-four strong E.C. drew up a short-list of six nominees, of whom three were sponsored and one partially sponsored. The short-list was:

Mr Andrews, nominated by the Co-operative party and four other organizations, and sponsored by the Co-operative party.

Mr Edwards, nominated by a ward party.

Mr Evans, nominated by a ward party and four other organizations.

Mr Johnson, nominated by a ward party, and partially sponsored by A.S.S.E.T.

Mr Richards, nominated by the E.T.U. and two other organizations, and sponsored by the E.T.U.

Mr Robinson, nominated by the T.G.W.U. and three other organizations, and sponsored by the T.G.W.U.

In addition to the formal notice of the selection conference, the delegates also received a covering letter containing the following paragraph:

no delegate should consider himself under a Mandate to vote for any particular candidate. We are there to listen impartially to the six people on the short-list. It is then our responsibility to choose the *best candidate* – one who will win the confidence of the majority of the electors: who will have the ability and forcefulness to press the urgent claims of this constituency in Westminster and who will work with the Constituency Labour Party both to retain the seat for Labour and to serve local needs with a true Socialist spirit.

The delegates were also reminded that only those of their number who had heard all the nominees would be allowed to vote at the selection conference. Each delegate was supplied with the nominees' biographical details. These were similar to those supplied in the first case-study, but no questionnaire was sent to the nominees *by the C.L.P.* Generally speaking, each nominee's biographical details occupied a single quarto sheet: the biographies of Andrews and Johnson were the largest and most detailed, that of Richards the shortest and most perfunctory.

The selection conference was attended by 105 delegates. The N.E.C. was represented by the regional organizer, and the chairman of the C.L.P. presided. Each nominee was introduced by the regional organizer, who read brief biographical details, including, if appropriate, the fact that the nominee was sponsored. Each candidate would be seen for

Table 9(16): Details of speeches given by the nominees

Robinson	Edwards	Evans	Andrews	Johnson	Richards
Electoral experience	Socialism	Personal	Electoral experience	Attacking opposition	Personal
Local problems	Economy	Local problems	Consumers	Social services	Unemployment
Local government	Attacking opposition	Housing	Transport	Education	Industrial conditions
Unemployment	Education	Nationalization	Foreign affairs	Foreign affairs	Social services
Housing	Socialism	Attacking opposition	Defence	Local problems	Defence
Attacking opposition			Economy	Unemployment	Attacking opposition
Education				Socialism	Nationalization
Personal					Attacking opposition

a total period of thirty minutes, of which twenty minutes would be devoted to a speech and ten to questions. There would be a break of ten minutes after the third candidate had been seen.

There was much more variety in the speeches given at this selection compared with those at both the conferences in the first case-study. All six nominees had had experience as parliamentary candidates, and Andrews was a former junior Minister, but only two, Robinson and Andrews, chose to refer to this experience. All six nominees, with the exception of Andrews, came from the north-west: three made direct reference to local problems, and all five emphasized the importance of selecting an M.P. with local knowledge. In contrast, Andrews laid great stress on his political experience and allowed his speech to range widely over foreign affairs and defence, as well as home affairs. Of the remaining five, only Johnson made any reference to foreign affairs and only Richards to defence (Table 9(16)).

Table 9(17): *Questions asked by delegates per nominee*

Nominee	Number of questions
Robinson	5
Edwards	4
Evans	5
Andrews	9
Johnson	5
Richards	3

The average number of questions per nominee was 5·2. Andrews received nearly twice and Richards nearly half the average. In Andrews's case this was a clear reflection of his experience as an M.P. and junior Minister, and probably, also, a reflection of the delegates' desire to question him fairly closely.[18] In Richards's case it was simply a reflection of his inability to deal effectively with questions.

Of the four conferences described in this chapter, only here were any questions asked about local problems. At the time of the conference there was a great deal of discussion about local transport developments and proposed changes in local government, a discussion in which the constituency found itself at odds with most of the other local authorities concerned. Feelings on these issues were therefore particularly

18. There appeared to be some suspicion of Andrews, both as the Co-operative nominee and the only 'carpet-bagger'.

sensitive. Apart from this, however, questions on home affairs predominated.

In the author's view, the order of nominees in terms of performance was as follows: Andrews and Johnson (equal first), Evans, Robinson, Edwards, and Richards. Three ballots were held:[19] Robinson and Edwards were eliminated in the first ballot, Richards was eliminated in the second, and in the third Johnson had a clear majority. By the third ballot, two of the sponsored candidates, Robinson and Richards, had

Table 9(18): Subjects of the questions asked by delegates

Subject	Number of questions
Foreign affairs and defence	2
Home affairs	15
Local problems	9
Personal	1
Miscellaneous	4

been eliminated, and one, Andrews, and the partially sponsored Johnson, remained, together with the unsponsored Evans. There were two interesting features in the balloting: the failure to reject Richards until the second ballot, and Johnson's ability to defeat two other nominees in the third ballot.

There can be little doubt that Richards was by far the poorest of the nominees: he was hesitant in his speech, then he forgot it and had to read it; he seemed unable to introduce any cohesion into his address and his attempt to ridicule the then Prime Minister by suddenly producing a newspaper photograph of him failed because he temporarily mislaid it. Richards's success in surviving the first ballot is probably attributable to his being the only *industrial* trade unionist among the six nominees. Robinson, who is a member of the T.G.W.U. and on its parliamentary panel, was asked why he, a solicitor, belonged to the T.G.W.U., and an attempt was made to put a similar question to Evans, a barrister and member of the N.U.G.M.W. It seems reasonable to suggest that Richards was the beneficiary of a substantial union vote based, not on his own union, which had only two delegates, but on his position as the only working class trade unionist on the short-list.[20]

Johnson's success in the third ballot was perhaps surprising against

19. The voting figures were not announced.
20. This was the opinion of the secretary of the C.L.P.

a man of Andrews's experience and the presence of a third nominee. Johnson, however, had a strong advantage in age – he was ten years younger than Andrews – and he had had wide academic, industrial, and political experience combined with a knowledge and appreciation of local problems. Andrews was less well qualified academically and industrially, and, although possessing considerable political experience, could not match Johnson's local connections. He was, moreover, the Co-operative nominee, and there had been some recent anti-Co-operative feeling in the C.L.P.[21] Andrews himself also felt that he had not made a good impression on the delegates. Johnson undoubtedly impressed the conference with his fervour and sincerity, and although one delegate did ask the regional organizer to repeat the terms of Johnson's partial sponsorship when he was first introduced, it is extremely doubtful whether the question of sponsorship had any substantive influence in his selection.

The chairman then moved the formal motion approving Johnson's selection, and the regional organizer asked for a formal resolution approving the financial arrangements for the candidature. *Before* this resolution was passed, however, a delegate again asked for details of Johnson's partial sponsorship. This was a technical infringement of the 1957 amendment of the Hastings Agreement, although no action was taken by the Chairman nor the regional organizer, and the selection was not subsequently invalidated by the N.E.C.[22]

The selection in this case was decided largely on the merit of the nominees, but the delegates were subject to a number of cross-pressures, some positive, some negative. Some delegates at least gave consideration to financial factors; some felt bound to vote for the only industrial trade unionist; others resented Andrews as the Co-operative nominee; others resented Robinson as a non-industrial member of the T.G.W.U.; whilst a substantial proportion of delegates placed much importance on local considerations. By and large it was a fair selection, but it illustrated many of the problems of selection as reflected in the words of the secretary of the C.L.P.: 'The whole method of selection, I feel, is hit and miss, a bit like being thrown in the deep end to learn to swim.'[23]

21. Andrews was asked two hostile questions: one on the Co-operative attitude towards the nationalization of insurance, and the other on the failure of the Co-operative party to affiliate to the Labour party at national level.

22. A complaint to the N.E.C. would have been necessary, of course.

23. It is significant that at one point during the selection conference the author's advice was asked on a procedural matter.

Part Four

CHAPTER TEN

The Selection of Parliamentary Candidates in the Conservative and Labour Parties: Conclusions

The distribution of power within the British political parties is primarily a function of cabinet government and the British parliamentary system. So long as the parties accept this system of government effective decision-making authority will reside with the leadership groups thrown up by the parliamentary parties; and they will exercise this authority so long as they retain the confidence of their respective Parliamentary parties. The views of their organized supporters outside Parliament must inevitably be taken into account by the party leadership because of the importance of the role these supporters play in *selecting candidates*, raising funds, and promoting the cause of the party during elections. But, whatever the role granted in theory to the extra-parliamentary wings of the parties, in practice final authority rests in *both* parties with the parliamentary party and its leadership. *In this fundamental respect the distribution of power within the two major parties is the same.*[1]

Robert McKenzie's summary of his thesis stresses the importance of recognizing the similarities which exist between the Conservative and Labour parties, similarities which he attributes to the common framework which both parties accept and within which both must therefore work. This is reflected not only in the *distribution of power* within the two parties, however, but in their organization and procedures. Neither party can function successfully without adequate local organization within the framework of territorial parliamentary constituencies, each

1. McKenzie, op. cit., p. 635. (Author's italics.)

returning a single Member. Despite the fact that approximately two thirds of the seats in Parliament may be regarded as safe for one or other of the two major parties, uncontested elections are rare[2] and each local party must normally go through the motions of a formal election campaign, however bleak the prospects of its candidate.

A candidate must therefore be found and some form of selection procedure, formal or informal, elaborate or simple, must be employed. For the local party, whether it is merely selecting a standard-bearer or, more especially, an M.P.-designate, this is a moment of real power, perhaps the only time when its decision can make an impact beyond the bounds of the constituency. It is a power that the local parties guard most jealously, especially where their choice involves the selection of an M.P.-designate. It would be misleading to regard the power of local parties over selection as entirely contrary to McKenzie's thesis, however, for a measure of control lies with the national party. It is true, of course, that this control is only negative: neither party can ensure the selection of a particular individual, but both can veto a selection should circumstances demand it. It is not unreasonable to argue that *local autonomy over selection is the prize which the national parties must pay for adequate local organization*.

It is not surprising, therefore, to find that the Conservative and Labour parties have much in common in the selection of candidates. For instance, both use a combination of selection and election: a relatively small body examines the applicants or nominees for the vacancy and makes certain recommendations to a larger body, which in turn normally elects one of the recommended candidates. Similarly, selection remains in the hands of comparatively few people, not only within the constituency but within the local party itself. At national level both parties maintain lists of approved candidates which are available to local parties. And the most important similarity of all is the existence of local autonomy over selection, in spite of the fact that representatives of the national organization normally attend selection meetings.

Nevertheless, there are important, perhaps fundamental differences, both in the formal procedures and the factors which influence selection in the two parties.

Selection in the Labour party is subject to the rules laid down in the Party and C.L.P. constitutions and no C.L.P. may depart from the prescribed procedure. Under this procedure no individual may *apply*

2. In the four general elections between 1955 and 1966 all constituencies were contested.

for the vacancy; he must be nominated by a party or affiliated organization. There is no formal procedure for interviewing nominees prior to their appearance before the selection conference and, apart from the general adoption meeting held shortly before the election campaign (which for obvious reasons must be a formality), the decision of the selection conference is final as far as the C.L.P. is concerned. The N.E.C. may overrule the G.M.C. and refuse to endorse its choice, but this is the exception rather than the rule. At no time, therefore, is the selected candidate submitted to the approval of the general membership of the C.L.P., other than when the withholding of such approval would be virtually unthinkable.

There is no *formal* selection procedure in the Conservative party, however, although a fairly detailed advisory[3] pamphlet is made available by Central Office and most local associations follow a basically similar procedure. At the same time, variations in procedure are not only permissible but fairly common. Individuals may apply for vacancies and there is no system of nomination by party bodies. The interviewing of applicants prior to short-listing is normal, after which successful applicants appear before a body similar in form and composition to the Labour G.M.C. The decision of the executive council is subject to the approval of a general meeting of the association. A *second* general meeting is held at the beginning of the election campaign, when the candidate is formally adopted. The selection is *not* subject to the *formal* endorsement of the national party, since approval is sought prior to selection.

These procedural differences are important and offer a partial explanation of the factors which influence selection in the two parties. For instance, the federative nature of the Labour party is reflected in its selection procedure and many of the cross-pressures which affect the selectors are the direct result of the formal divisions within the Labour party. In this sense the Labour party is very much concerned that, to adapt a tenet of natural justice, not only should democracy be done, but it should be seen to be done. It is not therefore unusual to find greater concern with the *democratic* nature of the selection procedure than with its *efficiency*.

The lack of any formal procedure renders Conservative party selection more flexible and more amenable to local considerations and

3. The selection pamphlet occasionally adopts an authoritative tone, in fact, with the use of words like 'should' (p. 5) and 'must' (p. 9), and phrases like 'It must be clearly understood . . .' (p. 4), 'should be severely discouraged . . .' (p. 7) and 'the Party does not approve . . .' (p. 7).

the circumstances in which the selection is taking place. It is generally more exhaustive than Labour procedure (partly because the selectors have to consider a larger number of names initially) and is much more concerned with producing a satisfactory *result* than a patently satisfactory *method*. Similarly, the rejection of a nomination procedure in favour of applications from individuals gives added flexibility to the procedure by widening the initial choice, whereas the Labour system of nomination is unduly restrictive and places a heavy responsibility on party and affiliated organizations which they are often poorly equipped to undertake.

Furthermore, because it has formalized its divisions, both in nomination and representation, the Labour party invariably has built-in cross-pressures in selection which militate against the efficiency of the selection procedure. Cross-pressures are inevitable – each delegate may have his own idea of what sort of candidate is required, and each may be justified, but all too often these are over-shadowed by sectional considerations. Similarly, the financial problems which face many C.L.P.s may play an undue part, especially in the early stages of selection, and the temptation to short-list or select a sponsored candidate is strong. The question of sectional and financial considerations come together, moreover, when the sponsoring body is a powerful group in the C.L.P. These are problems which the Labour party has been unable to solve, if only because their solution probably threatens the very existence of the Labour party in its present form.

Ability, of course, counts for a great deal, but it should count for much more in the Labour party. It is doubtless possible to make out a case for certain constituencies to be represented by individuals with a certain background – this has always been the argument of the miners – but no political party can afford to discourage men of talent because their antecedents are not to the taste of those they seek to represent.

The Conservative party has solved many of these problems, though not always by design; in many respects the Labour party is the victim whereas the Conservative party is the beneficiary of its history. Neither party can claim to be a microcosm of the nation and both are affected by social factors in the selection of candidates. Although the selection procedure used by the Conservative party is normally efficient, it cannot however, eradicate the social background against which selection takes place. The most efficient part of Conservative selection procedure is the selection committee, which will normally produce a short-list of the ablest and, in its view, most suitable applicants. It is inevitable that suitability becomes a criterion of selection when the latter is unaffected by built-in divisions, and concepts of what constitutes suitability vary. When it comes to the executive council stage, therefore, it is not surprising that suitability should sometimes overshadow ability. Seldom is ability enough: a candidate must be suitable and selection becomes a matter of judgement tinged by personal preference. A man's appearance, his demeanour, his personality, his marital status, his wife (if he has one), his religion may all render an applicant more or less suitable in the eyes of the selectors. It may be right, and indeed wise, that the selectors should choose an applicant with whom they feel they can work, but there are times when a local association stops short of selecting a young and able applicant who perhaps lacks the orthodoxy of his rivals: the temptation to play safe is often strong. The question of suitability is sometimes applied to unequal rivals, to the detriment of the more able applicant, instead of as a means of resolving a deadlock between applicants of equal merit.

It is against these considerations that the following conclusions should be seen.

The Conservative Party

1. The selection of parliamentary candidates is primarily the concern of local Conservative associations. The national party, whilst retaining overall surveillance of the standard of candidates, and, to some extent, the functioning of selection machinery, can normally influence a particular selection only in a negative sense.

2. Only a small proportion of the total membership of a local association is directly involved in the selection of a candidate and it is doubtful whether this is ever more than the most active 1 per cent. Furthermore, this normally means that only officers of the association, branch officers, or members of the executive council play a *substantive* part in selection: persons who are simply *members* of the association are involved only in the general meeting at which the recommended candidate is adopted.

3. Although there is a general uniformity of selection procedure, regardless of the electoral status of the seat, this is the result of practice and advice and is not imposed by *formal* party rules enforced by sanctions emanating from national level.

4. Because there is no *nationally imposed* uniformity or procedure there is considerable variation in *detailed* procedure. This means that a local association, having selected one candidate, will not

necessarily follow exactly the same procedure the next time it selects a candidate.

5. Associations in Conservative-held constituencies or non-Conservative marginal seats are fully aware that they either are or may be selecting an M.P.; associations in hopeless seats know that they are merely looking for a candidate, a standard-bearer.

6. The system of *applying* for vacancies rather than nomination by local party bodies provides a local association with a wide initial choice. The foundation of this process is the willingness of local associations to accept lists of possible candidates from the national party organization.

7. The individual most likely to be in a position to exert personal influence in a selection (especially before and during the selection committee stage) is the chairman of the association rather than the constituency agent.

8. As a method of reducing a large number of applicants to a manageable number, the selection committee is probably an efficient method, and any shortcomings are probably attributable to the prejudices and preconceptions of the selectors.

9. Within the context of social background, the nature of the constituency and any arbitrary criteria it may have laid down, the primary consideration of the selection committee is one of ability. Political considerations seldom have any bearing on the deliberations of the selection committee.

10. Short-lists are normally minimized in order to assist the executive council in its final choice.

11. Once the selection is beyond the short-list stage, neither the selection committee nor the officers of the association can normally influence the course of the selection.

12. The applicants' biographical details supplied to members of the executive council are generally adequate, given that they are normally systematically presented and given the criteria on which the council bases its decision.

13. Most applicants' speeches are political in content and are usually delivered in the form of an election campaign speech. Personal references are common, but they do not normally constitute a major part of a speech. Although the speeches may provide some indication of an applicant's ability, or lack of it, they are principally a test of his effectiveness as a platform speaker.

14. The questions put to applicants usually concern recent political

events and current party policy. There is usually an emphasis on home compared with foreign affairs and defence, and national problems normally take precedence over local problems.

15. Council members are clearly influenced by the performance of applicants and it is probably upon this that they base their decisions. In fact, the absence of built-in sectional divisions and political considerations makes it more likely that this is the case.

16. The most important *single* factor is probably personality, the assessment of which is based almost entirely on the performance of the applicants.

17. Both performance and personality are viewed within the context of suitability for the particular constituency.

18. Council members are subject to a number of cross-pressures, among them age, marital status, religion, occupation, political and non-political experience, all or some of which may affect a particular selection, but each will normally be seen as rendering an applicant more or less suitable for the constituency rather than as an isolated factor.

19. The primary consideration in non-Conservative seats is to find a candidate who can fulfil the demands of the election campaign and all other factors are subordinate to this.

20. The general meeting of the association, which must approve the executive council's choice, is normally a formality.

21. There is no reason to believe that the selection of Conservative candidates is *procedurally* inefficient and any failings of the system are probably due to the attitudes of the selectors.

The Labour Party

1. The selection of candidates is primarily the concern of constituency Labour parties. The national party, whilst retaining overall surveillance of the standard of candidates and the proper functioning of selection machinery, can normally influence a particular selection only in a negative sense.

2. Whether the constituency is held by Labour or not, and regardless of the majority of the incumbent party, the *formal* selection procedure does not vary.

3. C.L.P.s in Labour-held constituencies or non-Labour marginals are fully aware that they either are or may be selecting an M.P.; C.L.P.s in hopeless seats know that they are merely looking for a candidate, a standard-bearer.

4. The process of nomination is usually haphazard: nominating bodies, with the possible exception of some trade unions and the Co-operative party, find it difficult to choose a nominee, both in terms of method and criteria.

5. Nomination probably limits the choice of a C.L.P. since there is no machinery for dealing with direct applications for a vacancy: these can be indirect and informal only.

6. An experienced agent is in a potentially powerful position to influence nominations, either by judicious advice or the judicious withholding of information.

7. It is the E.C. rather than the G.M.C. which is more likely to be concerned with financial considerations, since the former is more conversant with the C.L.P.'s financial position.

8. In drawing up the short-list, the E.C. may pay considerable attention to the feelings of affiliated organizations, to the number of nominations received by each nominee, to local susceptibilities, and, furthermore, is more open than the G.M.C. to pressure from forceful individuals among its members. C.L.P.s therefore tend to have larger short-lists than Conservative associations, since the cross-pressures are normally greater.

9. Once the selection is beyond the short-list stage, the E.C. has little control over it.

10. Attendance at the selection conference is likely to be fairly high compared with a normal G.M.C. meeting.[4]

11. The nominees' biographical details supplied to delegates are generally inadequate and poorly presented. It is often difficult to compare the paper qualifications of the nominees because there is no systematic form of presentation.

12. Although personal references are common, most nominees' speeches are essentially political in content, invariably taking the form of an electoral campaign speech. On the whole, the speeches tend to illustrate the nominees' effectiveness as platform speakers rather than their suitability as M.P.s and/or candidates.

13. Delegates' questions to the nominees are usually related to recent political events and discussion, and there is a marked emphasis on home affairs compared with foreign affairs and defence. Questions

4. The average attendance at G.M.C. meetings in the C.L.P. in the first case-study is twenty-five to thirty, compared with eighty-four at the first selection conference and sixty-five at the second. The rise in attendance is generally attributed to the higher turnout of trade union delegates.

on local matters are normally important only when there is a current local problem of some dimensions.

14. It is unlikely that delegates are unaffected by the performance of the nominees on the platform, but this is probably only one of a number of cross-pressures.

15. Nominees who appear before the conference early in the proceedings may be at a disadvantage since delegates appear to have difficulty in distinguishing between nominees.[5] This is partly a time factor,[6] but it also suggests that short-lists of six or more are too long.

16. Normally trade union delegates will support their own nominee as long as he remains in the ballot. The *general* union support for one nominee in the final case-study was probably exceptional in so far as it is unusual for there to be only one industrial trade unionist on a short-list in a Labour-held seat.

17. The political views of nominees may be of great importance, but it is difficult to establish that this is always the case.

18. Sectional considerations are at least as important as political considerations, but these vary according to the constituency, the short-list, and the quality of the nominees.

19. The most important *single* factor is probably quality, but the assessment of quality is based almost entirely on the performance of the nominees, and may be pre-judged by sectional and political considerations.

20. The cross-pressures to which delegates are subject alter from predominantly sectional to predominantly qualitative considerations as the short-list is reduced, unless there is an overriding political schism in the G.M.C.

21. In non-Labour seats the primary consideration is to find an adequate candidate and the selection is governed by the needs of the forthcoming election campaign. None the less, sectional and political cross-pressures may still affect the selection.

5. Before the ballot at the second selection conference in the first study, delegates requested that the nominees appear again for purposes of identification.

6. In the first study, the first selection conference lasted 3 hours, 45 minutes (six nominees); the second conference, 4 hours, 15 minutes (eight nominees). In the second study, the conference lasted 2 hours, 5 minutes (six nominees). In the third, 4 hours, 10 minutes (six nominees). These times, however, must be seen in the context of the minimum time possible for each conference, i.e. the total time made available for nominees' speeches and delegates' questions: this was 3 hours at the first and 2 hours, 40 minutes, at the second conference in the first study; 2 hours, 30 minutes in the second study, where the time was reduced by the failure of delegates to utilize the full period for questions; and 3 hours in the third. This meant that at the first conference in the first study procedural matters and balloting took only 45 minutes, compared with an hour and a half at the second conference and just over an hour in the third study.

Statistical Notes

The statistics for this study are based on the period 1950–66, excluding the General Election of 1950, but including that of 1966, and also including every by-election which fell between those two dates. In effect, therefore, this meant that the selection of every Conservative and Labour candidate between 1950 and 1966 was examined. This realized a total of 3,760: 1,850 Conservative and 1,910 Labour candidates. A fundamental distinction was drawn between the candidates selected by incumbent parties and those selected by non-incumbent parties. Some adjustments were made to take into account the redistribution of seats which occurred in 1954 (this was why the General Election of 1950 was excluded – the 1948 Redistribution being so drastic that it was impossible to compare the majority of old and new constituencies), and where a sitting Member moved from one constituency to another, either as a result of redistribution or choice, he was included only if he was selected for an entirely new constituency; selection for a substantially reconstituted constituency was ignored. For analytical purposes, the Labour selections were divided into three groups according to the party or affiliated organization financially responsible for the candidature, that is the C.L.P., trade union, and Co-operative party candidates.

Each selection was examined on two broad bases: the constituency and the candidate.

The Constituencies

(a) Electoral classification

All constituencies were classified as follows: the majority of the incumbent party was expressed as a percentage of the total votes cast, thus enabling all constituencies to be compared on a common basis, regardless of the size of the electorate or the percentage poll in any one constituency. In each case the general election immediately preceding was used. Constituencies were divided into five categories:

(i) Marginal: majority less than 5 per cent of the total votes cast.
(ii) Semi-marginal: majority 5 to 10·9 per cent of the total votes cast.
(iii) Comfortable: majority 11 to 16·9 per cent of the total votes cast.
(iv) Safe: majority 17 to 30 per cent of the total votes cast.
(v) Impregnable: majority over 31 per cent of the total votes cast.

This classification was first used by Finer, Berrington, and Bartholomew (op. cit.), and was more recently used by B. R. Mitchell and Klaus Boehm in *British Parliamentary Election Results, 1950-64* (London, 1966), and *The Gallup Analysis of the Election '66* (London, 1966). Where the non-incumbent party's candidate had come third or lower in the poll at the preceding general election, an adjustment was made to the relative safeness or marginality of the seat.

(b) Urban and Rural Character

Following Mitchell and Boehm (op. cit), constituencies were divided into four categories according to the relative concentration of urban or rural population:

(i) Primarily urban: those with an urban proportion of the population of 75 per cent or over.
(ii) Mixed, with urban areas predominating: 50 to 74·9 per cent urban population.
(iii) Mixed, with rural areas predominating: 25 to 49·9 per cent urban population.
(iv) Primarily rural: less than 25 per cent urban population.

Urban population was defined as those people living in (a) boroughs or urban districts with a population of 5,000 or more; or (b) in smaller boroughs or urban districts which are contiguous with others with a total population of 5,000 or more; or (c) civil parishes (registration districts in Scotland) of an urban or suburban character which are contiguous with boroughs or urban districts with a population of 5,000 or more. Both the 1951 and 1961 Censuses were used according to which was the most appropriate.

(c) Region

All constituencies were divided into one of eleven groups, according to geographical location, as follows:

(i) North-East.
(ii) North-West.
(iii) Yorkshire.
(iv) Midlands.
(v) London.
(vi) Home Counties and South.
(vii) West Country.
(viii) Eastern England.
(ix) Wales and Monmouth.
(x) Scotland.
(xi) Northern Ireland.

Regions (i), (ii), and (iii) were also grouped together as the Northern Region.

The Candidates

Each candidate was classified according to electoral experience, age, sex, marital status, education, occupation, local connections, and local government experience. These are further explained where necessary.

(a) Age

Since the date of every candidate's selection is not known, candidates' ages were calculated according to the date of the relevant general or by-election, and candidates were divided into six categories:

(i) Under 30 years of age.
(ii) 30–39 years of age.
(iii) 40–49 years of age.
(iv) 50–59 years of age.
(v) 60 years of age or over.
(vi) Not known.

(b) Education

Candidates were divided into five categories:

(i) Elementary: candidates whose full-time education terminated at elementary school and including candidates who had further education at night school, adult education courses, etc.

(ii) Elementary/secondary plus: candidates who, after attending elementary or secondary schools, had some form of technical or teacher training.

(iii) Secondary: candidates whose full-time education terminated at secondary level.

(iv) University: all graduates, including attendance at the Inns of Court and various military colleges.

(v) Not known.

The public school background of candidates was also examined, including attendance at one of the nine Clarendon schools (as defined by the Royal Commission on Public Schools, 1864), i.e. Eton, Harrow, Winchester, Charterhouse, Shrewsbury, Rugby, Westminster, St Paul's, and Merchant Taylors'. Public schools in general comprised members of the Headmasters' Conference and the Association of Governing Bodies of Public Schools, together with the list of overseas public schools and the list of principal girls' schools published annually in *Whitaker's Almanack*.

These were basically the categories used by Finer, *et al.* (op. cit.).

The university background of candidates was analysed according to whether they had attended Oxford or Cambridge on the one hand, or other universities or degree-awarding institutions on the other.

(c) Occupation

Candidates were divided into five categories:

(i) Workers: self-explanatory, but including all full-time trade union officials.

(ii) Professional: lawyers, doctors, dentists, school, university and adult education teachers, retired officers of the regular forces, and all recognized professions.

(iii) Business: all employers, directors of public and private companies, business executives, stockbrokers, farmers and landowners, and small businessmen.

(iv) Miscellaneous: housewives, professional politicians, welfare workers, local government officers, insurance agents and estate valuers, journalists, party publicists, professional party organizers, and miscellaneous administrators.

These are the categories used by D. E. Butler in the Nuffield Election Studies and by Finer, *et al.*, op. cit., but following the latter's practice of classifying by the subject's current or most recent occupation rather than the former's practice of using the earliest or formative occupation.

(d) Local Connections

Candidates were divided into four categories:

(i) Direct connections: including born in the immediate locality, a member of a local government body within the constituency, or within which the constituency lies, known to live or work in the locality, a member of the local party.

(ii) Area connections: including membership of a local government body in an area adjacent to or within the same county as the constituency – generally similar but less specific connections than (i) above.

(iii) Regional connections: known to have connections with a wider area in which the constituency lies, e.g. midlands, north-west, etc.

(iv) None known: self-explanatory.

Labour candidates were also classified according to their membership of trade unions affiliated to the Trades Union Congress and according to the length of their party membership. Sponsored candidates in particular were classified according to whether they had held union or co-operative office on a part-time or full-time basis. Finally, all candidates selected by non-incumbent parties were grouped according to whether they had been re-selected for the same constituency or not.

The Scottish Conservative and Unionist and the Ulster Unionist Parties

Although a Conservative Prime Minister or Leader of the Opposition is accepted as party leader by both the Scottish Conservative and Unionist party[1] and the Ulster Unionist party, the party organization based on Central Office in London has no jurisdiction over either party. This applies equally to selection: 'Neither the Vice-Chairman [of the party organization] nor the [Standing Advisory] Committee has any jurisdiction over candidates in Scotland or Northern Ireland.'[2] Apart from the strong tendency for Scottish and Ulster constituency associations to select Scotsmen and Ulstermen respectively, and the marked absence of electoral experience among Ulster Unionist candidates, the factors which influence their selection differ very little from those which pertain in English and Welsh constituencies. There are some procedural differences, however.

The Scottish Conservative and Unionist Party

At national level there is a Scottish equivalent of the S.A.C.C., but responsibility for parliamentary candidates is in the hands of the party chairman, *not* the vice-chairman. The party chairman is, of course, appointed by the Leader of the party. It is therefore the chairman who maintains a list of potential candidates. Apart from this, the procedure is basically similar.[3] To qualify for the list, applicants must satisfy the

1. Until 1965 known as the Unionist Party in Scotland.
2. Selection pamphlet, p. 2.
3. The Scottish Conservative and Unionist Central Office publishes a brief outline of procedure, *Notes for Guidance in the Selection of Candidates*, similar in many respects to the Central Office (London) pamphlet quoted above, though less detailed.

Candidates' Interview Board, which checks an applicant's references and interviews him. As in England and Wales, the chairman assists constituency associations by supplying a list of suitable applicants, but takes no other part in selection, which remains the prerogative of the local association.

The Ulster Unionist Party

There is no Ulster equivalent of the S.A.C.C. and no official list of potential candidates. The Ulster Unionist Council plays no part in selection and a candidature is entirely a matter for the constituency association.[4] It is also largely a personal relationship between the candidate and the association: most of the election expenses are still borne by the candidate, for instance.[5] Applications for a candidature are made direct to the association chairman, usually in response to a newspaper advertisement. The number of applicants will not normally be high by Conservative standards, and this means that, provided no applicant is patently unsatisfactory, all applicants will be interviewed by the selection committee. The recommendation of the selection committee will then be placed before an extraordinary general meeting of the association, and there is, therefore, no equivalent of the executive council stage found in England, Wales, and Scotland.

4. For instance, the Council does not publish any literature on selection procedure.
5. *Daily Telegraph*, 14 June 1963.

The Selection of Trade Union Parliamentary Panels

Between 1950 and 1966, thirty-six unions were financially responsible, under the terms of the Hastings Agreement with the Labour party, for one or more candidates. Inevitably the methods by which these candidates were selected by their respective unions vary considerably, whilst the qualifications demanded vary from nominal union membership to strictly enforced rules concerning age, length of membership, place of work, and so on.

Similarly, the size of union panels varies considerably, from the A.E.U., with an actual panel of nearly forty and a potential panel of fifty (the maximum it is prepared to sponsor), to a number of small unions which are limited to a single candidate. Limits are sometimes laid down in union rules: this is the case with the N.U.R., A.S.L.E.F., C.A.W.U., and A.S.W., for example. In other cases the maximum size of the panel is based on financial considerations – the number of candidates a union feels it can afford to support.

It follows, of course, that in the case of most of the smaller unions any branch which wishes to nominate a member of the parliamentary panel is likely to be severely limited in its choice. A few unions are willing to consider sponsoring any member of the union who first secures a seat, but the majority insist on sponsored candidates being drawn from the panel; and one, U.S.D.A.W., even imposes a system of seniority[1] on its panel, although this does not always work out in practice. The larger unions, however, provide a wider choice, and although the union executive will normally have a right of veto, the choice is usually left to the branch: the executive will be far more

1. U.S.D.A.W. Rules, 1961: Parliamentary Representative Scheme, Section 2.

concerned with the *constituency* than the candidate. Some of the larger unions hold a local 'selection conference' in order to select someone from the panel: this practice is widespread in the N.U.M., where the local miners' lodges normally choose the nominee; others, such as the A.E.U., leave the selection of the nominee to the union's district committees: thus among the candidates sponsored by the A.E.U. the majority have held union office at district level or above.

The majority of unions allow their full-time officials to become members of the panel, although several unions, among them the A.U.B.T.W., C.A.W.U., N.U.G.M.W., T.G.W.U., and T.S.S.A., discourage officials from seeking parliamentary candidatures, largely because of the serious effect this may have on union administrative resources. Only a few unions (e.g. the N.U.R. and the Patternmakers) have rules which make officials ineligible for consideration. Whilst often preserving union administrative resources, this practice of discouraging officials from seeking parliamentary careers has cut off a useful source of recruitment to union panels, as the N.U.G.M.W. found when it introduced this policy before the 1950 election.

The majority of unions do not impose any age limits on members of the panel, but members of the panels of D.A.T.A., the A.E.U., N.U.R., and T.S.S.A. must retire from the panel at sixty, provided they are not sitting M.P.s or prospective candidates, and of the A.U.F.W., N.U.G.M.W., A.S.L.E.F., the Tobacco Workers' Union, and the Durham and Derbyshire Areas of the N.U.M. at sixty-five. All these unions, except the A.E.U. and A.U.F.W., also impose an age limit of sixty-five on M.P.s, after which the union ceases to sponsor them. On the other hand, most unions demand a minimum period of union membership as a basic qualification for the panel. This ranges from one year in the U.P.W. to seven in the A.E.U., with most unions favouring a period of five years.

Within these limitations, any member of a union is eligible for membership of its parliamentary panel, provided, of course, he or she pays the union's political levy. The area qualification imposed by the N.U.M. has already been mentioned,[2] and the only comparable condition laid down by another union is that of the N.U.R. which stipulates that all members of the panel must be employed by the British Transport Commission.[3]

In spite of the fact that the means by which candidates are chosen

2. See Chapter Six, page 173, above.
3. N.U.R. Rules, Rule 20, Clause 10.

by unions is subject to important variations, it is possible to divide the methods used into four groups:

1. Unions which have no regular panel

This group includes trade unions whose panels have lapsed completely, those whose panel has lapsed temporarily, those who leave the initiative to individual members of the union, and those who select a candidate only when necessary. A number of smaller unions have allowed their panels to lapse completely, with the result that sponsorship has either ceased or has been restricted to one, or possibly two, candidates. Others, such as the South Wales and Durham Areas of the N.U.M., only select a candidate when a vacancy occurs in a constituency in the area, whilst the N.U.R. selects union members from the Labour party's 'B' List of candidates.

2. Nomination by branches followed by a ballot of the union

Within this broad category practice varies widely: some unions select annually, some biennially, some after each general election, and others at irregular intervals. Examples of trade unions in this category are the U.T.F.W.A., T.S.S.A., U.S.D.A.W., the Lancashire and Yorkshire Areas of the N.U.M., C.A.W.U., A.S.L.E.F., and A.S.W.

3. Nomination by branches and selection by committee

These fall into two groups: those in which the committee's decisions are subject to ratification by the union conference, and those in which they are not. For example, the E.T.U., N.U.G.M.W., T.G.W.U., D.A.T.A., and the Derbyshire and Nottinghamshire Areas of the N.U.M.

4. Nomination by branches and selection by committee and examination

Only four unions use examinations to select candidates: B.I.S.A.K.T.A., the A.E.U., the Scottish Area of the N.U.M. and the Boot and Shoe Operatives. In 1962 B.I.S.A.K.T.A.'s examination consisted of five essay questions to be answered in two sessions of two hours each. The questions were all entirely political in content, with one exception which could be described as industrial-political.

The A.E.U.'s selection procedure is more elaborate and candidates are examined over a period of two days. They are divided into two groups, one of which is interviewed whilst the other takes part in a debate. This is followed by individual speeches from the candidates. The following day the candidates are subjected to a two-hour written examination – this was the position in 1963. Since then the A.E.U. has adopted more sophisticated methods of testing applicants, although the basic format remains the same.[4]

It is very difficult to assess the efficiency of these various methods of selection. None the less, however democratic it may be, there is little to be said, from the point of view of efficiency, for a ballot of the union. This normally means that nominees must be known nationally, and this is not necessarily a sufficient recommendation for membership of the panel. It often leads to odd results, such as the selection of a particular area's 'favourite son' merely because the area has the largest number of votes; or, as happened to one union, the 'wrong' candidate is selected because confusion arises over identification. It is probable that selection by interview or examination, or both, is far more likely to produce suitable candidates, or at least eliminate the most unsuitable. The success of the A.E.U. in securing so many constituencies may be due to the efficiency of its methods of selection (though the subsequent training of candidates probably plays its part), but it is difficult to be certain. The use of examinations by other unions does not appear to have produced conspicuous results, though this may be due to other factors, such as the size and nature of the union. This in itself suggests that the A.E.U. training programme is an important factor in securing nominations in Labour selections. It certainly seems of some significance that the larger and more general unions have greater success than the smaller craft unions, but this too can be attributed to the size and nature of the unions concerned, and it may be that the part played by the selection of parliamentary panels is one of emphasis rather than cause.

4. See D. M. Heap, 'The Trade Union M.P.', *A.E.U. Journal*, March 1967.

Index

Aberdare, 189
Aberdeenshire, West, 3
Abertillery, 238, 242
Accrington, 65, 67
Adoption, *see under* Candidates, adoption of
Age: influence of in Conservative selection, 72–3, 96, 115; influence of in Labour selection, 208–9, 221
Agents, Conservative party: role of in selection, 36, 49, 104, 108, 115, 118, 123, 280
Agents, Labour party: eligibility for nomination, 133–4; role of in selection, 246–7, 282
Agricultural Workers, National Union of (N.U.A.W.), 169, 234, 236, 243, 244
Aitchison, Craigie, 144
Alford, R. R., 84n
Altrincham and Sale, 13n
Anderson, D. C., 24–5
Anderson, Miss M. B. H., 64n
Antrim, and the O'Neill family, 77
Arundel and Shoreham, 178
Astor, J. J., 77
Astor, M., 102n
Astor, W. W., 77

Bacon, Miss Alice, 150
Bailey, Jack, 185n
Baird, John, 163
Baker, W. H., 80n
Banbury, 61–2
Barber, A. P. L., 13n
Barker, Sara, 242n
Barons Court, 147, 189n
Bartholomew, D. J., 100
Bartlett, Vernon, 139
Basingstoke, 46n
Battersea South, 197
Baxter, William, 162–3
Beckenham, 54n, 218
Belfast West, 70
Bell, E. P., 138
Bell, P. I., 68n
Benn, Anthony Wedgwood, 146
Benney, M., 84n
Benson, Sir George, 174

Berkeley, Humphrey, 68n
Berrington, H. B., 100
Bevan, Aneurin, 148, 162, 239
Bevin, Ernest, 144–5
Biffen, John, 90
Billericay, 198n, 237
Bilston, 189n
Birmingham, Conservative selection in, 75–6
Birmingham (Edgbaston), 54
Birmingham (Hall Green), 45n, 47n
Birmingham (Northfield), 227n
Birmingham (Small Heath), 140, 189n, 240
Birmingham (Yardley), 198n
Bishop Auckland, 155
Bishop, E. S. D., 140
Blondel, J., 29n
Bolton East, 140
Bonham, J., 84n
Boot and Shoe Operatives, National Union of (N.U.B.S.O.), 169
Bootle, 161n, 228
Bournemouth East and Christchurch, 33, 35, 36, 55, 100–1
Bowes, R. W., 136, 141–2
Bowles, Frank, 145
Braddock, Mrs Bessie, 162–3
Braddock, Tom, 139
Bray, Jeremy, 182
Bridgwater, 139, 170
Brighton (Kemptown), 35, 50, 56, 150n
Bristol Central, 194n
Bristol East, 144
Bristol South-East, 46n, 146
Bristol West, 53, 142
British Iron, Steel and Kindred Trades Association (B.I.S.A.K.T.A.), 134, 149n, 169, 239–40, 293
British National party, 20
Bromley, 35, 38, 40, 45n, 153, 157n
Bryan, P. E. O., 17n, 21
Buck, P. W., 9n, 59
Buckingham, 142–3
Buckinghamshire North, 115n

affiliate to, 184–6; Labour party, relations with, 184–95; marginal constituencies, sponsorship of, 196, 197–8; membership of, 184; non-Labour constituencies, sponsorship of, 196–8; parliamentary group, 184n, 189n; parliamentary panel, 200–4; success in selection, 188–91, 234, 236, 237; and trade unions, 166, 182, 189–91; women, sponsorship of, 222

Co-operative and trade union sponsorship, comparison of, 195–7, 200, 202–4

Country Landowners' Association, 33

Cousins, Frank, 145

Cripps, Sir Stafford, 144

Critchley, J., 75, 90n

Crosby, 54

Cross, Sir R., 72

Cross-pressures: in Conservative selection, 89–92, 100–2, 279, 281; in Labour selection, 205, 207–12, 232–42, 255–6, 283

Croydon North-East, 37n, 38, 39, 40, 62

Croydon North-West, 140

Cunningham, S. Knox, 55

Dagenham, 38

Dalton, Hugh, 155, 229

Darlington, 194

Dartford, 189n

Davies, D. H., 134

Davies, Stella, 240

d'Avigdor-Goldsmid, Sir Henry, 70n

de Ferranti, B. Z., 86n

Derbyshire Miners' Association (D.M.A.), 158, 174–6, 292, 293

Derbyshire North-East, 147, 153, 174

Derbyshire West, 218

Devon North, 3

Divorce, influence of in Conservative selection, 67, 109, 115, 117

Donnelly, Desmond, 141n

Dorset North, 157n

Dorset South, 46n

Douglas-Home, Sir Alec (formerly Earl of Home), 24, 25, 55, 94n, 101

Dover, 140, 226n

Draughtsmen's and Allied Technicians' Association (D.A.T.A.), 140–1, 178, 236, 244 and n, 249, 256, 292, 293

Driberg, Tom, 148, 225

Dumfries, 24

Dundee, 238

East Grinstead, 13, 36, 38, 40

East Ham North, 190

East Ham South, 189n

Ebbw Vale, 40, 153, 157, 239–40

Edelman, Maurice, 161

Eden, Sir Anthony (Lord Avon), 101, 125

Edinburgh North, 24

Edinburgh (Pentlands), 24

Education, influence of in Labour selection, 180–1, 206–7, 208–9, 221

Education and social background, influence of in Conservative selection, 82–5, 86–92, 96–7, 98–9, 280

Edwards, Alfred, 141

Edwards, J. K. O'N. (Jimmy), 56n

Edwards, L. J., 146n

Electoral behaviour, relative stability of, 7

Electoral gains, 5, 6–8, 98–9, 178, 197, 220, 241–2

Electoral gains, Labour-Co-operative candidates benefiting from, 197

Electoral gains, trade union candidates benefiting from, 178

Electoral Reform, Speaker's Conference on, 1944, 30

Electoral status of constituencies: Co-operative party, attitude towards, 195–200; defined, 284–5; and educational and social background of Conservative candidates, 86–92; and local connections of Conservative candidates, 87; and occupations of Conservative candidates, 86–7; selection, influence on, 4–9; trade unions, attitude towards, 170–8;

Electoral swing, 6–8

Electrical Trades Union (E.T.U.), 139, 178, 182, 236, 256, 266, 268, 293

Elliott, Walter, 25

Williams, R. W., 173n, 176n
Williams, Shirley, 227n
Williams, W. T., 147, 240n
Willson, F. M. G., 9n
Wilson, Harold, 3, 214, 232
Wilson Report (Report of the Sub-
  Committee on Labour party
  organization), 186, 214, 230–2
Wimbledon, 139
Withdrawals of candidature. *See
  under* Candidates
Wives, screening of by Conservative
  associations, 51–2, 64–6, 114–26
Wolrige-Gordon, Patrick, 55, 70
Wolverhampton North-East, 157n, 163
Women candidates. *See under*
  Candidates
Women M.P.s. *See under* Members
  of Parliament
Women, role of in Conservative
  selection, 61–7, 107, 124–5

Woodford, 22, 35, 36, 37n, 38, 39,
  40, 44, 46n, 62, 139
Wood Green, 189n, 222
Wood Green and Southgate, 138
Woodworkers, Amalgamated
  Society of (A.S.W.), 190n, 235,
  266, 291
Woolwich West, 35, 184n
Woolton, Lord, 20, 26–7
Worcestershire South, 36, 37n, 38,
  40, 62, 89
Worthing, 35, 37n, 38, 39, 40, 46n,
  62, 73
Wyatt, Woodrow, 148, 161
Wylie, N. R., 24
Wynn, H. W., 175

Younger, George, 25

Zilliacus, Konni, 139, 146, 240n